People
of the
HOLOCAUST

People of the HOLOCAUST

VOLUME 1
A-J

LINDA SCHMITTROTH
and
MARY KAY ROSTECK

DETROIT • NEW YORK • LONDON

People of the HOLOCAUST

Edited by Linda Schmittroth and Mary Kay Rosteck

Staff

Julie L. Carnagie, *U·X·L Developmental Editor*
Carol DeKane Nagel, *U·X·L Managing Editor*
Thomas L. Romig, *U·X·L Publisher*

Shanna P. Heilveil, *Production Assistant*
Evi Seoud, *Production Manager*
Mary Beth Trimper, *Production Director*

Tracey Rowens, *Art Director*
Cynthia Baldwin, *Product Design Manager*
Barbara J. Yarrow, *Graphic Services Supervisor*

Jessica L. Ulrich, *Permissions Associate*
Margaret A. Chamberlain, *Permissions Specialist*

Library of Congress Cataloging-in-Publication Data

Schmittroth, Linda.
    People of the Holocaust / by Linda Schmittroth.
      p.   cm.
    Includes bibliographical references and index.
    Summary: Profiles sixty women and men who were caught up in the Holocaust, including Nazi perpetrators and their victims, world leaders and policy makers, and those who showed their humanity and courage by resisting Hitler's reign of genocidal terror.
    ISBN 0-7876-1743-1 (set: alk. paper). — ISBN 0-7876-1744-X (v. 1.: alk. paper). — ISBN 0-7876-1745-8 (v. 2: alk. paper).
    1. Holocaust, Jewish (1939-1945)—Juvenile literature. 2. Jews—Biography—Juvenile literature. 3. Nazis—Biography—Juvenile literature. 4. War criminals—Germany—Biography—Juvenile literature. 5. Righteous Gentiles in the Holocaust—Biography—Juvenile literature. [1. Holocaust, Jewish (1939-1945) 2. Jews—Biography. 3. Nazis. 4. War criminals—Germany. 5. Righteous Gentiles in the Holocaust.] I. Title

    D804.34.S36 1998
    940.53' 18—DC21

                          98-4988
                          CIP AC

 ™ This book is printed on acid-free paper that meets the minimum requirements of American National Standard for information Sciences—Permanence Paper for Printed Library Materials, ANSI Z39.48-1984.

Printed in the United States of America
10 9 8 7 6 5 4 3 2

Contents

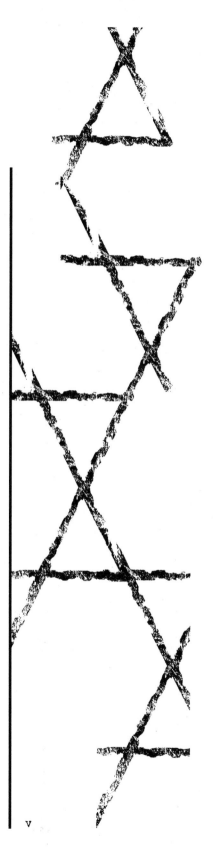

Volume 1: A–J

Volume 2: K-Z

Index xxxi

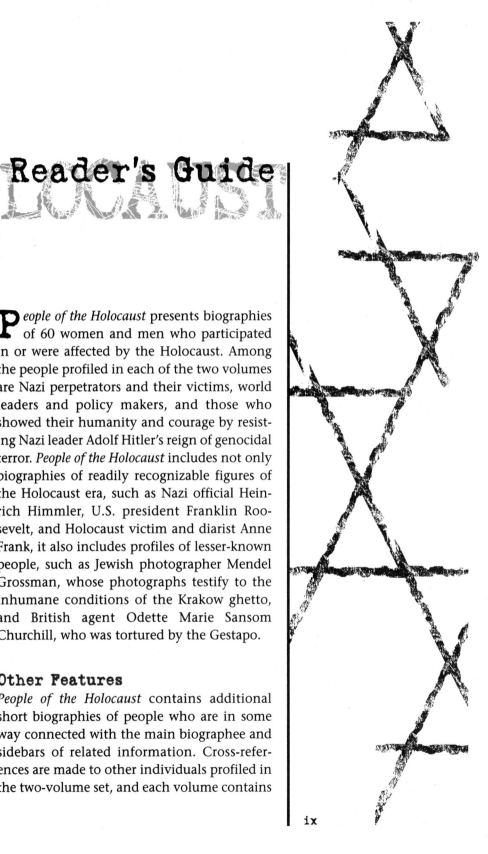

Reader's Guide

People of the Holocaust presents biographies of 60 women and men who participated in or were affected by the Holocaust. Among the people profiled in each of the two volumes are Nazi perpetrators and their victims, world leaders and policy makers, and those who showed their humanity and courage by resisting Nazi leader Adolf Hitler's reign of genocidal terror. *People of the Holocaust* includes not only biographies of readily recognizable figures of the Holocaust era, such as Nazi official Heinrich Himmler, U.S. president Franklin Roosevelt, and Holocaust victim and diarist Anne Frank, it also includes profiles of lesser-known people, such as Jewish photographer Mendel Grossman, whose photographs testify to the inhumane conditions of the Krakow ghetto, and British agent Odette Marie Sansom Churchill, who was tortured by the Gestapo.

Other Features
People of the Holocaust contains additional short biographies of people who are in some way connected with the main biographee and sidebars of related information. Cross-references are made to other individuals profiled in the two-volume set, and each volume contains

"Words to Know" and "Further Reading" sections. A cumulative subject index concludes each volume.

Comments and Suggestions

We welcome your comments and suggestions on *People of the Holocaust* as well as your suggestions for people to be included in future editions. Please write: Editors, *People of the Holocaust,* U•X•L, 835 Penobscot Bldg., Detroit, Michigan 48226-4094; call toll free: 1-800-877-4253; or fax: 313-961-6347.

Acknowledgments

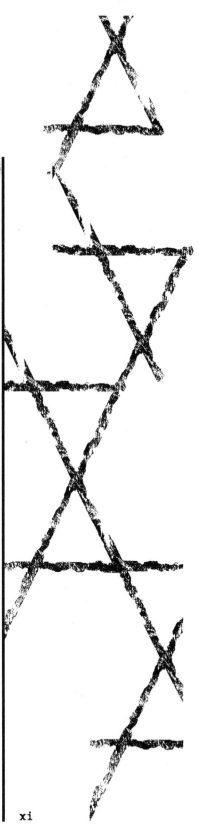

Special thanks are due for the invaluable comments and suggestions provided by U•X•L's Holocaust Reference Library advisors:

Jonathan Betz-Zall, Children's Librarian, Sno-Isle Regional Library Systems, Edmonds, Washington

Ruth Fox, Department Chairperson, Great Neck South Middle School

Linda Hurwitz, Director, The Holocaust Center of Greater Pittsburgh, Pennsylvania

Debra Lyman Gniewek, Library Services Coordinator, Office of Information Technology, School District of Philadelphia, Pennsylvania

Max Weitz, Director, Holocaust Resource Center of Minneapolis, Minnesota

HOLOCAUST Timeline

1923 Adolf Hitler is in charge of the Munich Beer Hall Putsch, the Nazis' armed attempt to seize power of Germany.

1926 Antisemitic Catholic priest Charles Coughlin broadcasts his first radio sermon.

1931 Vidkun Quisling cofounds the Nordic Folk Awakening movement in Norway, which believes in many of the same ideas and principles of Germany's Nazi Party.

1933 Adolf Hitler becomes chancellor of Germany and appoints Joseph Goebbels as Reichminister of Propaganda.

1933 Homosexual researcher Mangus Hirschfeld's Institute for Sexual Science in Berlin, Germany, is destroyed by the Nazis.

1934 Adolf Hitler orders the murder of SA leader Ernst Röhm and his supporters in what has become known as the "Night of Long Knives."

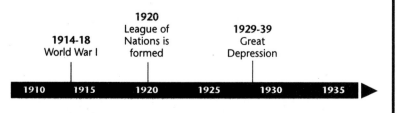

1914-18
World War I

1920
League of
Nations is
formed

1929-39
Great
Depression

| 1910 | 1915 | 1920 | 1925 | 1930 | 1935 |

1937 Karl Koch becomes commandant of Buchenwald concentration camp, and his wife Ilse, known as "the Beast of Buchenwald," begins to terrorize the prisoners.

1938 Jewish psychotherapist Bruno Bettelheim is arrested by the Nazis and placed in the Dachau concentration camp.

1938 Herschel Grynszpan assassinates Nazi official Ernst vom Rath at the German Embassy in Paris, France, which leads to *Kristallnacht* ("Crystal Night").

1938 Italian dictator Benito Mussolini adopts the Jewish laws of his ally Adolf Hitler.

1939 Nazi doctor Karl Brandt implements the Nazi euthanasia program.

1939 Adolf Hitler appoints Hans Frank governor general of the central section of Poland; Frank requires Jews to wear the Star of David on their right sleeves for identification purposes.

1939 Nazi Minister of Foreign Affairs Joachim von Ribbentrop signs the Munich Pact with the Soviet Union, which provides for the division of Poland between the Germans and the Soviets.

1940 The Lódz ghetto in Poland is created, and Jewish photographer Mendel Grossman begins to capture ghetto life with pictures.

1940 Odette Marie Sansom Churchill, a mother and wife, becomes a spy for Great Britain; she is later confined to a concentration camp and tortured by the Nazis.

1941 Rudolf Höss, commandant of Auschwitz concentration camp, oversees the first experiments using poisonous gas for the extermination of masses of human beings.

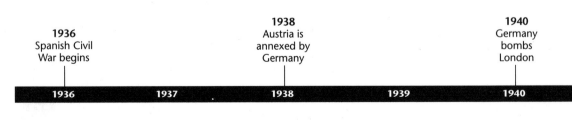

1936
Spanish Civil
War begins

1938
Austria is
annexed by
Germany

1940
Germany
bombs
London

| 1936 | 1937 | 1938 | 1939 | 1940 |

1941 Rudolf Hess makes a flight to Britain with the hope of persuading the British to side with Germany during World War II.

1941 Jewish physchotherapist Viktor E. Frankl remains in Vienna with his parents and is sent to the first of three concentration camps.

1941 U.S. president Franklin Roosevelt believes that the only way to save the prisoners of the German concentration camps is to win the war against Germany, Italy, and Japan as quickly as possible.

1941 Josip Broz Tito leads a group called the Partisans to resist the Germany occupation of Yugoslavia.

1942 A small group of high-ranking Nazi Party and government officials meet to discuss the "Final Solution," a code name for their plan to eliminate all European Jews.

1942 *Judenrat* official Adam Czerniaków commits suicide after the Nazis order him to hand over 9,000 Jews from the Warsaw ghetto for deportation.

1942 Jewish orphanage director Janusz Korczak and his 200 orphans are deported from the Warsaw ghetto in Poland to the Treblinka concentration camp, where they are all murdered in gas chambers.

1942 Polish-Jewish couple Shimson and Tova Draenger join other Jewish youths in forming the Jewish Fighting Organization to work against the Nazis' aims.

1942 Reinhard Heydrich, head of the SD, is assassinated in Prague, Czechoslovakia.

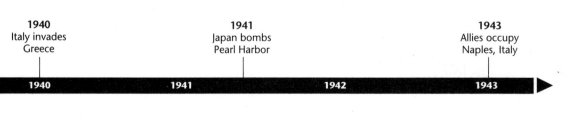

1940
Italy invades
Greece

1941
Japan bombs
Pearl Harbor

1943
Allies occupy
Naples, Italy

| 1940 | 1941 | 1942 | 1943 |

1943 Hans and Sophie Scholl are arrested on a Munich University campus for distributing pamphlets for the White Rose resistance group.

1943 Jewish resistance leader Mordecai Anielewicz is killed during the Warsaw ghetto uprising.

1943 German Jewish rabbi Leo Baeck is sent to the Theresienstadt concentration camp in Czechoslovakia, where he remains until the camp is liberated by the Soviets at the end of World War II.

1943 British spy Noor Inayat Khan is captured and tortured by the Nazis in occupied France.

1944 After living undetected for 25 months, Anne Frank and her family are discovered by the Nazis and sent to Auschwitz concentration camp.

1944 Hannah Senesh, a Jew living in Palestine, parachutes behind enemy lines as part of a British-sponsored rescue mission to reach Jews and other resisters.

1944 A young Swedish businessman named Raoul Wallenberg arrives in Hungary to help save the surviving Jews trapped in Budapest.

1944 Industrialist Oskar Schindler seeks permission from the Nazis to spare Jewish prisoners from death by employing them at a munitions factory in Czechoslovakia.

1944 Concentration camp prisoner Róza Robota participates in the inmates' revolt at Auschwitz, leading to the destruction of one of the crematoriums.

1944 German army commander Erwin Rommel is believed to be involved in a failed attempt to assassinate Adolf Hitler and is forced to commit suicide as a result.

1943
Battle of
Bismark

1944
D-Day

1945
V-E Day

| 1943 | 1944 | 1945 | 1946 |

1945 Swedish diplomat Folke Bernadotte negotiates a deal with Nazi official Heinrich Himmler that allows 10,000 women to be released from the Ravensbrück concentration camp.

1945 German Protestant minister Dietrich Bonhoeffer is executed for his participation in a plot to assassinate Adolf Hitler.

1945 Eva Braun marries Adolf Hitler in his Berlin bunker the day before they commit suicide.

1945 Chief of the SS Heinrich Himmler orders the destruction of the concentration camps and their inmates.

1945 U.S Army general George Patton and the Third Army liberate the Buchenwald concentration camp in Germany.

1945 Survivor Simon Wiesenthal forms the Jewish Historical Documentation Center in Austria to track down Nazi war criminals.

1946 Hermann Göring, one of the highest Nazi officials to be accused and convicted of war crimes, gives testimony on his behalf during the Nuremberg Trials.

1946 Brigadier General Telford Taylor becomes chief counsel for the remaining Nuremberg Trials after U.S. Supreme Court Justice Robert H. Jackson resigns.

1949 American radio personality Mildred Gillars ("Axis Sally") goes on trial for treason.

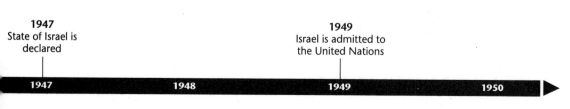

1947
State of Israel is
declared

1949
Israel is admitted to
the United Nations

| 1947 | 1948 | 1949 | 1950 |

1959 German industrialist Alfried Krupp is made to pay reparations to former concentration camp inmates who were forced to work at Krupp's munitions factories.

1960 Elie Wiesel publishes *Night,* an autobiographical account of his experiences during the Holocaust.

1962 Former Nazi official Adolf Eichmann is executed after being found guilty of war crimes for his part in the murder of hundreds of thousands of Jews.

1967 Franz Stangl, the former commandant of the Sobibór death camp where more than 100,000 people were gassed during his first two months there, is taken to Germany to stand trial for war crimes.

1971 Beate and Serge Klarsfeld discover that former Nazi officer Klaus Barbie is living in Bolivia.

1983 Donald Carroll publishes "Escape from Vichy," an article about American writer Varian Fry, who saved between 1,500 and 4,000 Jews in German-occupied France.

1985 Human remains found in Brazil are confirmed to be those of Nazi doctor Josef Mengele, who performed inhumane experiments on the prisoners of Auschwitz concentration camp.

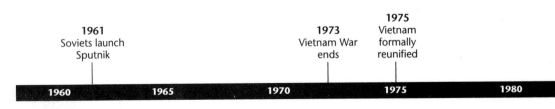

1961
Soviets launch
Sputnik

1973
Vietnam War
ends

1975
Vietnam
formally
reunified

1960   1965   1970   1975   1980

1987 Former SS soldier Klaus Barbie is found guilty of crimes against humanity and is sentenced to life in prison.

1987 Miep Gies publishes her book *Anne Frank Remembered.*

1990 Gypsy Holocaust survivor and artist Karl Stojka opens an exhibit titled *The Story of Karl Stojka: A Childhood in Birkenau,* which displays more than 100 paintings depicting his life in a concentration camp.

1992 Survivor Isabella Katz Leitner publishes *Isabella: From Auschwitz to Freedom* and *The Big Lie,* both of which describe her experiences during the Holocaust.

1993 The Israeli Supreme Court overturns the death sentence of former Nazi John Demjanjuk and acquits him.

1998 The Vatican issues a letter stating that Pope Pius XII, leader of the Catholic Church during the Holocaust, did all he could to save the Jews.

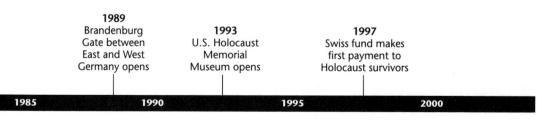

1989
Brandenburg
Gate between
East and West
Germany opens

1993
U.S. Holocaust
Memorial
Museum opens

1997
Swiss fund makes
first payment to
Holocaust survivors

1985   1990   1995   2000

Words to Know

A

Allies: The countries of Great Britain, the United States, the Soviet Union, and France, who fought against Germany, Italy, and Japan during World War II.

Antisemitism: The hatred of Jews, who are sometimes called Semites.

Aryans: A term originally used for the peoples speaking the languages of Europe and India. The Nazis used the term to mean anyone who was non-Jewish and of Germanic background.

B

Bliztkrieg: The military strategy of troops in land vehicles making quick, surprise strikes against the enemy with support from airplanes.

C

Chancellor: Head of the German government.

Collaborators: People who turned their own friends, families and neighbors over to the Nazis.

Communism: An economic system that promotes the ownership of all property by the community as a whole.

Concentration camps: Places where the Nazis confined people they regarded as "enemies of the state."

Crematoriums: Buildings that held large ovens used to dispose of the bodies of dead concentration camp inmates.

Crimes against humanity: Murder, extermination, enslavement, deportation, and other acts committed against the nonmilitary population of a country.

D

Death march: The process of forcing long rows of prisoners to walk great distances without the proper food or clothing.

Deportation: The process by which Nazis forcibly removed people from their normal place of residence to a labor, concentration, or death camp.

Depression: An economic downturn.

Dictator: Holding absolute ruling power in a country.

E

Einsatzgruppen: Special mobile units of the SS and SD that followed the German army into the Soviet Union; they shot at least one million Jews.

Euthanasia: The act of killing people that the Nazis considered "unfit to live."

F

Final Solution: The code name given to the Nazi plan to totally eliminate the Jews of Europe.

Führer: The German word meaning "leader."

G

Gassing: The Nazi process of locking people in sealed rooms and then filling the rooms with poisonous gas in order to suffocate the people to death.

Genocide: The deliberate, systematic destruction of a racial, cultural, or political group.

Gentiles: Non-Jewish people.

Gestapo: An abbreviation for *Geheime Staats Politzei* or Secret State Police.

Ghettos: Crowded, walled-sections of cities where Jews were forced to live in inferior conditions.

Gypsies: Dark-haired, dark-skinned, nomadic people who are believed to have originated in India. They are sometimes also called Roma or Sinti.

H

Holocaust: The period between 1933 and 1945 when Nazi Germany systematically persecuted and murdered millions of Jews, Gypsies, homosexuals, Jehovah's Witnesses, and other innocent people.

I

Isolationist: A country's policy of non-involvement in other countries' affairs.

J

Jehovah's Witnesses: A religious group whose beliefs did not allow them to swear allegiance to any worldly power.

Judenrat: The German term for Jewish Council. Nazi leaders ordered the formation of Jewish Councils in the ghettos.

K

Kapos: Prisoners who worked for the Nazis.

N

Nazi: The abbreviation for the National Socialist German Worker's Party.

Neo-Nazis: People who idolize the Nazis and their policies today.

O

Occupation: Control of a country by a foreign military power.

P

Pogroms: Mass attacks against a particular group of people.

Propaganda: Official government communications to the public that are designed to influence opinion. The information may be true or false.

R

Reichstag: Germany's parliament or lawmaking body.

Resistance: Working against an occupying army.

S

SA: An abbreviation for *Sturmabteilungen,* or Storm Troopers. They were members of a special armed and uniformed branch of the Nazi Party.

SD: An abbreviation for *Sicherdienst,* or Security Police. This unit served as the Intelligence (Spy) Service of the SS.

Selection: The process by which the Nazis decided who would be spared to work and who would be killed immediately.

Sonderkommando: Jewish prisoners who were forced to dispose of bodies of gassed inmates by cremation.

SS: An abbreviation for *Shutzstaffeln,* or Security Squad. This unit provided Adolf Hitler's personal bodyguard and provided guards for the various concentration camps.

Star of David: A Jewish religious symbol that the Nazis forced Jews to wear for identification purposes.

Swastika: The Nazi symbol of a black, bent-armed cross that always appeared within a white circle and set on a red background.

Synagogue: A Jewish place of worship.

T

Third Reich: The name Adolf Hitler gave to his term as Germany's leader. It means "Third Empire."

U

Underground: Engaged in secret or illegal activity.

W
War crimes: Violations of the laws or customs of war.

Y
Yiddish: A language spoken by Eastern European Jews.

Photo Credits

Photographs and illustrations for *People of the Holocaust* were received from the following sources:

Bildarchiv Preussischer Kulturbesitz. Reproduced by permission: pp. 1, 51, 158, 245, 325; Leah Hammerstein Silverstein/ USHMM Photo Archives. Reproduced by permission: p. 3; The Library of Congress: pp. 9, 43, 112, 222, 236, 384, 392, 394; Archive Photos, Inc. Reproduced by permission: pp. 19, 47, 56, 123, 251, 291, 317, 354, 467, 474, 478, 492; Hulton-Getty/Tony Stone Images. Reproduced by permission: pp. 26, 117; National Archives/USHMM Photo Archives. Reproduced by permission: p. 29; Yad Vashem Photo Archives/USHMM Photo Archives. Reproduced by permission: pp. 35, 371; AP/Wide World Photos, Inc. Reproduced by permission: pp. 37, 73, 79, 84, 95, 101, 147, 151, 164, 168, 172, 175, 180, 185, 205, 208, 214, 238, 271, 275, 280, 297, 357, 381, 455, 494; Main Commission for the Investigation of Nazi War Crimes/USHMM Photo Archives. Reproduced by permission: pp. 65, 226, 257, 437; Stadtarchiv Nuerenberg/USHMM Photo Archives. Reproduced by permission: p. 69; USHMM Photo Archives: pp. 77, 264, 464;

National Museum of American Jewish History/USHMM Photo Archives: p. 91; Photograph by Rudolph Hess. Archive Photos, Inc. Reproduced by permission: p. 121; Lena Fagen/USHMM Photo Archives. Reproduced by permission: p. 128; Rijksinstituut Voor Oorlogsdocumentatie/USHMM Photo Archives. Reproduced by permission: p. 131; Bilderdienst Suddeutscher Verlag. Reproduced by permission: pp. 137, 144, 231, 321, 362, 365; Photograph by Bernard Gotfryd. Archive Photos, Inc. Reproduced by permission: p. 155; Ghetto Fighters' House/USHMM Photo Archives. Reproduced by permission: p. 189, 283, 286; YIVO Institute for Jewish Research/USHMM Photo Archives. Reproduced by permission: p. 193; Morris Rosen/USHMM Photo Archives. Reproduced by permission: p. 197; Morris Rosen/USHMM Photo Archives. Reproduced by permission: p. 201; KZ Gedenkstatte Dachau/USHMM Photo Archives. Reproduced by permission: p. 218; Roland Klemig/USHMM Photo Archives. Reproduced by permission: p. 234; Reproduced by permission of Ms. Leitner: p. 301; Photograph by Bernhard Walter. Yad Vashem Photo Archives/USHMM Photo Archives: p. 305; State Museum of Auschwitz- Birkenau/USHMM Photo Archives. Reproduced by permission: p. 311; Gale Research, Inc: p. 328; Eliyahu Mallenbaum/ USHMM Photo Archives. Reproduced by permission: p. 373; Photograph by H. Hoffmann. Bildarchiv Preussischer Kulturbesitz. Reproduced by permission: p. 378; UPI/Corbis-Bettmann. Reproduced by permission: p. 408; Prof. Leopold Pfeffergerg-Page/USHMM Photo Archives: pp. 415, 421; Photograph by George J. Wittenstein. Reproduced by permission: p. 430; Beit Hannah Senesh/USHMM Photo Archives. Reproduced by permission: pp. 443, 447; American Jewish Archives/USHMM Photo Archives. Reproduced by permission: p. 451; Photograph by T/4 Hewitt. Hedy Epstein/USHMM Photo Archives. Reproduced by permission: p. 470; UPI/Bettmann. Reproduced by permission: p. 483; Lena Kurtz Deutsch/USHMM Photo Archives. Reproduced by permission: p. 487; UPI/Bettmann Newsphotos. Reproduced by permission: p. 500; Reuters/Bettmann. Reproduced by permission: p. 504.

Mordecai Anielewicz

Born 1919 or 1920
Warsaw, Poland

Died May 8, 1943
Warsaw ghetto, Poland

Jewish anti-Nazi resistance leader

Led uprisings in the Warsaw ghetto

World War II (1939–45) began when Adolf Hitler (see entry) invaded Poland. Hitler, the leader of the National Socialist German Workers' Party (Nazi for short), hated Jews. He blamed the Jews for Germany's humiliating loss of World War I (1914–18). It was Hitler's intention to eliminate the entire Jewish population in the lands controlled by the Nazis. The first step in achieving this end was to force the Jews to live in special areas called ghettos, which were small, crowded parts of a city, full of disease and poverty. Mordecai Anielewicz was one of the young Polish-Jewish men and women who put themselves at great risk to supply the Warsaw (Poland) ghetto with food, medical supplies, and weapons for defense, and who tried to stop the Nazis' evil plans for the Jews who lived there. He participated in the Warsaw Ghetto Uprising in 1943, the most famous of the Jewish attempts to resist Nazi rule.

"The Germans
will have
to fight
for months
on end . . .
the enemy
will pay
with a sea
of blood."

Childhood in Warsaw

Mordecai Anielewicz (pronounced More-da-keye On-yell-a-wits) was born into a very poor family in the slums of Warsaw, Poland, in 1919 or 1920. When he was growing up some of the young boys in the neighborhood used to beat up little Jewish children. As a result, Anielewicz learned how to defend himself at a very early age. After finishing high school, he became one of the leaders of a Zionist group, young people who wanted to establish a Jewish homeland in Palestine (now Israel).

Escape and Return to Warsaw

World War II began in 1939 when German Nazi soldiers attacked and eventually conquered Poland. The Nazi Party, which took over Warsaw, Poland's capital, bombed the railroads and destroyed towns and villages. Many people lost their homes and were left to wander the streets. Anielewicz and some of his friends left Warsaw for southern Poland to help create an escape route for Polish Jews who wanted to go to Palestine. However, at that time Soviet (Russian) troops occupied the area of southern Poland, and Anielewicz was captured and put in prison. After his release, he went to the former Polish city of Vilna, which by then had become part of the country of Lithuania. A large number of Jewish youths from Warsaw had sought refuge there.

Anielewicz organized the return of a group of young people to Warsaw to set up underground political and educational activities (underground means engaged in secret or illegal activity). He and his fiancée, Mira Furhrer, decided that it was their duty to return to Poland and do what they could to help other Jews. They volunteered to become part of the teaching efforts in Warsaw.

Jews Restricted to Ghetto

Beginning in October 1940, the Nazis required the Jews of Warsaw to live together in an old section of the city that came to be called the Warsaw ghetto. The Nazis enclosed the section with nine-foot brick walls that were topped with barbed wire. All the Jews of Warsaw and nearby areas, more than 400,000 people, had to leave their belongings behind and move into the ghetto with only what they could take on

their backs. This included mainly pots and pans, blankets, clothing, and various supplies. In addition to Warsaw, additional Jewish ghettos were established in other Polish cities.

Early Underground Activities

Once he had relocated to the Warsaw ghetto, Anielewicz taught classes, organized political activities, and made secret trips to visit underground groups in the ghettos that had been established in other parts of Poland. He was involved with an early resistance (worked against the Nazis) effort headed by Pinya Kartin, a former soldier. The group believed that, being vastly outnumbered, the best approach for Warsaw's Jews was to undertake secret missions to destroy military buildings and disrupt transportation. Anielewicz worked on an underground newspaper so that important information could be shared among the members of the resistance. The paper encouraged the people of the ghetto to take up arms in opposition to Nazi rule. It declared, "Jewish workers! Jewish youth! Gather your forces and pool them for battle. Stand united shoulder to shoulder." Before long, Kartin was identified as a spy and shot to death by Nazis. His followers disbanded because of the loss of his leadership and their fear of the Nazis.

Resistance Efforts As Leader

Anielewicz continued urging the Jews of the Warsaw ghetto to join together in resistance groups and refuse to surrender to the will of the Nazis. In 1940, he became head of the ZOB, an acronym for *Zydowska Organizacja Bojowa,* or Jewish Fighting Organization. The other main resistance group was called the Jewish Military Union. The two groups, made up mostly of people in their teens and twenties, soon began working together. Some of the young women, especially those with fair skin and light eyes, became messengers, bringing information, goods, and money to and from the ghetto. Because they did not have the dark coloring of many of the Jews, the women were more easily able to travel through the city without arousing suspicion.

During 1940 and 1941, Anielewicz put his efforts into strengthening the defenses of the people who lived in the ghetto. He sought help from a group of Polish citizens who remained loyal to the former Polish government, which was in exile in London, England. Unfortunately, these efforts failed.

In 1942, the Nazis commanded large groups of people to leave the Warsaw ghetto and go to a nearby concentration camp called Treblinka. Concentration camps were places where the Nazis confined people they regarded as "enemies of the state." The inmates were forced to perform hard labor for very little food, and many were put to death. When Anielewicz found out what was happening at Treblinka, he knew it was time for members of the resistance to arm themselves.

Life in the Warsaw Ghetto

In November 1940, the National Socialist German Workers' Party (Nazis for short) closed the gates of the Warsaw ghetto. No Jews were allowed out and no non-Jews were allowed in. The Jews found ways to fight the destruction of their culture by the Nazis. Even though people were forbidden to study, secret schools were started, libraries were formed, and occasionally musical events were held. The following year the Nazis decreed that any Jews found outside the gates of the ghetto were to be killed.

At this time the Warsaw ghetto was divided into four sections: the main center section where the majority of people lived, the brush maker's ghetto, the productive ghetto, and the little ghetto. Jews were put to work making Nazi uniforms, as well as leather goods and fur products. According to the author Karen Zeinart, "others produced textiles [fabric], shoes, furniture, bedding, rushes, and wooden door and window frames . . . . Workers were not paid, but they were given some food during their twelve-hour shifts." People were required to live in the section near their place of work. The inhabitants were isolated, and the area of the walls dividing the four sections was supposed to remain free of people. The Nazis believed that this would make the inhabitants easier to control.

Still, people managed to slip in and out of the ghetto to obtain food and other needed supplies. The sewer system offered the most common route used by smugglers to leave and return to the ghetto. The pipes, high enough for an adult to walk through if bent over, extended all over the city and provided an effective way to go about undetected. Bunkers, or small caves, were dug under the buildings and connected one to another so that people could pass underground secretly. Food and water were stored in the bunkers.

By 1941, conditions within the ghetto had become extremely bad. The Nazis had torn down the brick wall outlining the ghetto and made the Jews' living area even smaller. Food was in very short supply and there were almost no medicines. People slept several to a cot, intestinal infections and diseases caused by the unsanitary conditions ran unchecked, the smell of human waste filled the air, and people were dying at the rate of 4,500 per month. Families of beggars lined the streets. People sold any objects of value in exchange for money.

The Germans announced in July 1942, that the ghetto was to be emptied. They said that Jews were going to be sent eastward by train to work camps where the living conditions were much better. However, as many people suspected, this was untrue. In fact, the Jews were being transported to the Treblinka concentration camp, 60 miles from Warsaw, where most would be killed. By mid-September more than a quarter of a million of the Jews had been sent away. Only 60,000 to 70,000 remained at the time of the Warsaw Ghetto Uprising in 1943.

As of 1943, only about one-sixth of the Jews originally sent to live in the Warsaw ghetto remained there. By then, most of the ghetto inhabitants believed that death was their ultimate fate under Nazi rule, and they vowed to resist at all costs.

The two major resistance groups organized members of the underground to protect the various sections of the ghetto. In order to get the weapons they needed, the resistance groups collected money and dealt with various smugglers and Nazi deserters. Money, sometimes contributed by American and European supporters to purchase food, was used to buy arms. In order to maintain security, Jewish resistance leaders ordered that many of the Nazi spies and thieves who preyed on the Jews should be killed.

The Jews Fight Back

On January 18, 1943, members of the Nazi SS (the abbreviation for the *Shutzstaffeln* or the Security Squad) surrounded three sections of the ghetto and ordered the Jews to come out. Much to the surprise of the SS, the Jews remained inside. Under Anielewicz's command, gunfire and grenades greeted the Nazis. SS members who broke down doors to reach their intended victims encountered Jews swinging clubs and chairs. At other entrances the Nazis found empty rooms, as the Jews had escaped to underground passageways. Several Nazis were killed that day and the SS retreated.

The next day, the Germans returned and, though they were able to capture 6,000 people, the soldiers left in fear of their lives. After four days of confrontation, the Nazis stopped the deportation (forcibly removing people from their city or country) of the Jews. The people in the ghetto believed that their armed resistance had caused the Germans to back down. For three months the ghetto was relatively quiet, and Anielewicz and the ZOB continued their defense preparations.

Responding to the strong show of Jewish resistance, Heinrich Himmler (see entry), head of the SS, came to investigate. He decided that the ghetto was becoming dangerous and unmanageable for the Germans, and that it had to be destroyed.

The Conflict Resumes

On April 19, 1943, German tanks rolled into the Warsaw ghetto. The Nazis chose to attack on the first day of Passover, the holiday that commemorates the Jews' escape from Egypt during biblical times. The Jews had been preparing as best they could for the possible return of the Nazis. They bravely defended themselves, although they had very few weapons.

The writer Seymour Rossel describes the arms used by the resistance fighters to fend off more than two thousand fully armed Germans. "They had three machine guns, about eight rifles, some hand grenades, some Molotov cocktails (bottles filled with gasoline-soaked rags that would be ignited and thrown) and perhaps three hundred pistols and revolvers."

During the first conflicts, led by Anielewicz, the Jews pushed back the Germans. The Germans later returned with more soldiers, and the fighting got even more intense. Jews were driven from their dwellings, and many escaped in underground passageways.

The Nazi SS general in charge, Juergen Stroop, used planes, tanks, and artillery to attack the ghetto. Soldiers with dynamite and flame throwers went house to house looking for Jews. Even very young Germans, part of the Hitler youth group, were instructed to kill any Jew on sight.

Stroop, who reported his progress to Berlin (the city where the Nazi Party headquarters was located) each day, was shocked that the Jews preferred to be burned alive rather than surrender. In one of his reports he said: "With their bones broken, they still tried to crawl across the street into buildings which had not yet been set on fire. . . . Despite the danger of being burned alive, the Jews . . . often preferred to return into the flames rather than risk being caught by us." Women used both hands to fire heavy pistols at the Nazis. Some people waiting to be searched pulled hand grenades out of their clothing, burning up both their captors and themselves.

After two weeks, the Nazis were still unable to stop the fighting of the ghetto inhabitants. In a letter to a member of the resistance, Anielewicz wrote: "I have no words to describe to you the conditions in which the Jews are living. Only a few chosen ones will hold out; all the rest will perish sooner or later. The die is cast. . . . The main thing is: My life's dream has come true; I have lived to see Jewish resistance in the ghetto in all its greatness and glory."

On May 8, the Germans were able to take over the bunker on Mila Street that served as Jewish headquarters. Many of the resistance leaders took their own lives that day so that they would not fall into German hands. Anielewicz was killed in the fighting. In June, the conflict came to an end. The

Germans burned the entire ghetto down to the ground. At Himmler's order, the ghetto's historic Tlomackie synagogue (Jewish place of worship) was blown up. Himmler was reported as saying, "The Jewish quarter of Warsaw is no more."

Mordecai Anielewicz is memorialized by a monument in Israel at the site of the Kibbutz Yad Mordecai, which was named in his honor. A kibbutz is a collective farm found in Israel.

Where to Learn More

Adler, David A. *Child of the Warsaw Ghetto*. Holiday House, 1995.

Gilbert, Martin. *The Holocaust: A History of the Jews of Europe During the Second World War*. Holt, Rinehart and Winston, 1985.

Haas, Gerda. *Tracking the Holocaust*. Runestone Press, 1995.

Korczak, Janusz. *Ghetto Diary*. Holocaust Library, 1978.

Mark, Ber. *Uprising in the Warsaw Ghetto*. Schocken Books, 1975.

Marrin, Albert. *Hitler*. Viking Kestrel, 1987.

Rogasky, Barbara. *Smoke and Ashes: The Story of the Holocaust*. Holiday House, 1988.

Skipper, G. C. *World at War: The Invasion of Poland*. Children's Press, 1983.

Zeinert, Karen. *The Warsaw Ghetto Uprising*. Millbrook Press, 1993.

Leo Baeck

Born May 23, 1873
Lissa, Germany

Died November 2, 1956
London, England

World-renowned rabbi, leader of the German Jews in World War II, concentration camp survivor

Wrote two important books about the Jewish faith

Leo Baeck (pronounced Bek) grew up in an era in which antisemitism (hatred of Jews, who are sometimes called Semites) was very much kept secret. With the defeat of Germany in World War I (1914–18), he witnessed the widespread growth of anti-Jewish feelings and eventually the persecution and murder of millions of his fellow Jews during what has become known as the Holocaust. (The Holocaust refers to the period from 1933 to 1945 when millions of Jews and other innocent people were systematically persecuted and murdered.) Throughout the ordeal, he realized the necessity for keeping one's faith and putting it into action.

A Happy Childhood

According to Baeck family history, their ancestors settled in Moravia, part of today's Czech Republic. Many of Baeck's ancestors were rabbis (leaders of Jewish congregations), including his father, Samuel. By the time Baeck was born in 1873, the family had moved to Germany. Baeck was one of eleven children of a German-Jewish middle-class family. The town they grew up in was peaceful and pleasant and a center of Jewish learning.

Student Life in Germany

Baeck was an outstanding student in high school, where he graduated at the top of his class. As a young man he studied to become a rabbi, first in Breslau, Germany, and later in Berlin, Germany. Life was not easy for Baeck, as he had very little money for food and had to borrow the books he needed. He received both excellent religious training and a fine German non-religious education. He earned his Ph.D. in philosophy in 1895 and was ordained a rabbi in May 1897 at the age of 24.

First Appointment as Rabbi

Baeck first served as a rabbi to a congregation near Breslau, where he stayed for ten years. During that time he met and married Natalie Hamburger, a shy and kind woman who gave birth to their daughter, Ruth, and offered him the stability of family life. Baeck was popular with both adults and students, whom he frequently invited to his house for lively discussions. When people had disputes they came to Baeck to mediate. During these years, he began his lifelong practice of having dialogues (two-way conversations) with Gentiles (non-Jews). His education at German universities gave him the ability to present his ideas effectively in non-Jewish circles.

In 1905, Baeck published his first book, *The Essence of Judaism*. He wrote that it was the responsibility of the Jew to do God's will on Earth. He emphasized that Judaism had not died with the coming of Christianity, but that it was very much alive and thriving. The Christian religion derived from the Jewish religion.

Moves to Dusseldorf and Berlin

In 1907, Baeck was invited to become a rabbi in the prosperous German city of Dusseldorf. There he initiated question-and-answer sessions with students. He also began to talk about the importance of education for women. He was well known throughout the city as a result of interfaith lectures in which he participated.

"We Jews know that the commandment of God is to live."

In 1912, after five years in Dusseldorf, Baeck became a rabbi to Berlin's Jewish community. Over the next thirty years, he was assigned to various synagogues (Jewish houses of worship) throughout the city. He became an expert on the Jewish sources of Christianity, especially the Jewish origins of the New Testament.

Serves as Chaplain to Soldiers

When World War I (1914–18) began, Baeck volunteered to serve as a chaplain for the Jewish troops who were fighting for Germany. The 41-year-old rabbi brought food to wounded soldiers in field hospitals, wrote letters to their families, and offered services for the dead.

The Rise of Antisemitism

Following Germany's defeat in World War I, both the soldiers and the common people felt a sense of betrayal. Many Germans considered themselves to be a special people, "God's chosen." As such, they had to come up with a reason for why Germany had lost the war. Over time, blaming the loss on the Jews became widespread, even though many Jews had fought bravely alongside their German countrymen. Military leaders and business leaders united in denouncing the Jews, whom they accused of causing Germany to lose the war. The accusations were based on fiction, not fact, as well as a history of antisemitism that stretched back over centuries.

A Popular Rabbi

Shortly before the end of the war, Baeck had returned to Berlin to resume his duties as a rabbi. Throughout the 1920s, the city's Jews often chose the tall, dignified rabbi to be their spokesman before the Christian majority. His lectures were known for their excellence, clarity, and spiritual insight. Baeck served as president of the German B'nai Brith organization, which raised money for scholarships, hospitals, and other charitable Jewish institutions. By the late 1920s, Baeck was one of the most prominent Jews in Berlin.

The Rise of Hitler

In 1929, just as Germany was beginning to experience economic recovery, the world was hit with a global depression (an economic downturn). Unemployment rose dramatically in Germany and the people began to listen to the hate-filled speeches of Nazi Party leader Adolf Hitler (see entry), who preached that the Jews were responsible for the country's difficult economic conditions. (Nazi is the abbreviated term used to refer to the National Socialist German Workers' Party.)

In 1933, Hitler assumed power in Germany, and the Nazis stepped up their anti-Jewish activities. Hitler made laws forbidding Jews to work as lawyers or as members of the civil service (the people who carried on the work of the government). As antisemitism grew, the Jews established an organization headed by Baeck. The Representative Council of Jews in Germany supervised educational and charitable programs and provided aid to Jewish people wishing to leave the country.

Between 1934 and 1935, the Nazis enacted the Reich Citizenship Laws that took away citizenship from all Jews, banned marriages between Jews and non-Jews, and permitted the Gestapo (the Secret State Police) to arrest and imprison Jews in concentration camps without cause. Concentration camps were places where the Nazis confined people they regarded as "enemies of the state." Jews were also forbidden to use public beaches, telephones, hospitals, colleges, barbershops, and dining or sleeping cars on trains.

Protests Nazi Policies

In response to a declaration by Hitler that German children should be taught "the necessity of blood purity," Baeck wrote a special sermon. In that sermon he said "the lies uttered against [the Jews], the false charges made against [their] faith and its defenders are hateful. Let us trample these falsehoods beneath our feet. . . . " As a result of the sermon, the Nazis imprisoned Baeck. However, because a British reporter threatened to tell the world about the arrest of this prominent man, Baeck was released.

Helps Fellow Jews Flee Germany

As conditions for the Jews in Germany became worse, Baeck used his influence to obtain as many visas (travel documents) as possible to enable German Jews to leave for other countries. Although he could easily have left Germany himself, Baeck chose to stay and help his fellow Jews. He urged his wife, Natalie, and his daughter, Ruth, to leave, but they refused. In October 1937, Natalie became ill and died from a stroke (the rupture of a blood vessel in the brain). After her death, Baeck began to devote all of his time and energy to helping the Jews of Germany survive the Third Reich (meaning "Third Empire," the name Hitler gave to his term as Germany's leader).

Baeck Helps Protect and Rescue Children

On November 7, 1937, a young Jewish man named Herschel Grynszpan (see entry) shot a Ernst vom Rath, a low-level Nazi official, at the German Embassy in Paris, France, for deporting his father to Poland. (Deporting is the forcible removal of people from their city or country.) The Nazis used the incident as an excuse to carry out pogroms, or mass attacks, against German Jews two days later. *Kristallnacht,* (meaning "Crystal Night") or the "Night of Broken Glass," as the event is known because of the tons of broken glass in the streets, resulted in the deaths of more than 90 Jews, and the destruction of 300 synagogues and 7,000 Jewish shops. Baeck traveled throughout the city that night helping Jewish children escape the violence.

Continues Work Helping Jews

By 1939, two-thirds of Germany's Jews had fled the country. That year, the Nazis attacked Poland, and in a short time they conquered Denmark, Norway, Holland, and Belgium. Baeck arranged for a trainload of Jewish children to be rescued from Berlin and sent to safety in London, England. When asked how long he would be staying in Germany, Baeck replied: "Until the last Jew is saved."

As the savagery of World War II increased, Baeck insisted that his daughter and her family leave the country for England. His organization for the welfare of Jews was taken over by the Nazis, who were interested in making money on the sale of the life-saving visas for which people were willing to spend large sums of money. Baeck decided to remain with the now Nazi-run group because he felt he could do more for the Jews from the inside than from the outside.

By 1940, Hitler had intensified his efforts to rid Europe of the Jews, whom he referred to as "vermin." Jews were forbidden to drive cars, walk on city streets, go to the movies, buy new clothing, or own radios or any other appliances. They were required to wear yellow stars (a Jewish religious symbol) on the outside of their clothing for identification. Baeck's was the only seminary (school for religious training) for Jewish youth that was allowed to stay open. However, in September 1941, the Gestapo barged into the seminary and declared that from then on it would serve as a center for the deportation of Jews.

In mid-1941, Hitler began to implement a secret plan that was called the Final Solution, the code words the Nazis used to refer to the complete elimination of all European Jews. All of Europe's Jews were to be rounded up and sent to concentration camps. There they were to be gassed to death. Gassing was the Nazi process of locking people in a sealed room and then filling the room with poisonous gas in order to suffocate them to death.

Although the horrors that took place at Auschwitz (one of the largest and deadliest of the concentration camps) and other camps were not yet known by Baeck, he was aware of many other cruel acts. Adults and children were starving in the Jewish ghettos. (Ghettos were crowded, walled sections of cities where Jews were forced to live in inferior conditions and apart from non-Jews.) Every day thousands of Jews began to disappear as they were sent from the ghettos to what the Nazis called labor camps (inmates were actually worked to death or gassed). At first Baeck intended to meet with every Berlin Jew whose name appeared on lists to be sent away. When that became impossible, he took to meeting people in the streets and alleys and carrying messages from them to their loved ones.

Arrest and Imprisonment at Theresienstadt

On January 27, 1943, the Nazis arrested Baeck and sent him to the concentration camp in Theresienstadt (Ter-rays-en-shtott), Czechoslovakia. This camp was the least harsh of all the camps. It housed Jews who were World War I veterans, artists, spouses of non-Jews, and other prominent Jews.

Theresienstadt, with its bakeries, medical rooms, and shops, was totally unlike any of the other camps, in which people lived under terrible conditions. The Nazis used it as a model to show foreign representatives how humanely Jews were supposedly being treated in all the camps. Baeck was photographed there in order to add credibility to Hitler's claims. The houses and barracks at Theresienstadt, originally built as a military installation to house 10,000 people, now held six times that number. Adults and children were forced to sleep in wooden bunks stacked five high. Dysentery (a painful intestinal infection) and diarrhea contributed to the filth and foul smells.

Life in the Camp

Baeck was assigned to be a garbage collector. He and his partner were strapped to a heavy wagon and went around the camp carrying away the rat-infested trash. During his rounds Baeck met and comforted people. He was fond of saying, "The soul and the hour meet each other. What is given to us, we have to do."

At the camp, Baeck organized prisoners to nurse victims of a typhus (an infectious disease caused by unsanitary conditions) epidemic. He also found time to write parts of a book that would later be published. It was only because of mistaken identity that Baeck stayed alive in the camp. Adolf Eichmann (see entry) had ordered him to be killed. However, Eichmann saw the name of another rabbi named Beck on the death rolls and assumed that Baeck was dead, even making an announcement to that effect.

In mid-1943, Baeck learned the truth of the horrible mass murders that were taking place at Auschwitz and other camps. After much soul-searching he chose not to share the information with other prisoners. He believed that to do so would be devastating to them, and that hope must be kept alive.

By 1944, information coming from Germany became very difficult to obtain and the fate of Baeck was unknown. But in early 1945, it became obvious that the Allies (the United States, Great Britain, the Soviet Union, and France) were winning the war. Some Nazis hoped to receive mercy from the victorious Allies by freeing Jews in concentration camps. In February 1945, Baeck's daughter, Ruth, received a letter from a freed Dutch Jew. He told Ruth that Baeck had been told he could leave too, but that her father preferred to stay and be of help.

The Story of a Dignified Death

Before Leo Baeck was a prisoner at Thereseinstadt, another Jewish man, Jacob Edelstein, served there as head of the Council of Elders. The council was made up of a group of Jewish leaders who managed Jewish affairs as best they could within the camp. One day in 1938, Edelstein and three other men were accused of having given false daily reports to the Nazis. As a result, Edelstein was sent to the death camp called Birkenau in Poland. A year after Edelstein's death in June 1944, an eyewitness, Yossl Rosensaft, recalled the events of that day. Rosensaft's report appears in the book *The Holocaust: A History of the Jews of Europe During the Second World War* by Martin Gilbert. Here is what he had to say:

"Jacob was in the same barracks as I was—number 13—on that Monday morning. It was about nine a.m. and he was saying his morning prayers, wrapped in his prayer shawl. Suddenly the door burst open and [a Nazi lieutenant] strutted in, accompanied by three SS men. He called out Jacob's name. Jacob did not move. [The lieutenant] screamed: 'I am waiting for you, hurry up.'

"Jacob turned round very slowly, faced [him] and said quietly: 'Of the last moments on this earth, allotted to me by the Almighty, I am the master, not you.' Whereupon he turned back to face the wall and finished his prayers. He then folded his prayer shawl unhurriedly, handed it to one of the inmates, and said to the lieutenant, 'I am now ready.'

"[The lieutenant] stood there without uttering a word, and marched out when Edelstein was ready. Edelstein followed him and three [Nazi soldiers] made up the rear. We have never seen Jacob Edelstein again."

On April 30, 1945, knowing that the war was over for Germany, Hitler committed suicide in order to escape falling into the hands of approaching Soviet troops. At Hitler's request his body and that of his new wife Eva Braun (see entry) were burned. The Nazis' rule came to an end with their surrender to the Allies on May 7, 1945.

Life After Liberation

In May 1945, one week after the suicide of Hitler, the camp at Theresienstadt was liberated. The Soviets (now called Russians) and representatives of the Red Cross came there to supply food and medical needs. Trainloads of very sick people from other camps arrived for treatment. Baeck nursed the sick, in some cases cleaning maggots (insects) from their infected wounds. He also wrote letters for former prisoners, informing their loved ones that they had survived.

In May 1945, a U.S. Army major was dispatched to Theresienstadt to transport Baeck, who had become known as "the pope of the German Jews," to join his family in England. The esteemed rabbi refused to leave for two months until "every Jew [in the camp] ha[d] a destination."

A New Life

In early July 1945, Baeck, now a bit bent over and fifty pounds lighter than before his imprisonment, was reunited with his daughter, son-in-law, granddaughter, and three sisters in London, England. Throughout his seventies Baeck lived in London and continued his work. He was elected president of the British Council for the Protection of the Rights and Interests of the Jews from Germany. In 1947, he visited the United States, met President Harry S Truman at the White House, and gave talks to various liberal Jewish groups. He was also the first famous German Jew to return to Germany after the war. He helped families in trouble and shared funds he had received from his book royalties.

In 1948, Baeck was offered a half-year job as visiting professor at Hebrew Union College in Cincinnati, Ohio. He kept this post for several years, traveling during breaks to Britain where he became a British citizen. Baeck completed his second book, *This People Israel,* in 1956. Later that year, he was hospitalized in London with intestinal cancer. He refused to dwell on his illness but insisted on talking with his family about their futures.

Death and Memorialization

Leo Baeck died on November 2, 1956. Eulogies were given for him around the world. In his honor, the new German government in Berlin issued a postage stamp with his image. His books were translated into many languages.

Leo Baeck Institutes were opened in London, New York, and Israel. They offer extensive collections on German-Jewish history and scholarship. Schools and colleges are named after him. When asked before his death if he could forgive the Germans, Baeck replied, "I forgive the Germans? It is for the Germans to forgive themselves."

Where to Learn More

Baeck, Leo. *This People Israel: The Meaning of Jewish Existence.* Translated by Albert H. Friedlander. Holt, Rinehart and Winston, 1965.

Baker, Leonard. *Days of Sorrow and Pain: Leo Baeck and the Berlin Jews.* Macmillan, 1978.

Boehm, Eric H. *We Survived.* Yale University Press, 1949.

Friedlander, Albert H. *Leo Baeck: Teacher of Theresienstadt.* Holt, Rinehart and Winston, 1968.

Gruenewald, Max. "Leo Baeck: Witness and Judge." *Judaism,* Autumn 1957.

Neimark, Anne E. *One Man's Valor: Leo Baeck and the Holocaust.* E.P. Dutton, 1986.

Stadtler, Bea. *The Holocaust: A History of Courage and Resistance.* Behrman House, 1974.

Nikolaus (Klaus) Barbie

Born October 25, 1913
Bad Godesberg, Germany

Died September 25, 1991
St. Joseph Prison, France

Soldier, head of German secret police in Lyon, France

Known as "The Butcher of Lyon"

Klaus Barbie was a German soldier sent to France after Germany conquered it during World War II (1939–45). He ordered the arrest and sometimes the imprisonment of thousands of French Jews. He was particularly known for his active involvement in the brutal torture of prisoners, which earned him the nickname "The Butcher of Lyon." Long after the war ended, he was discovered hiding out in South America. He was brought back to France, tried, and convicted on 341 counts of crimes against humanity, including murder, extermination (complete destruction of a group of people), enslavement, deportation (forcibly removing people from their city or country), and other acts committed against a nonmilitary population.

Unhappy Childhood in Germany

Nikolaus (called Klaus) Barbie was born in 1913, the first of two sons born to Nikolaus

Barbie and Anna Hees. Both his parents were Catholics and schoolteachers descended from farming families. The couple married when Klaus was three months old.

Nikolaus Senior was badly wounded in World War I (1914–18) when Barbie was just an infant. Although he did not die from the wound until 1933, it caused him so much pain that he took to drinking heavily for relief. When he was drinking, he was often physically abusive to his sons. It is quite possible that young Barbie developed a lifelong hatred for the French because his father had been wounded in the war against them.

Barbie attended the same school where his father taught until he was 11 years old. From 1923 to 1925, he attended boarding school and greatly enjoyed the independence of that experience. For recreation he favored swimming and fencing. In 1925, his family moved to the city of Trier, where Barbie attended secondary school. He was disappointed at having to once again live with his family in their unhappy home. His teachers found him to be an intelligent boy who avoided conflicts. He may have felt drawn to the priesthood at a young age, but this ambition eventually died. He did not pass his school exams until 1934, when he was 20 years old. A year earlier, both his father and brother had died and there was no money for Barbie to attend college. Instead, he volunteered for a work camp run by the National Socialist German Workers' Party (Nazi for short), the political organization headed by Adolf Hitler (see entry), who had just risen to power.

Hitler hated the Jews. He believed that they had caused Germany's defeat in World War I. He also believed that they were a "poisonous" race that did not deserve to live. His ultimate goal was to eliminate all the Jews of Europe. Many of the Nazi Party members agreed with Hitler's feelings toward the Jews and were willing to carry out the means to the Jews destruction.

Begins SS Career

In 1935, not yet 22 years old, Barbie joined the SS, the abbreviation for *Shutzstaffeln* or Security Squad. The unit was orginally formed to act as bodyguards for Hitler. In a book about Barbie, a German newspaperman was quoted by author Ladislas de Hoyos: "All the SS men have this in common: cold eyes like those of fish, reflecting a complete absence of inner life, a complete lack of sentiments." Barbie became a dedicated follower of Hitler. He was an ambitious man whose ultimate goal was the SD, which stands for *Sicherdienst* or Security Police. The SD served as the intelligence (spy) service of the SS. Barbie began a slow but steady rise through the SS ranks. He attended a spy school set up by the Nazis and became an enthusiastic persecutor of Jews in Berlin, Germany's capital city.

Sometime in the late 1930s, Barbie became engaged to Regine Willms, a loyal Nazi Party member who was employed in a Nazi Women's Association nursery school. She was an accomplished cook who liked painting and music. The couple had to pass complicated medical tests devised by SS Chief Heinrich Himmler (see entry) to make sure they were "racially pure," meaning they had no Jewish blood. After a thorough investigation of his background, Barbie passed the tests; it was noted he had been born the "perfect SS baby." In April 1940, Regine promised to attend the Nazi School for Mothers, in which should would learn to raise children obdient to the Nazis. That month, the couple was finally allowed to marry, eight months after World War II began.

Barbie Goes to War

Almost immediately after his wedding ceremony, Barbie was called to active military duty and sent to Amsterdam, Holland. There his primary task was to round up and torment Jews and to keep an eye on Jewish and Christian groups to make sure there was no resistance to Nazi Party policies. Witnesses in Amsterdam later remembered Barbie for his coldness and cruelty. He soon fell out of favor with his supervisor, who complained of Barbie's overfondness for wine and women. He was sent to fight in the Soviet Union (now Russia) and then transferred to France in mid-1942. It was in France that his brutality reached its peak.

Because of his training in espionage (spying), Barbie was given the assignment of hunting down leaders of the French resistance, who were French patriots acting secretly to weaken Germany's army in France. Barbie was especially interested in Jean Moulin, who was known to be the right-

Charles de Gaulle, Resistance Leader

Charles de Gaulle (1890–1970) (pronounced duh Gawl) was one of the most famous French leaders of the twentieth century. Among his many accomplishments was his role as head of the Free French Resistance during World War II (1939–45). Resistance groups struggled to free their country from occupying Nazi troops.

De Gaulle had a history of military activities dating back to his graduation at the head of his 1911 class at France's premier military school. He was made a general when Germany invaded France in 1940. When France surrendered to Germany in June of that year, de Gaulle refused to accept the surrender and fled to London, England. There he led a group of Free French forces and eventually was accepted by the Allies (the United States, Great Britain, and the Soviet Union) as the leader of the "Fighting French." He also delivered radio addresses in which he kept alive the spirit of his countrymen, proclaiming that "France has lost a battle, but she has not lost the war."

When the Allies entered Paris–France's capital—in triumph in August 1944, de Gaulle marched with them.

De Gaulle served briefly as president of France after the Nazis were driven out. He was called back once again in the 1950s to serve as president, a position he held until 1969. He died in 1970.

It was de Gaulle who convinced the French Parliament to adopt the concept of bringing a person to trial charged with "crimes against humanity." Crimes against humanity include murder, extermination (complete destruction of a group of people), enslavement, deportation (forcibly removing people from their country), and other pitiless acts committed against the nonmilitary population of a country. Previously such acts committed during wartime had not been recognized as crimes. Because of de Gaulle's work, France was finally able to try, convict, and imprison Klaus Barbie for his crimes against humanity.

hand man of French resistance leader Charles de Gaulle (see box). Because French resistance efforts centered around the city of Lyon, Barbie went there to capture Moulin.

Barbie in Lyon

While ordinary citizens in Lyon were living on rationed food, SS officers lived like kings. Barbie and other Nazis took over a large hotel and began their activities of arresting, interrogating, beating, and torturing suspected resistance leaders and Jews. Finally, so many people had been placed under arrest that the SS had to move into larger quarters, where an underground network of cellars and thick-walled rooms muffled the screams of SS victims. When Barbie could not convince his prisoners to talk, he kidnapped their family members and threatened to kill them. He was said to be especially fond of kicking and hitting his victims. Sometimes, he let his dogs attack them.

Magnus Linklater and his coauthors offered this portrait of Barbie: "[He] considered himself a civilized German: he played the piano, though badly, and enjoyed long...discussions about German history and the consequences of the war. He prided himself on his knowledge of France and the French language, and he felt at home in the city of Lyon. He particularly enjoyed his daily walks...with his Alsatian, Wolf.... Without [his wife], who was for most of the war in [the German city of] Trier, he behaved much like any other unattached officer, eating out in expensive restaurants, getting drunk, and frequenting the nightclubs..."

In February 1943, under Barbie's command, a raid was carried out against the offices of a local Jewish organization. Eighty-four people were seized and sent to a concentration camp, where the Nazis confined people they regarded as "enemies of the state." Only two of the eighty-four survived. One of the most hideous crimes Barbie was said to have committed occurred in April 1944; Barbie was later to deny responsibility for the act. It involved a raid carried out on a Jewish children's home in the town of Izeu, in which forty-three children aged three to fourteen years and ten Jewish workers were rounded up and sent to concentration camps. All of the children and nine of the ten workers died in the camps.

Captures Famed Resistance Leader

Barbie clinched his reputation as "The Butcher of Lyon" with his torture and murder of Jean Moulin, who was the highest-ranking member of the French Resistance ever captured by the Nazis. Moulin was known throughout France as a hero for his bravery in defying the Germans. Barbie, who admired Moulin's courage, considered his capture to be a great personal challenge. In 1943, with the assistance of some French men who betrayed their own leader, Barbie captured Moulin and personally conducted the interview with him.

Despite beatings and torture, Moulin refused to reveal the names of his comrades. Barbie had hoped that his handling of Moulin would ensure a promotion, but he went too far in his "interrogation." On the way to Berlin for further questioning, Moulin died. Barbie later claimed Moulin had killed himself by hurling himself "with incredible violence, head first, against the wall."

In spite of his superiors' disapproval over Moulin's death, Barbie received a medal and was recommended for promotion for his "cleaning out of numerous enemy organizations." But Barbie, himself, was unhappy with his handling of the Moulin affair, and he became moody and unpredictable. He often flew into rages, and his conduct toward prisoners was unspeakably brutal. He began going out into the countryside on surprise raids, rounding up prisoners for questioning. On their way to carry out such a raid in August 1944, Barbie and his men were ambushed, and he suffered several gunshot wounds. He was taken back to Germany and hospitalized.

Barbie just missed the liberation of Paris, France from the Germans that took place on August 25, 1944. Allied soldiers entered the French capital in a victory that was celebrated around the world. (The Allies were the United States, Great Britain, the Soviet Union, and France.) While Barbie was recovering in the hospital, Germany suffered several more defeats in battle and finally surrendered in May 1945. The war in Europe was over. Barbie was released from the hospital shortly after the surrender, and he was soon rounded up by victorious U.S. troops. In the chaos that surrounded the end of the war, however, Barbie convinced the Americans that he was a French "displaced person." He was given a bicycle and pedaled away.

Postwar Activities

Although there was a warrant out for his arrest, Barbie was able to hide himself from the Allies until 1947. By then, the Allies had found a new enemy—the Soviet Union (now Russia) and its economic and social system called communism. Communism aimed for a classless society and was considered a graver threat to world peace than the now-defeated Germans.

Maurice Papon

In what will probably be one of the last trials for World War II war crimes, former French Cabinet minister Maurice Papon was found guilty of crimes against humanity in April 1998. A former official of the pro-Nazi regime in Vichy, France, he was sentenced to ten years in prison for ordering the deportation of 1,560 Jews, including 223 children, between 1942 and 1944.

In an emotional speech before his conviction, the 87-year-old Papon told the court that he was innocent of all charges. He claimed that he was just relaying orders from his superior, and that he had no idea of Adolf Hitler's plan to eliminate all the Jews of Europe. Prosecutors had insisted that instead of just following orders, Papon could have resigned. In response, Papon noted that "staying in one's post sometimes takes more courage than resigning."

After the verdict was handed down, Papon's lawyer stated that he will file an appeal. It is likely that Papon will never serve any time in prison since he would not actually go to jail until all his appeals are exhausted, and that could take years.

The Allies decided they were willing to overlook the crimes of former Nazi leaders to take advantage of their knowledge and skills against the new threat of the Soviet Union. Barbie, still in Germany, was hired as a spy for the United States. Soon he had recruited many of his former Nazi comrades and was running a vast spy ring on the U.S. payroll.

In 1949, Barbie's continued presence in Europe became known to the French, who demanded that he be turned over to them for trial for war crimes (violation of the laws and customs of war). The United States, wishing to conceal the extent of Barbie's secret work for them, arranged for Barbie to escape to South America. He was given false identity papers under the name of Klaus Altmann, which he chose himself. He had known a man by the name of Altmann in the city of Trier, a Jew who later died in the gas chamber at Auschwitz. (A gas chamber is a sealed room that was filled with poisonous gas in order to kill the people locked inside.) In March 1951, the

"Altmann family"—Klaus, Regine, their daughter Ute Marie, age nine, and their son Jorge, age four—set sail on an Italian ship for Buenos Aires, Argentina. From Argentina the family soon moved to Bolivia, where Barbie supported himself as an auto mechanic, having been given a quick training course by the American Counter Intelligence Corps (CIC).

Barbie in South America

But Barbie had too many other "talents" to be satisfied working as a mechanic. South America was a continent at war, and Barbie knew well the ins and outs of war. It was not long before he was involved in theft, fraud, forgery, drug running, arms selling, spying, and politics. He was able to live in luxury once again. He was befriended by Bolivia's president and carried out spy work for him. Barbie also obliged his new friend by training his soldiers in the art of torturing prisoners. All the while he was living openly, dining out in restaurants, and hobnobbing with fellow German exiles.

Finally, in 1971, someone grew suspicious of this German who held Bolivian citizenship and got in touch with the Nazi-hunter Simon Wiesenthal (see entry). But it was Nazi-hunter Beate Klarsfeld (see entry) who actually made the case by identifying "Klaus Altmann" as the notorious "Butcher of Lyon." It was to be twelve years before Barbie was finally brought to justice. In 1983, with a new government in place in Bolivia, Barbie was expelled and sent to France. He was 69 years old and in poor health. He kept insisting that what he had done was "my duty."

Back in France

Barbie's return to France for trial caused a sensation. The French were still trying to come to terms with the fact that the Nazis had been aided by thousands of French men and women who were collaborators—people who had turned their own friends, families, and neighbors over to Nazis.

The ailing Barbie sat in jail for four years before his case finally came to trial. Showing no signs of remorse, Barbie claimed to have no knowledge of what had happened to the Jews he had rounded up and deported (forcibly removing people from a city or country). Witnesses testified that he most certainly did know. A telegram he had sent announcing the murder of the children of Izeu was also used as evidence against him.

Finally, on July 4, 1987, Klaus Barbie was found guilty of crimes against humanity and was sentenced to life imprisonment. In 1990, he sought to be released from prison because he had cancer of the blood; his request was refused. He died in prison in 1991. While his victims saw his trial and imprisonment as simple justice, others have asked whether any point was served in bringing this old, sick man—who said he was only following orders—back to France to stand trial.

Where to Learn More

Chevrillon, Claire. *Code Name Christiane Clouet: A Woman in the French Resistance*. Translated by Jane Kielty Stott. Texas A & M University, 1995.

Dabringhaus, Erhard. *Klaus Barbie: The Shocking Story of How the U.S. Used This Nazi War Criminal as an Intelligence Agent*. Acropolis Books, 1984.

De Hoyos, Ladislas. *Klaus Barbie: The Untold Story.* Translated from the French by Nicholas Courtin. McGraw-Hill, 1984.

Dowell, William. "A Verdict on the Butcher: After a Final Scuffle with History, Barbie Is Convicted." *Time* 130 (July 13, 1987): p. 40.

Linklater, Magnus, Isabel Hilton, and Neal Ascherson, et al. *The Nazi Legacy: Klaus Barbie and the International Fascist Connection.* Holt, Rinehart and Winston, 1984.

Murphy, Brendan. *The Butcher of Lyon: The Story of Infamous Nazi Klaus Barbie.* Empire Books, 1983.

Folke Bernadotte

Born January 2, 1895
Stockholm, Sweden

Died September 17, 1948
Jerusalem, Israel

Member of Swedish royal family, diplomat

Negotiated the exchange or release of an estimated 30,000 prisoners during World War II (1939–45)

Between five and six million Jews were murdered during the Holocaust (1933–45) by members of the National Socialist German Workers' Party (Nazi for short). They were killed because the Nazis hoped to establish a pure German "master race." One of the most unlikely and unsung heroes of the Holocaust was Count Folke Bernadotte. His early life gave little indication of the dedication and courage he would later display. As a member of the Swedish royal family and the husband of a woman who was heir to millions of dollars, Bernadotte could have devoted himself to trivial pursuits. Instead, he worked on behalf of war victims and developed a liking for helping others that carried on after the war was over. Unfortunately, his postwar work led to his assassination.

"The object is to save human life and to try to [lessen] human suffering and any means to this end is legitimate."

A Modest Upbringing for Royalty

Folke Bernadotte was born in 1895 in Stockholm, Sweden, one of five children of Prince Oscar and Ebba (Munck) Bernadotte. His father was the son of King Oscar and Queen Sophia and gave up his claim to the throne to marry the woman he loved, a commoner. The event caused a worldwide sensation.

Bernadotte's father was a simple, good, and religious man who avoided the trappings of palace life and worked to help Sweden's poor people. About his childhood Bernadotte wrote: "My upbringing was strict. I remember that my father often said a child should learn to obey before it reached two years of age. My parents very much insisted on honesty, obedience and punctuality. Already when we were small our thoughts were directed towards trying to help others."

Ralph Hewins, a longtime friend and Bernadotte's biographer, wrote that life in the Bernadotte household was so dull that "the Bernadotte children's friends rather dreaded an invitation" to their home. A lot of time was devoted to attending church services, gathering for family prayers, and studying. Despite the hours spent on his studies, however, Bernadotte was described as a boy "of limited cleverness," not especially bright but enthusiastic and willing, handsome, and unselfish.

His parents took him to England for the summer when he was nine years old. While there he quickly learned English, a skill that proved valuable in his future career (later he mastered German and French). In the fall after his return from England, Bernadotte was sent to a school where he attended classes with members of Sweden's upper middle class. He excelled at athletics and was popular with the other students and his teachers. He also enjoyed history and religion classes. Once, when asked his ambition, he declared: "I shall be a Papa." Overall he was an "ordinary small boy" who did not display any particular qualities that one might expect in a future world figure. When he graduated at age eighteen, wrote Hewins, he was "an outdoors boy and not at all 'bookish.'" He was somewhat shy and reserved.

Seeks His Destiny

After graduation, Bernadotte was not quite sure what to do with himself. In fact, he was to be well into adulthood before his career came together in a way that would prove satisfying to him. He entered the Royal Swedish Military Academy, where he performed well and graduated tenth in his class in 1915. He became an accomplished horseman, too, but he had problems seeing himself as a professional soldier. He suffered from hemophilia, a rare blood disorder that sometimes caused spontaneous bleeding and would most likely have resulted in death if he had received even a minor wound in battle. He also had a problem giving orders, which he would naturally be required to do as an officer. According to Hewins: "His main trouble was a tendency to see every order from the men's as well as the officers' side."

At age 33, he was still a military officer and vacationing in France when he met his bride-to-be, the American heiress Estelle Manville, in 1928. Estelle's father, Hiram Manville, had made millions in the manufacture of asbestos products. Although Estelle's mother was delighted that her daughter wished to marry a man with a royal title, her father wished to know more about him. Hiram Manville was dismayed to find that "his daughter's beloved had spent his entire adult life in the Swedish Royal Life Guards Dragoons, riding horses and preparing for battles everyone knew would never occur [because Sweden had a longstanding policy of remaining uninvolved in European conflicts]. Despite a history that implied great honor, the Royal Life Guards Dragoons was by Bernadotte's time essentially a gentleman's club . . . a way to claim a career without ever doing meaningful work," wrote Ted Swarz.

After a lavish wedding that cost $250,000, a fortune in 1928, Hiram Manville arranged for his new son-in-law to work for six months as a clerk in a New York bank. Since Bernadotte would one day inherit the Manville millions, Hiram Manville wanted him to learn money management. As was characteristic of him, Bernadotte willingly and enthusiastically accepted the job, but he simply could not master it. The Bernadottes, who by then were expecting their first child, decided to move to Sweden.

Becomes Boy Scout Leader and Diplomat

Between 1929 and 1936, the Bernadottes had four sons. Both parents were devoted to their family and were devastated by the tragic and unexpected deaths of two of the young boys. Bernadotte resigned from the Swedish Army and began to devote time to the Swedish Boy Scouts. In 1939, he was proud to be made head of the Swedish Scout Union of the Boy Scout Association. With his military training and his jolly personality, Bernadotte shone in his role as Boy Scout leader.

In 1933, Bernadotte was asked to travel to Chicago, Illinois, to represent Sweden at a huge festival being organized by Americans of Swedish ancestry living there. While in the United States, Bernadotte also visited several cities with large Swedish populations. His tour was a great success, and the newspapers were full of stories about his charming personality. Over the next several years, he tried several business ventures and failed, but when asked to perform roles requiring diplomacy, he showed exceptional skill. Meanwhile, Europe was gearing up for war, but Bernadotte was largely unaware of it.

War in Europe

Nazi leader Adolf Hitler (see entry) had assumed power in Germany in 1933. Hitler's plan for Germany was to create a "master race" of pure Germans, who would rule for a thousand years. There would be no place for Jews in this German Empire. Hitler began a campaign of persecution against the Jews in Germany. He also began to build up the German army in preparation for taking over Europe and making it part of his empire. In 1939, he signed an agreement with the Soviet Union (now Russia), in which the two countries agreed to divide eastern Europe between themselves. Soon after the Soviet-German nonaggression pact was signed, Hitler attacked Poland, and World War II began.

In 1939, Bernadotte was once again in the United States, this time working on the Swedish Exhibit at the New York World's Fair, when the Soviet Union, long his country's enemy, launched a surprise attack against neighboring Finland. Bernadotte was torn. He felt that "it was my duty as a soldier to be home in Sweden in case my country should become drawn into war"; on the other hand, he still had the Swedish Exhibit to run. That matter was decided for him by a telegram from Swedish leaders asking him to remain in the United States to enlist a group of Scandinavian-American volunteers to help Finland. Scandinavia is the name given to

Norway, Sweden, and Denmark; the name is sometimes applied to Iceland and Finland as well.

The U.S. government was not willing to permit Bernadotte to train an army to serve in another country. In any case, before his plans had gotten very far, Finland had made peace with the Soviet Union, but Germany had swept into Norway and Denmark. Sweden was now almost entirely surrounded by Germans. Sweden hoped to remain uninvolved in the conflict but was at first inclined to offer some assistance to its longtime friend Germany. As the war dragged on, and news spread of German mistreatment of both Scandinavian prisoners and Jews, Sweden's attitude changed. Stories circulated of prisoners and Jews confined in concentration camps, where they were forced to labor long hours under crowded, unsanitary conditions, with little food.

Bernadotte's War Work

Bernadotte's life and career entered a new and grander phase after the war began. He was placed in charge of a group that cared for airplane pilots and other military personnel seeking refuge in neutral (uninvolved) Sweden—regardless of what side they were fighting on. He arranged for medical treatment, food and clothing, and even for entertainment. According to Hewins, between 1940 and 1945, Bernadotte's organization showed forty thousand movies to six million military moviegoers and arranged for theatrical performances for two million servicemen and women. He proved to be such an organizational genius that his wartime responsibilities increased.

In 1943, Bernadotte was named vice-chairman of the Swedish Red Cross (in 1946 he became president). By then the extent of German brutality—and its ambition to control Europe—were becoming widely known. If Sweden were to be overtaken by the Germans, Red Cross assistance would be vital. Bernadotte also saw a role for the Red Cross assisting war victims in neighboring countries.

One of Bernadotte's first accomplishments as a representative of the Red Cross was to oversee the first successful exchange of prisoners between Germany and Great Britain. After as many as four years' imprisonment by the Germans, more than five thousand British invalids and others landed

The Red Cross and the Holocaust

The Red Cross is an international organization that works to relieve human suffering. Its name comes from its flag (a red cross on a white background), which is patterned after the flag of Switzerland, where the Red Cross was founded in 1863.

Red Cross volunteers and staff members in each of the more than 135 countries that have branches carry out tasks according to the country's needs. The Red Cross has been instrumental in preventing untold misery to people all over the world in times of war and peace. During World War II (1939–45), members of the International Committee of the Red Cross, including Count Folke Bernadotte, worked as go-betweens for the protection of prisoners and victims of war. In spite of Bernadotte's activities, however, the International Committee finally came to believe that it had not done enough to help during the Holocaust when approximately six million Jews were killed by the Nazis.

In 1997, the International Committee of the Red Cross admitted "moral failure" in keeping silent. A spokesman for the committee, which is based in Geneva, Switzerland, indicated that the organization could and should have done more.

The Red Cross had an opportunity to save Jewish lives as early as 1940. The opportunity was missed when the International Committee concluded (on the basis of a German report) that tales of the mass murder of Polish-Jewish prisoners of war were unfounded. The Red Cross was also responsible for providing travel papers to Nazi criminals such as Josef Mengele, who was responsible for hundreds of thousands of deaths at the Auschwitz concentration camp. Mengele escaped to South America after the war.

on Britain's shores in an emotional homecoming witnessed by thousands. "I never had a task which interested me more than this," wrote Bernadotte.

In 1945, with Germany under constant siege by Allied bombers, Bernadotte went to Berlin, Germany's capital. (The Allies were the United States, Great Britain, the Soviet Union, and France.) He persuaded the Nazi official Heinrich Himmler (see entry) to release more than 7,000 Scandinavians being held in concentration camps. Among them were more than 400 Danish Jews. Shortly afterwards, Bernadotte arranged for the release of 10,000 women, including 2,000 Jewish women, being held in the Ravensbrück concentration camp. They were taken to Sweden. At Bernadotte's request their rescue was given no publicity so as not to endanger other rescue efforts by bringing them to Hitler's attention.

According to biographer Hewins: "Bernadotte and the Swedish Red Cross [never got] deserved credit for the magnitude of their achievement at Ravensbrück. One only had to stare at the . . . living corpses as they were carried on to the Swedish hospital trains to realize the hell on earth from which Bernadotte . . . had saved them at the last flickering moment between life and death."

Bernadotte has been credited with helping to save approximately 32,200 concentration camp victims and prisoners of war, at risk to his own life. Hewins wrote: "Among the saved were people from 30 different nations—including one Chinese—and blessed was the name of Bernadotte the whole world round."

A Death in Jerusalem

Having earned a worldwide reputation, Bernadotte continued his efforts on behalf of peace after the war. In 1948, the United Nations, newly formed to help resolve interna-

Bernadotte negotiating with Heinrich Himmler on behalf of the Swedish Red Cross.

tional disputes, chose Bernadotte to go to the then-new Jewish nation of Israel and help mediate a dispute there. The dispute was between Israel and the neighboring Arab countries. While traveling in a car flying the United Nations flag in Israel, Bernadotte was assassinated by members of a Jewish terrorist organization. He was 53 years old. Bernadotte's assassins were never brought to justice, so their motives cannot be known for sure. They may have believed that the compromises Bernadotte was urging Israel to accept were unfair. The issues between Israel and its neighbors had still not been resolved as the twentieth century drew to a close.

Bernadotte's body was returned to Stockholm, Sweden. At the funeral his casket was carried by 48 Boy Scouts; the procession included 2,500 more Boy Scouts. Floral tributes came from around the world and included those from people he had rescued from the concentration camps. A hero in his own time, Bernadotte's contributions had largely been forgotten by the 1990s.

Where to Learn More

Hewins, Ralph. *Count Folke Bernadotte: His Life and Work.* T.S. Denison and Company, 1950.

Marton, Kati. *A Death in Jerusalem.* Pantheon Books, 1994.

Swarz, Ted. *Walking with the Damned: The Shocking Murder of the Man Who Freed 30,000 Prisoners from the Nazis.* Paragon House, 1992.

Bruno Bettelheim

Born August 28, 1903
Vienna, Austria

Died March 13, 1990
Silver Spring, Maryland

World-renowned psychotherapist, author, concentration camp survivor

Headed the Orthogenic School in Chicago, Illinois

Bruno Bettelheim was a clever, insightful man who survived nearly a year in the Nazi concentration camps. Concentration camps were places where members of the National Socialist German Workers' Party, or Nazis, confined people they regarded as "enemies of the state." Relocating to the United States, Bettelheim became a world-famous authority on the treatment of emotionally disturbed children. His death provoked a storm of controversy about his beliefs and practices that makes it difficult to untangle the truth about the man and his teachings.

Childhood in Vienna

Bruno Bettelheim was brought up in a non-religious Jewish family in Vienna, Austria, at the beginning of the century. His father, Anton Bettelheim, the son of a wealthy family, was a lumber merchant. He married Bruno's mother, Pauline Seidler, in an arranged marriage. Bruno Bettelheim's sister, Margarethe, was four years older, and the two shared a longstanding rivalry. Although he was sometimes taken care of by nannies and maids, young Bettelheim also spent a lot of time with his mother, who enjoyed telling him fairy tales. Bettelheim's parents were kind and gentle with him, and he often spoke of his appreciation for having the emotional support of a family.

Bettelheim was a short, slight, sensitive boy who liked to daydream. As a child, he suffered from a number of illnesses, including measles, mumps, scarlet fever, diphtheria, and intestinal disorders. He was a good student but clumsy at sports, in part because the lenses of his glasses were improperly made. When Bettelheim was only four, his father was diagnosed with an incurable disease. His father suffered a stroke when Bettelheim was thirteen. This made life more difficult both for Bettelheim and for his family.

Perhaps in part because of the stress of his father's illnesses on the family, Bettelheim himself suffered from depression. This is a disease which causes a person to feel unhappy and pessimistic about life. The condition was to plague him on and off for the rest of his life.

Bettelheim entered high school in 1914. Along with friends, he joined a group that spent much of its time hiking and picnicking in nearby forests, and discussing what the future would be like. He graduated near the top of his class and decided that in college he wanted to study philosophy—that is, the study of the laws and causes that underlie reality.

Forced to Leave College

During his first years at Vienna University, Bettelheim became interested in psychoanalysis, a system of examining a person's emotional states that was devised by a doctor named Sigmund Freud. Bettelheim also studied Latin, German literature, music, philosophy, and dramatic readings. At the same time, he enrolled in an international trade school to learn accounting and business management. His grades at both schools were excellent.

In 1926, Bettelheim's father, Anton, experienced a slow, painful death. For the last two years of his life, it was primarily 23-year-old Bruno and his mother who took care of Anton.

"Being one of the very few who were saved when millions like oneself perished [entails] a special obligation to justify one's luck and very existence."

Upon his father's death, Bettelheim was forced to stop his studies at the university and take over the family lumber business.

First Marriage

During that period Bettelheim fell in love with an attractive young woman named Gina Alstadt. Like Bettelheim, Alstadt suffered from depression. In the Vienna of the 1920s, many young people were optimistic about a future that they believed would see the development of a society built upon the equality of individuals. Although many of his friends felt this way, Bettelheim experienced a dread of what lay ahead for the world.

Bettelheim married Alstadt on March 30, 1930, and they moved into a beautiful apartment in Vienna that they decorated with contemporary art. Although they shared similar interests, the couple never seemed to get along very well.

Child Lives with Couple

Bettelheim's lumber business prospered, and he expanded it to include furniture manufacturing. In the late 1920s, Gina Bettelheim and a friend opened a kindergarten to serve the children of the many Americans who had come to Vienna to study psychoanalysis. Around 1932, they opened a summer camp for children with behavioral problems. Eventually, a little girl named Patsy Crane, one of the children who was being treated there, moved in with Gina and Bruno Bettelheim. Her mother, Agnes, believed the couple could help Patsy with her emotional problems. Agnes seemed to have no knowledge of the strain that was then occurring in the Bettelheim marriage.

In 1936, Bruno Bettelheim met a young Swiss woman named Trude Weinfeld, who listened carefully to his ideas, even encouraging him to return to the university to earn a Ph.D. He grew increasingly fond of her. That same year, Gina Bettelheim met a successful young dentist and gradually fell in love with him.

During the 1930s, the Nazi Party was gradually building up its strength and numbers. By 1933, the Nazis, under the leadership of Adolf Hitler (see entry), had taken control of the German government. The Nazis referred to Jews as "parasites" and "degenerates" who poisoned German society. The aim of the Nazis was to build a new social order in the country, with no Jews. They wanted to prepare the German people to fight and prove themselves worthy of establishing a new German empire that would rule all of Europe.

Arrested By Nazis

In the spring of 1937, Bettelheim returned to Vienna University to study philosophy and psychology, while continuing his work as a lumber merchant. Bettelheim received his Ph.D. in February 1938. One month later, Hitler, facing no armed opposition, took over Austria. This event is known as the Anschluss. The Bettelheims feared for their safety from the anti-Jewish Nazis. Gina fled to the United States with little Patsy. Bettelheim decided to stay in Vienna because he felt he could not abandon his mother and his sister. Soon full-scale persecution of the Jews began. Jewish people were seized by the police and attacked, and their shops were looted. Bettelheim's car was confiscated by the Nazis. He then tried but was unable to obtain a visa (travel documents) to go to the United States.

In May 1938, Bettelheim was twice arrested and twice released by the Nazis. In June, along with thousands of other so-called "enemies of the state," he was arrested a third time and deported (forced to leave his country) to Dachau concentration camp in Germany. Concentration camps were places where the Nazis confined people they regarded as "enemies of the state." On the train ride there Jews were struck, punched, and kicked by the Nazis. Wounded on the head, Bettelheim was taken to a clinic by a sympathetic guard and allowed to stay for a week and recover.

Upon his release from the clinic, Bettelheim's hair was cut short, and he was placed in a crowded, wooden barrack. The inmates worked long hours digging gravel pits and building roads, while being verbally abused by the guards. Prisoners were mercilessly whipped and hung up on trees by their shoulders for small infractions of the rules. Dreadful though it was, conditions at Dachau were not as bad as at some of the other camps. Though the food was crude and bad tasting, it was enough to sustain a person's health. Occasionally, sporting matches and concerts were put on by the prisoners. They could also receive small amounts of money sent by loved ones outside the camp.

Bettelheim's Thoughts on Concentration Camps

Throughout his lifetime Bettelheim gave a great deal of time and thought to life in the concentration camps. Writer Nina Sutton explained the three stages in his thinking about this subject. First there was a positive stage, in which he strove to derive lessons from his experience. Next there was a stage in which he acknowledged the guilt he felt in being a survivor. He called this "the morally unacceptable feeling of happiness" that wells up when a person discovers that it is the next man who has drawn the unlucky number. Finally, there is a stage in which the silence of the rest of the world in the face of the Nazis' persecution of their victims led him to despair and to give up on life.

Back in Vienna, Bettelheim's company was closed down on July 7, 1938. It was reopened one week later with a new Nazi owner. Bettelheim received a vastly smaller sum in return for the firm than it was worth. Such takeovers of businesses took place all over Austria at the time. With the support of Agnes Crane (Patsy's mother), the U.S. government approved a visa application on Bettelheim's behalf, which was to be issued at once upon his release from Dachau.

Deportation to Buchenwald

In September 1938, Bettelheim and other prisoners were taken on a cramped train ride to the Buchenwald concentration camp. With filthy trenches for toilets, the camp was much worse than the one at Dachau, and even more violent. Bettelheim wrote that he was assigned a job indoors mending stockings, where he stayed relatively safe and warm. His version of his experiences at the camp cannot be verified, however, because he failed to name fellow prisoners in his writings, who could later be interviewed.

In fact, any attempt to write a complete and accurate biography about Bettelheim is very difficult. He sometimes embellished the truth. Some coworkers from his past have even referred to him as a liar. Most accounts support the notion that he liked to describe events in the form of stories, and often the stories were exaggerated in order to make them more interesting or to make him look better. This problem will be discussed further below.

Release and Relocation

In 1939, the contagious disease typhus had become a major problem in the concentration camps. Typhus is usually caused by unsanitary conditions like those in the camp. To decrease the incidence of typhus, Hitler reduced the number of prisoners at Buchenwald by ordering the release of some—including Bettelheim. He was warned that if he did not leave Germany within one week he would be rearrested. Bettelheim traveled to Antwerp, Belgium, where he boarded the S.S. *Gerolsein* for the United States.

Second Marriage

After arriving in the United States, Bettelheim moved to Chicago, Illinois, where he became a research assistant at the prestigious University of Chicago. After a short visit, both he and his wife concluded that their marriage was at an end. Within the year his mother, his sister, and Trude Weinfeld joined Bettelheim in the United States. In May 1941, Bettelheim was divorced from Gina and married Trude Weinfeld. Later, Gina also remarried.

The Beginning of Fame

Bettelheim got a teaching job at Rockford College, 90 miles from Chicago, to which he commuted for several years. Trude gave birth to his first child, Ruth, in 1942. They later had another daughter, Naomi, and a son, Eric. In 1943, Bettelheim wrote a famous article titled "Individual and Mass Behavior in Extreme Situations" that won him acclaim in academic circles. The article used his experiences in the concentration camps to examine how human beings adapt to stress.

Becomes Head of School

In 1944, Bettelheim became both assistant professor of psychology at the University of Chicago and head of its Sonia Shankman Orthogenic School. The latter was a residential treatment center for emotionally disturbed children ages six to fourteen. Bettelheim specialized in the treatment of autis-

Bettelheim giving a speech about emotionally disturbed children.

tic children. These are children who withdraw from everyday life and fail to respond normally to outside stimulation. Bettelheim once said that his dedication to the school resulted from his experience in the concentration camps, and his anger at the prospect that lives should be wasted "whether trapped behind metal or emotional barbed wire." He became an associate professor at the university in 1947 and was appointed a full professor in 1952.

The staff he headed at the Orthogenic School was said to idealize him and sometimes fear him. It was largely made up of young women who seemed to have blind trust in Bettelheim's authority and what they saw as his genius. Many have reported that Bettelheim was very understanding, while at the same time he could be cruel and bullying.

A Prolific Writer

Over his lifetime Bettelheim wrote nearly 20 books. Some of the best-known are *Love Is Not Enough, The Children of the Dream, The Uses of Enchantment, The Informed Heart,* and *A Good Enough Parent.* He became widely respected as one of the foremost authorities on the treatment of autistic children. Bettelheim believed that a major cause of a child's autism was having a "deficient" mother and that the best treatment was the removal of the child from the family. He wrote extensively about the relationship between social health and family life, as well as countless articles that were published in popular magazines.

Critics of Bettelheim

Bettelheim's ideas are opposed by people who point out that some mothers of autistic children have raised a number of perfectly normal ones, and by people who believe that autism may have a genetic component. Bettelheim got a reputation for sometimes treating the parents of his young patients in a disrespectful manner. It has been said that he viewed the parents as the source of the children's problems and himself as their defender.

Richard Pollak, whose younger brother spent years in treatment with Bettelheim, wrote a critical book about him in 1997 called *The Creation of Dr. B.* According to Pollak, Bettelheim's power to terrorize those under him and his talent for telling stories contributed to his international success. He contends that Bettelheim made false claims about his training in Vienna, which made him appear to be a legitimate expert in psychoanalysis, when in fact he was not.

According to critic Lev Raphael: "Bettelheim also falsified the success rate of patients at his Orthogenic School in Chicago . . . [where he treated] children . . . who weren't severely disturbed, while making exaggerated claims of their illness."

Christopher Lehmann-Haupt pointed out that "despite [Bettelheim's] insistence that hitting the children was strictly forbidden, he evidently smacked and punched his charges, sexually abused several of the girls, and relied in general on threats to intimidate his staff."

In Bettelheim's defense, writer Nina Sutton pointed out that in dealing with disturbed children, Bettelheim's aim was to "get them gradually to understand . . . that even the most miserable of lives . . . is valuable as soon as one succeeds in giving it meaning. This is what . . . being cured meant for him: finally to acknowledge the value of one's own life." And, said Sutton, "He saved my life" . . . is the statement that occurred most often in the testimonies of the former students and counselors she spoke to about Bettelheim.

Old Age and Death

Bettelheim retired from the Orthogenic School in the early 1970s. He continued writing books about his experiences at the school and taught occasional classes. He took several trips to Europe and to Israel. He and his wife moved to California in 1973. His connection to the Orthogenic School was cut off when he had a disagreement with the new director in the early 1980s. In May 1986, the University of Chicago held a conference honoring him and his work; Bettelheim was invited and attended. Bettelheim became seriously depressed after the death of his wife from cancer in 1984 and because of his own ailments. He committed suicide in 1990 at a home he had moved to in Silver Spring, Maryland. Years after his death, the controversy about the man and his methods still continues.

Where to Learn More

Bandler, Michael J. "The Good Enough Parent's Parent." *Parents' Magazine,* 62 (November 1987): p. 189.

Bettelheim, Bruno. "Individual and Mass Behavior in Extreme Situations." *Journal of Abnormal and Social Psychology,* 38 (October 1943): pp. 417-52.

Bettelheim, Bruno. *The Informed Heart: Autonomy in a Mass Age.* Free Press, 1960.

Bettelheim, Bruno. *Love Is Not Enough: The Treatment of Emotionally Disturbed Children.* Free Press, 1950.

Feig, Konnilyn G. *Hitler's Death Camps: The Sanity of Madness.* Holmes & Meier, 1979.

Pollak, Richard. *The Creation of Dr. B: A Biography of Bruno Bettelheim.* Simon and Schuster, 1996.

Sutton, Nina. *Bettelheim: A Life and a Legacy.* Basic Books, 1996.

Dietrich Bonhoeffer

Born February 4, 1906
Breslau, Germany

Died April 9, 1945
Flossenburg concentration camp

German Protestant minister and writer

*Imprisoned and executed by the Nazis for an
assassination plot against Hitler*

Dietrich Bonhoeffer became famous after his death as a powerful religious leader who courageously acted according to his conscience. Once he realized the evil of the system of government headed by Adolf Hitler (see entry) and his National Socialist German Workers' Party (Nazi for short), Bonhoeffer dedicated himself to the struggle to overthrow the Nazi government. Throughout World War II (1939–45), he engaged in several unsuccessful attempts to assassinate Hitler.

Childhood and Youth

Dietrich Bonhoeffer (pronounced Deetrick Bon-hoffer) was the son of a prominent German family that can be traced back to the fifteenth century. His father was a respected professor, and his mother was a homemaker who influenced her children to become virtuous and idealistic. Dietrich Bonhoeffer and his

"In the long run, human relationships are the most important thing in life."

twin sister, Sabine, born in 1906, were the sixth and seventh of eight children. The family lived in a spacious and comfortable house in Breslau, Germany, with two servants and a nanny for the children. Summers were spent at a house in the Harz Mountains where the children played among the hills and forests.

When Bonhoeffer was six years old, his family moved to Berlin, Germany, and his father began teaching at Berlin University. Bonhoeffer began to attend school at age seven, and by the age of ten he had begun to read great German literature. In his teens, he played music with friends, organized parties, and wrote plays. He considered becoming a professional musician but thought the late-night schedule of travel and performing did not suit him. His brother Walter was killed in 1918 during World War I (1914–18). This incident made Bonhoeffer think a great deal about the meaning of death, and he and his sister had long talks about it.

At age 14, Bonhoeffer began to consider becoming a Protestant minister. His sister Sabine wrote about his "open and considerate nature." She said that Bonhoeffer had "the gift of perfect assurance of manners; he listened attentively and attached great value to dealing politely with other people and keeping a certain distance . . . from respect of the other's personality on which he did not want to [intrude]."

Studies for the Ministry

Bonhoeffer's family experienced food shortages, as did many Germans after World War I. By 1923, inflation (a sharp and continuing increase in the general price of goods and services, caused by an increase in the amount of money in circulation) had become so serious that people had to carry bags full of paper money to purchase a loaf of bread. That year, Bonhoeffer began his religious studies at the University of Tubingen. Bonhoeffer was then a powerful-looking young man, over six feet tall, with blond hair and intense blue eyes.

Writer Mary Bosanquet pointed out that Bonhoeffer had great energy, a quick mind, and robust health. He was also a very sensitive person. It was then the German custom for a student to attend more than one university to gain experience. An excellent student, Bonhoeffer attended several. He completed his studies and earned the equivalent of a doctoral degree from the Berlin University in 1927 at age 21. He studied German liberal theology, and later became attracted to the teachings of a famous German religious scholar named Karl Barth. Bonhoeffer spent 1928 serving a small congregation in Barcelona, Spain. In 1930, he traveled to the United States where he studied at the Union Theological Seminary in New York as an exchange student.

Ordination and Early Career

Bonhoeffer was appointed a lecturer at the University of Berlin and was made chaplain (a clergyman who conducts religious services) at the Technical College in Berlin in 1930. At the university, his income depended entirely upon his ability to attract students to voluntarily attend his classes. He was ordained a minister in November 1931.

According to Mary Bosanquet: "A remarkable feature of Bonhoeffer's life at every stage was the amount that he contrived to pack into his days. . . . He contrived to live the broad and rich life which humanists admire with what was little more than the overflow from his deeper spiritual energies."

Rise of Nazism

Ever since Germany's defeat in World War I, unemployment in the country was very high and the economy was in turmoil. The streets were filled with the angry, hungry, and poor, and bloody street battles were an everyday occurrence. The citizens of Germany were looking for some way out of their predicament.

Dozens of new political parties arose at that time, all promising solutions to the Germany's many problems. One such group became the Nazi Party. Its leader, Adolf Hitler, was a hypnotic speaker. He talked of returning Germany to economic stability. He also blamed the Jews for the loss of the World War I, and demanded that Germany be allowed to return to a position of strength in the world. He preached the superiority of the Aryan (white, non-Jewish) race, a message the "Aryan" Germans were eager to hear.

When a punishing, worldwide depression (economic downturn) began in the late 1920s, Hitler took advantage of the desperation felt by many people. He used brilliant tactics and his outstanding speaking skills to convince people to get behind the Nazi Party.

Hitler became dictator (ruled with absolute authority) of Germany after the 1933 election. His grand scheme for building a mighty German Empire required that he take control over every aspect of people's lives. One way he planned to accomplish this was to use the German Protestant Church. He wanted to enlist people in his cause in such a way that they would believe the church was behind him. So began the so-called "Faith Movement" in Germany.

Bonhoeffer Rejects Nazism

Bonhoeffer was very concerned about the growth of Hitler's "Faith Movement." It held that every nation should develop its own form of the Christian faith, rooted in the "soil of the country and the blood of its people." Leaders of the pro-Nazi faith movement in Germany believed that God wanted the German people to unite under a powerful leader (Hitler), to devote their energies for the common good of the nation, and to keep the Aryan race free from so-called "tainted alien" (Jewish and other "undesirable") blood.

Bonhoeffer became an opponent of these teachings. He denounced the theory that membership in a church can ever be based on race. In a sermon rejecting these ideas, Bonhoeffer said, "God shall rule over you, and you shall have no other Lord."

As a result of his opposition to these policies, Bonhoeffer was sent to London, England, from 1933 through 1935, where he served as a chaplain. He later returned to Germany, where he became a member of the anti-Nazi Confessing Church. He then went to a part of Germany called Pomerania to lead a new seminary, a religious school for like-minded young men.

Bonhoeffer's seminary was suppressed by the Nazis in 1937. They objected to the seminary's refusal to support their policies of violence and racial oppression. In fact, the Nazis rejected every aspect of traditional Christianity, partly because it interfered with the German people giving complete allegiance to Hitler, whom the Nazis treated as practically god-like. Bonhoeffer went on teaching anyway. However, he lost the right to teach at a university, the right to speak in public, and the right to publish his opinions.

Recruitment for Espionage

German admiral Wilhelm Canaris, leader of the Nazis' intelligence (spy) service, was secretly opposed to Hitler's policies and plotted with other people to oust him from power. The admiral requested that Bonhoeffer visit churchmen he knew in other countries. Although the official purpose was for Bonhoeffer to gather information for the Nazis, in fact Canaris wanted him to have secret conversations with these people to enlist their help in overthrowing Hitler and the Nazis. Bonhoeffer made trips to Sweden and Switzerland to try to accomplish these aims. In 1942, he brought plans to the British bishop George Bell, known as the patron of the oppressed Christians and Jews in Germany. The plans concerned possible terms of peace that would be enacted if the Germans who were plotting to overthrow the Nazis were successful.

Bonhoeffer was once asked by a fellow prisoner how, as a Christian and religious scholar, his conscience could permit

Bonhoeffer (fourth from the left) and the leaders of the Confessing Church.

him to take part in the resistance against Hitler. Bonhoeffer replied that if he, as a minister, witnessed a drunk driver speeding down the highway, he did not consider his main responsibility that of burying the victims of the drunken driver or comforting the family; rather, his chief duty was to wrench the steering wheel out of the hands of the driver.

Arrest and Imprisonment

Bonhoeffer was arrested and sent to prison to await trial in 1943. His arrest warrant charged him with "destruction of fighting power." In addition to a history of preaching against the Nazis' antisemitic (anti-Jewish) policies, he was jailed for his role in assisting Jews to escape from Germany. Various members of his family were also involved in these efforts. They too were put in jail and eventually executed.

Shortly before being sent to jail, Bonhoeffer became engaged to Maria von Wedemeyer. His fiancée's mother publicly announced their engagement on the day of his arrest. Bonhoeffer and von Wedemeyer communicated by letter and occasionally saw one another during his two-year imprisonment.

Bonhoeffer underwent months of interrogation about his trips throughout Europe, his professional duties as a pastor, and his loyalty to the Third Reich (meaning "Third Empire"; the name Hitler gave to his term as Germany's leader). For a while, Bonhoeffer was able to provide clever answers and avoid incriminating himself and others about many matters. However, he was eventually condemned to death when his role in the anti-Nazi plot was uncovered.

Character and Convictions

Bonhoeffer spent time at several prisons and prison camps, including Buchenwald concentration camp and camps at Regensburg and Flossenburg. (Concentration camps were places where the Nazis confined people they regarded as "enemis of the state.") In the several places in which he was imprisoned, Bonhoeffer was always able to establish good relationships with many of the guards. Fellow prisoner Fabian Von Schlanbrendorff wrote: "[He was] always of the same kindliness and politeness towards everybody, so that to my surprise, within a short time, he had won over his warders, who were not always kindly disposed."

Memorials to a French Hero

During the Holocaust (the period between 1933 and 1945 when the Nazis systematically persecuted and murdered millions of Jews and other innocent people), very few Jews were rescued in Nazi-occupied Europe, due to anti-Jewish sentiment, indifference, and fear on the part of those who might have rescued them. However, among those who did take the risk to help the Jews were some Christian members of the clergy, like Father Jacques de Jesus.

Born in France in 1900, Father Jacques, named Lucien Bunuel at birth, joined a Roman Catholic religious order. During World War II (1939–45), Father Jacques was head of a boys' school in Avon, France. He turned the school into a refuge for Jews and for young men who wanted to avoid being forced into doing labor for the Nazis.

In January 1943, he enrolled three Jewish boys in the school under false names to protect them from the Nazis. He also hid a fourth Jewish boy, claiming the boy was the school custodian. In addition, Father Jacques found shelter for that boy's father with a local family. He rescued a prominent Jewish scientist by appointing him to the school's faculty.

When the Nazi Secret State Police (called the Gestapo) discovered Father Jacques's actions, they arrested him and the three students he had sheltered, his mother and sister, and the scientist. All of those captured were sent to concentration camps (places where the Nazis confined people they regarded as "enemies of the state"); all but Father Jacques died. He was imprisoned in several Nazi concentration camps before being liberated by American troops in May 1945. Sickly, and weighing a mere 75 pounds, Father Jacques died a few weeks later.

In 1985, Father Jacques was memorialized at Yad Vashem, the Martyrs' and Heroes' Remembrance Authority in Jerusalem, Israel. His story was made into a film in 1987 by the late French director, Louis Malle. The film, *Au Revoir Les Enfants,* was Malle's tribute to his former headmaster.

While in prison he wrote a number of letters to various friends and members of his family discussing his experiences in prison and his thoughts about various religious and political matters. These inspiring writings were later published and read worldwide. The English edition is called *Letters and Papers from Prison.*

British captain Payne Best was captured on the borders of Holland in 1940 and sent to the same prison as Bonhoeffer. He wrote a letter to Sabine, Bonhoeffer's sister, in 1951, about the final days of Bonhoeffer's life. "[Dietrich]," he observed, "was different; just quite calm and normal, seemingly perfectly at his ease . . . his soul really shone in the dark desperation of our prison."

Bonhoeffer had a lot of time to consider the great questions in life while he was imprisoned. Concerning his detention behind bars Bonhoeffer once wrote: "If I were to end my life here, in these conditions, that would have a meaning that I think I could understand."

Execution and Legacy

On April 9, 1945, Bonhoeffer was executed by hanging along with others who had participated in efforts to assassinate Hitler. A prison doctor described what happened: "On the morning of the day, . . . between five and six o'clock, the prisoners . . . were led out of their cells and the verdicts read to them. Through the half-open door of a room in one of the huts I saw Pastor Bonhoeffer, still in prison clothes, kneeling in fervent prayer to the Lord his God. The devotion and evident conviction of being heard [by God] that I saw in the prayer of this intensely captivating man, moved me to the depths." Just three weeks after Bonhoeffer's death, Hitler committed suicide, knowing that the war was lost. One week after that Germany surrendered to the Allies (the United States, Great Britain, the Soviet Union, and France) and the war in Europe came to an end. The victims of the Nazis were freed.

Letters and Papers from Prison, Bonhoeffer's most widely read work, was first published in German in 1951 and later published in English in 1953. The book examines the problems that face Christians in the twentieth century. Bonhoeffer's other books were *The Cost of Discipleship,* written in 1937 and published in English in 1947, and *The Community of Saints,* which was written in 1929 and published in English in 1963.

Dietrich Bonhoeffer was a very ethical individual who was passionately opposed to violence. However, when he believed that there was no other recourse to stopping the evil of the Nazis, he was prepared to do what needed to be done to stop it. This young religious scholar, who showed so much promise, became famous after his death and continues to inspire succeeding generations.

Where to Learn More

Bethge, Eberhard. *Dietrich Bonhoeffer*. Harper and Row, 1977.

Bonhoeffer, Dietrich. *Letters and Papers from Prison*. SCM Press, 1959.

Bosanquet, Mary. *The Life and Death of Dietrich Bonhoeffer*. Harper and Row, 1968.

Goddard, Donald. *The Last Days of Dietrich Bonhoeffer*. Harper and Row, 1976.

Leibholz, Sabine. *The Bonhoeffers*. Sidgwick and Jackson, 1971.

Robertson, E. *The Shame and the Sacrifice: The Life and Martyrdom of Dietrich Bonhoeffer*. Macmillan, 1988.

Zimmermanm, Wolf-Dieter. *I Knew Dietrich Bonhoeffer*. Collins, 1966.

Martin Bormann

Born June 17, 1900
Halberstadt, Germany

Died May 2, 1945?
Berlin, Germany

German Nazi Party secretary

*Last right-hand man of
German dictator Adolf Hitler*

Martin Bormann was said to have been an unlikable man, completely without moral sense. He was one of the major planners of the Final Solution, which called for the total elimination of European Jews. By the end of World War II (1939–45), Bormann had become second only to Adolf Hitler (see entry) in the power he wielded. (Hitler was head of the National Socialist German Workers' Party—Nazi for short.) As Hitler's aide, Bormann worked in secret, so the extent of his power was little known outside the Nazi inner circle. Hitler trusted him absolutely, but Bormann was feared and hated by most others who knew him. Bormann's disappearance after the war remains the biggest unsolved mystery of the brutal reign of the Nazis.

An Unremarkable Childhood

Martin Bormann was born in 1900 in Halberstadt, an old and picturesque town in Germany. His father, Theodor, had played the trumpet in a military band before retiring from the army and taking a job as a clerk in a post office. Theodor died when Bormann was only four years old. Soon after, his mother married a bank director, and Bormann was brought up in a comfortable, middle-class home.

World War I began in 1914, when Bormann was only 14. As soon as he was old enough, in June 1918, he interrupted his studies at an agricultural trade school to go into the army. That was the end of his formal education. The war ended later that year without his seeing any combat action, and he left the army in 1920.

Joins Anti-Jewish Groups

Bormann took a position as the manager of a large farm. Like many other ex-soldiers, he was unhappy with conditions in Germany after the war. The German economy was in shambles and many people were unemployed. The Treaty of Versailles that ended the war imposed many unpopular conditions on Germany, including the disbanding of its mighty army. Germans felt humiliated, and blamed their problems on the Jews. Sharing in this frustration, Bormann joined an anti-Jewish organization. He also joined an organization headed by a man named Rossbach, which promoted the overthrow of the German government and the reestablishment of Germany as a great power. Bormann became the treasurer of the Rossbach organization.

By this time he was 23 years old. He had brown eyes, brown hair, and was about five feet seven inches tall. According to writer James McGovern, he had "a powerful build and a short thick neck from which derived his nickname, 'The Bull.'" He was good with figures, was a hard worker, and was soon to demonstrate his utter ruthlessness when it came to protecting his position.

Ready to Kill for His Beliefs

In 1923, another member of the Rossbach organization made the mistake of "borrowing" some money from the organization's treasury. The man was already under suspicion as a spy. Bormann, Rudolf Hess (see entry), and a few other men took the hapless thief to a forest, beat him, cut his throat, fired two bullets into his head, and buried him.

"[Hitler] towers over us like Mount Everest . . . [he is] the greatest human being we know of . . . his poise in the face of fantastic difficulties is marvelous; and so indeed is everything else about him . . . ."

Bormann was sentenced to prison for a year. Although his precise role in the crime was never determined, it appeared he was the instigator and provided the car. This became his typical way of operating—always manipulating behind the scenes.

While Bormann sat in prison, Hitler was building the Nazi Party into a major political force. He attracted large crowds, who listened with enthusiasm to his hate-filled, anti-semitic (anti-Jewish) speeches. He shouted accusations against the Jews, blaming them for the loss of World War I and charging them with holding Germany back from becoming a world power. His followers sometimes attacked and humiliated innocent Jews in the streets.

After his release from prison, Bormann joined the Nazi Party. He quickly rose through the ranks, and in 1933 he was chosen Chief of the Cabinet in Hess's office. He proved himself to be very efficient, a "model secretary." He never sought glory or titles. He has been described as coarse, brutal, and lacking in culture, and his slow and gradual rise in Hitler's esteem at first went unnoticed by other Nazi Party officials.

Marries a Pure German Girl

In 1929, Bormann married Gerda Buch, described as "the sturdy, pure-blooded Aryan [white, non-Jewish] daughter" of a high-ranking Nazi official. Gerda was noted for her hatred of religion in any form. The couple would have ten children; the first was named Adolf in honor of Hitler. Bormann had Gerda's support in making pregnant other German girls to populate the new German Empire that Hitler dreamed of creating. Gerda raised her children to believe that "every single child must realize that the Jew is the Absolute Evil in this world."

Becomes Hitler's Loyal Comrade

Throughout the 1930s, the Nazi Party worked toward its goal of building a powerful nation without Jews. Violence against German Jews escalated, and thousands were imprisoned for no reason other than that they were Jewish. Laws were passed denying German Jews all legal rights. Vast numbers of Jews fled the country, only to be turned away by the anti-Jewish governments of Germany's neighbors. Meanwhile,

Strong Opinions about Bormann Held by His Fellow Nazis

All of the high-ranking Nazis who surrounded Hitler had strong negative opinions about Bormann. One of them once said: "Next to [Heinrich] Himmler, the most sinister member of Hitler's [inner circle] was Martin Bormann." Another called him an "arch-scoundrel," and said that the word "hate" was "far too weak" to describe his feelings. Nazi criminal Hermann Göring was asked at his trial after the war if he knew where Bormann was. He replied: "If I had my say about it, I hope he is frying in hell."

At one time or another these men complained to Hitler about Bormann. On one occasion Hitler replied: "I know that Bormann is brutal. But there is sense in everything he does and I can absolutely rely on my orders being carried out by Bormann immediately and in spite of all obstacles." Albert Speer, another Nazi, said: "Even among so many ruthless men, Bormann stood out by his brutality and coarseness. . . . " Speer noted that if Hitler had voiced only a few critical words about Bormann, "all Bormann's enemies would have been at his throat." But Hitler never said those words.

Hitler had been building up the German army, in violation of the Treaty of Versailles. By 1939, Hitler felt that Germany was ready for war. He stated that all of the Jews in Europe would be done away with as the result of a world war. In September 1939, he invaded Poland. World War II had begun.

When Bormann's boss, Rudolf Hess, made a mysterious flight to England in 1941 and was taken prisoner, Bormann stepped into his shoes (some people say Bormann encouraged Hess to make the flight so he could have his job).

Bormann put Hitler's daily affairs in order and explained matters to him in a clear and simple way. Hitler began to appreciate and depend on Bormann more and more. As the war went on and Hitler's behavior became more peculiar, it was Bormann who calmed Hitler down and kept him from knowing the truth about how the war was being lost. According to some of the people who have studied Bormann, he actually became "more powerful than Hitler himself."

Bormann's duties were many and varied. He became Hitler's gatekeeper, controlling who was allowed to see Hitler and admitting them only after they told him their business. He filled jobs with people of his choosing. He controlled Hitler's finances and even saw to the construction of Hitler's vacation home in the mountains. His enemy, the Nazi Albert Speer, described how Bormann accomplished this task with the crudeness that was typical of him. Speer was a gifted architect, in charge of designing new buildings for Hitler's future German Empire. He called Bormann "this brutal contractor [who] ravaged the natural beauty of the place, forcibly buying up old farms, tearing down buildings, turning the forest paths into paved promenades and creating a complex of concrete buildings."

Bormann's Policies

Bormann did not actually kill people during the war, but he was aware that the killings were going on, and he approved of them. As Hitler's chief assistant, he played an important role in ordering the building of concentration camps throughout Europe. The camps were places where the Nazis confined (and later murdered) people they regarded as "enemies of the state."

Bormann was especially known for his hatred and persecution of Christian churches and for the extremely harsh measures he proposed for the treatment of Jews and the conquered peoples of Europe. He was also a supporter of the policy of euthanasia, the mercy killing program set up by doctor Karl Brandt (see entry).

Bormann opposed Christian churches because he believed they stood in the way of the Nazis assuming total control over people's lives. The influence of the churches "must be broken totally and forever," he declared. As for the Jews, Bormann decreed in 1942 that "the permanent elimination of the Jews from the territories of Greater Germany . . . [must be] carried out . . . by the use of ruthless force in the special [concentration] camps. . . . "

Attends Hitler's Suicide

By 1945, Hitler could no longer deny to himself that Germany had lost the war, and believed that he must commit suicide in order to escape capture. Bormann was with him right up until the end. He witnessed the wedding ceremony of Hitler and Eva Braun (see entry), even though Braun detested him. Bormann expressed the desire to commit suicide along with Hitler, but Hitler ordered him "to put the interests of the nation before his own interests," to live on and carry out the Nazi vision of a great German Empire.

Martin Bormann was the first person to enter the room after Hitler and Braun committed suicide on April 30, 1945. He was one of the six people who attended to the disposal of the couple's bodies in a garden, where they were set on fire with gasoline. As the bodies of Hitler and Braun burned, Bormann left the premises. Where he went, no one can say for sure.

Tried in His Absence

While the war was still raging, three of the Allies (Great Britain, the Soviet Union, and the United States) had issued a warning to Nazi leaders. They warned those responsible for the torture and murder of millions of innocent people that "[we] will pursue them to the furthest corners of the earth and deliver them to their judges so that justice may be done." Many were indeed caught, and some were sentenced to hang at the trial of Nazi criminals that took place in Nuremberg, Germany. But Bormann was nowhere to be found. What happened to him remained a mystery for many years. Because it could not be established whether he was dead or alive, the Nuremberg court tried and sentenced him to death in his absence.

The Biggest Unsolved Nazi Mystery

Martin Bormann was the subject of an intensive search by British and American agents who were anxious to bring him to trial for his crimes. Rumors about his whereabouts persisted for decades. It was said that he made his way to Italy, where his wife lay gravely ill, and from there to South America. (His wife died in 1946. By the terms of her will, all of the children of this anti-Christian couple were brought up

Nazi-Era Gold in Swiss Banks

A controversy that had been quietly simmering for half a century erupted in worldwide news headlines in the 1990s—the matter of Nazi-era gold still being held in Swiss banks. Swiss banks have long been known for their strict refusal to release any information about money held in secret bank accounts.

Switzerland declared a policy of neutrality (non-involvement) in World War II (1939–45). As Nazi persecution of Jews elsewhere in Europe grew worse in the 1940s, and the Nazis began to confiscate Jewish property, many Jews sent their money to be deposited in secret accounts in Switzerland. Many of those Jews, however, died in Nazi concentration camps, places where the Nazis confined people they regarded as "enemies of the state." The heirs of those victims are seeking the release of money held in the secret bank accounts. Jewish organizations seeking the gold on behalf of the heirs estimate it could be worth between $3 billion and $7 billion.

The controversy over the victims' gold has focused attention on Jewish valuables said to have been stashed in Swiss banks by high-ranking Nazis. Included in the loot are gold bars melted down from the teeth and jewelry of victims of the Nazi death camps. The gold was to be used to finance the escapes of Nazi officials if Germany lost the war. Martin Bormann would have had the authority to withdraw the funds from the Swiss banks.

Catholic. No one knows why she made this request in her will. Some people have suggested that the Catholic Church may have done her a favor and this was her way of repaying it.) Another version of the story is that Bormann tried to escape from the invading Soviet Union (now Russia). The tank in which he was riding was said to have been hit by Soviet anti-tank shells, and he was killed.

Bormann was a primary target of famed Nazi-hunter Simon Wiesenthal (see entry). At a 1967 news conference, Wiesenthal asserted: "Bormann travels freely through Chile, Paraguay, and Brazil. . . . He has many friends, money."

Author Says Bormann Alive

In 1972, a famous series of reports was published in European and American newspapers, written by Hungarian-born American writer Ladislas Farago, a former secret service agent. Farago claimed he had discovered Martin Bormann alive but ailing in South America. The story caused a sensation, because Bormann was still at the top of the "most-wanted" list of condemned Nazi criminals. Farago claimed that 50,000 Nazi criminals had found their way to South America and lived openly there.

Farago further claimed that South American leaders were not sheltering Bormann simply out of kindness. He said that Nazi leaders had been stashing away gold and other valuables stolen from Jews and others since as early as 1943 (see box). According to Farago, Bormann used the treasure to finance a new life in South America.

Shortly after Farago made his claim, a skeleton was unearthed in a railroad yard in Berlin, Germany. The German government declared that the body was that of Bormann. The cause of death was declared to be suicide, and the official death date was given as May 2, 1945, two days after the death of Bormann's idol, Adolf Hitler. Farago dismissed the report by the German government. He claimed that neither the Germans nor anyone else was interested in bringing Bormann to justice. "How convenient," he said. "The Germans have a big file on Bormann, and they've always looked for him where they were sure he wasn't."

Where to Learn More

Fennel, Tom. "Naming Names: Swiss Banks Issue a Long-sought List of Nazi-era Accounts." *Macleans'*, 110, no. 31 (August 4, 1997): p. 30.

Fest, Joachim C. *The Face of the Third Reich: Portraits of the Nazi Leadership*. Translated from the German by Michael Bullock. Pantheon Books, 1970.

Hirsh, Michael. "Nazi Gold: The Untold Story." *Time,* November 4, 1996, pp. 47-48.

McGovern, James. *Martin Bormann*. Morrow, 1968.

Nelan, Bruce W. "The Goods of Evil." *Time,* October 28, 1996, pp. 54-55.

Speer, Albert. *Inside the Third Reich; Memoirs by Albert Speer.* Translated from the German by Richard and Clara Winston. Macmillan, 1970.

Trevor-Roper. "Martin Bormann Was Last Seen Definitely in a Tank in Berlin on May 2, 1945. Does He Live?" *The New York Times Biographical Edition,* January 1973, pp. 23+. Or, *The New York Times Magazine,* January 14, 1973, pp. 12+.

Vincent, Isabel. *Hitler's Silent Partners: Swiss Banks, Nazi Gold, and the Pursuit of Justice.* Morrow, 1997.

Warren, Howard. "Writer in Detroit Tells of Nazi's Open Life in Brazil." *Biography News,* January/February 1975, p. 29.

Wilson, Victor. "Author Claims Nazi War Criminal Is Still Alive." *Biography News,* January/February 1975, p. 29.

Karl Brandt

Born January 8, 1904
Mulhouse, Alsace

Died June 2, 1948
Landsberg Prison, Lech, Germany

Surgeon, Hitler's personal doctor, head of Nazi euthanasia program

Set up a program that allowed German doctors to kill anyone they deemed "unworthy of life"; at least 200,000 deaths resulted

Karl Brandt was an intelligent man and a gifted surgeon who was chosen by Nazi (the term used for the National Socialist German Workers' Party) leaders to head a so-called "mercy-killing" program that began by killing "defective" children and expanded to include adults and Jews. (The Nazis used the term "defective" to refer to anyone with a physical or mental handicap.) With Brandt as overseer, the mercy-killing or euthanasia program led to murderous experiments on living human beings. After World War II (1939–45), Brandt was sentenced to hang for his crimes. Almost to the very moment the hangman's noose tightened around his neck, he insisted that his actions were justified in a time of war and what he had done was right.

Educated in Germany

Karl Brandt was the son of a German policeman. He was born in 1904 in Alsace, a

"Death
can mean
deliverance.
Death is life--
just as much
as birth. It
was never
meant to be
murder."

beautiful, fertile region of Europe that France and Germany had fought over for centuries. At the time of Brandt's birth, Alsace belonged to Germany, but when World War I (1914–18) ended, Germany was forced to surrender the region to France. As a result, a bitter Brandt, who considered himself German, felt that he had to leave Alsace to remain a German citizen.

In 1928, Brandt received his license to practice medicine and took a position at a clinic in Bochum, Germany. While still only in his twenties, he acquired a reputation among doctors as a talented surgeon with a gift for treating head and spinal injuries. He has been described by those who knew or observed him as tall, elegant, proud, intelligent, decent, idealistic, sincere, and ethical. He was also ambitious and easily influenced by people with stronger personalities.

Ironically, Brandt's first major role model had been Albert Schweitzer, a fellow citizen of Alsace, a humanitarian, missionary, and winner of the Nobel Prize for peace. Brandt had hoped to become a doctor and join Schweitzer at his mission in a French-controlled part of Africa. He was upset to learn that he would have to become a French citizen and serve in the French army before he could qualify as Schweitzer's assistant. Brandt felt strongly that it was a great wrong for his homeland to be in the hands of the French, and it was unthinkable that he should join the French army.

In 1932, Brandt decided to join the Nazi Party, which was promising its supporters many things to restore Germany to greatness after its humiliating defeat during World War I. One such promise was taking Alsace back from the French, a cause dear to Brandt's heart. Sometime in the 1930s, Brandt married a German swimming champion named Anni and fathered a child.

Launches Career as Nazi Doctor

Brandt came to the attention of Nazi Party leader Adolf Hitler (see entry) in 1933 when he was called to treat Hitler's niece and a companion for injuries from an auto accident. Brandt made a good impression on Hitler and was invited to become one of his personal doctors. Hitler, a man with a very strong personality, became Brandt's new role model. Brandt rose rapidly in Hitler's esteem and in the Nazi Party.

At least as early as 1935, Hitler had made no secret of his intention of one day doing away with the "incurably ill." He considered them unproductive and full of "bad genes." There was no place for them in his planned new "master race" of pure white, non-Jewish people who would one day rule the world. But Hitler also knew he could not begin a large-scale program of killing the handicapped unless Germany was distracted by war—decent people would protest. However, some people did not want to wait for an "official" euthanasia program to be put in place. By 1938, Hitler was actually receiving letters from the family members of mentally handicapped children requesting the "mercy death" of their loved ones.

Hitler was especially interested in a letter from a man whose child had been born blind and did not have a leg and part of an arm. Hitler told Brandt to examine the child and, if the father's description was correct, to kill her. Brandt obeyed, and Hitler was pleased. He gave Brandt permission to treat similar cases in the same way, and Brandt was happy to oblige.

World War II began when Hitler invaded Poland in 1939. He immediately implemented his official euthanasia program. He declared that in a time of war and hardship, it was not practical for the state to spend money to care for handicapped children in institutions. Naturally, his loyal friend Brandt came to mind as the logical choice to head up the official euthanasia operation. The operation enlisted loyal Nazi-sympathizing doctors to participate in the killing of their young patients.

The Killing of Children Begins

Brandt and several other physicians quickly established the Reich Committee for the Scientific Registration of Serious Hereditarily and Congenitally Based Illnesses. The Reich Committee drew up a list of medical conditions that would qualify for mercy killing. The conditions included impairments such as "idiocy" (mental handicaps), especially when it was associated with blindness and deafness; malformations of all kinds; and paralysis. All medical personnel who were present at the birth of a baby who had any of these conditions had to report the baby to the Reich Committee. Furthermore, the names of any children in institutions who were under the age of three and who had any of the listed conditions had to be reported to the committee.

Opposite page:
A reproduction of the letter
signed by Adolf Hitler
authorizing Brandt to
implement Operation T-4.

A medical panel set up by Brandt then examined the reports and made the decision whether each child would live or die. A plus sign indicated a "garbage child," who would be killed; a minus sign meant the child would be allowed to live. As the program went on, the age limit of the qualifying children moved up, and Jewish children were added to the list just for being Jewish. Five thousand children were killed by doctors who had taken an oath to "do no harm." The children were killed with overdoses of drugs, by injections of poisonous chemicals, or by starving in institutions dedicated to that task. Later, gas chambers were introduced. Gas chambers were sealed rooms that were filled with poisonous gas in order to kill the people locked inside.

Soon the program, which came to be known as Operation T-4, was expanded to include mentally or physically ill adults. Those people who were considered "lives unworthy of living" or "useless eaters" were rounded up by male nurses, who were members of Hitler's secret police. Wearing white uniforms and tall black boots and carrying stethoscopes, they escorted their victims by bus to special centers, where the victims were shot to death. Later, gas was used, because some of the secret policemen were upset at having to shoot their victims.

Wins Public Over

Although he had little to do actual carrying out the mass killings, Brandt was the top medical authority in charge of the secret program. One day he had the idea to test public opinion of the euthanasia program by way of a movie and an opinion poll.

The movie *I Accuse* was released in 1941. Its plot involved a doctor whose wife was incurably ill. She begged her husband to give her a deadly injection to relieve her pain and suffering. The film's message seemed to be that mercy killing was acceptable because the patient wanted it.

But another message of the film was that in cases where the patient was mentally ill, the state should step in and carry out the killing, as the Nazis were already secretly doing. The SD, the intelligence (spy) agency of the Nazi Party, then prepared a report saying the film had been "favorably received

ADOLF HITLER

Reichsleiter B o u h l e r   und

Dr. med. B r a n d t

sind unter Verantwortung beauftragt, die Befug -

nisse namentlich zu bestimmender Ärzte so zu er -

weitern, dass nach menschlichem Ermessen unheilbar

Kranken bei kritischster Beurteilung ihres Krank -

heitszustandes der Gnadentod gewährt werden kann.

[signature]

[handwritten annotation] Von Bouhler mir
übergeben am 27.8.40
Dr. Gürtner

and discussed" by the public. The report told Hitler that his hold over the German people was so great that the public accepted the program of mercy killing carried out by Brandt. After all, Brandt and other Nazi doctors were scientists, and what they were doing, they said, was science.

Operation T-4 Halted

Such a program could not remain secret for long. Some religious leaders and family members of the adult victims of medical killings protested. Oddly, no such protest had arisen over the killing of children. Heinrich Himmler (see entry), head of the SS, finally recommended to Hitler that the program be stopped. (The SS was an abbreviation for *Shutzstaffeln* or Security Squad.) He complained that it was stirring up unrest at a time when Germans needed to concentrate on winning the war.

In August 1941, Hitler told Brandt to end the practice of killing mental patients. But it was too late—the murder of the "unworthy" was beyond Brandt's control. A period known as "wild euthanasia" followed, when doctors all over Germany carried out the killings on a large scale. In some places the murders even continued after the war was over, before a halt was called by the victorious Allies (United States, Great Britain, the Soviet Union, and France). It is estimated that 200,000 innocent people were killed out of "mercy."

In 1942, Hitler placed Brandt in charge of all German medical facilities. In this new role, he was present at meetings where Nazi doctors discussed the horrible experiments they were conducting on human beings in the concentration camps (where "enemies of the state" were imprisoned) (see Josef Mengele entry). Brandt was also present at a demonstration where victims were killed by carbon monoxide gas and morphine injections to see how the two methods of killing compared.

Falls Out of Favor with Hitler

Brandt remained in Hitler's good graces until two weeks before Hitler killed himself. By then it was obvious that Germany was losing the war. Berlin, the capital city, was being bombarded. Many high Nazi officials had taken their families to places where they could surrender to the advancing Allied

The Nazis' Crimes Defined

The trials of the Nazi leaders by four of the Allied powers (the United States, Great Britain, the Soviet Union, and France) were unique events in human history. The several trials that were held were known as the Nuremberg Trials after the city of Nuremberg, Germany, where they took place. They marked the first time in history that a group of victorious powers had established an international court in which they could try their defeated enemies on charges of violations of criminal laws. The Nuremberg Tribunal, as the group of powers was known, made it known that a nation's conduct must be governed by laws *even during wartime.*

The Tribunal defined war crimes and crimes against humanity this way:

"War Crimes: namely, violations of the laws or customs of war. Such violations shall include, but not be limited to, murder, ill-treatment or deportation [forced removal from one's city or country] to slave labor or for any other purpose of civilian population of or in occupied territory, murder or ill-treatment of prisoners of war or persons on the seas, killing of hostages, plunder of public or private property, wanton [excessive] destruction of cities, towns or villages, or devastation not justified by military necessity";

"Crimes Against Humanity: namely, murder, extermination [total destruction], enslavement, deportation, and other inhumane acts committed against any civilian population, before or during the war, or persecutions on political, racial or religious grounds in execution of or in connection with any crime within the jurisdiction of the Tribunal, whether or not in violation of the domestic law of the country where perpetrated."

U.S. Brigadier General Telford Taylor made the opening statement at the Doctors Trial, which was the case that involved Karl Brandt. He described the charges against the doctors and scientists:

"The defendants in this case are charged with murders, tortures, and other atrocities committed in the name of medical science. The victims of these crimes are numbered in the hundreds of thousands. A handful only are still alive; a few of the survivors will appear in this courtroom. But most of these miserable victims were slaughtered outright or died in the course of the tortures to which they were subjected. . . . The victims of these crimes are numbered among the anonymous millions who met death at the hands of the Nazis and whose fate is a hideous blot on the page of modern history."

---

troops rather than be killed by bombs. When Hitler learned that Brandt had placed his family in the path of the Allies, he was furious. He was also not in his right mind by this time. He accused Brandt of sending secret documents to the Allies by way of his wife. He ordered that Brandt be killed. The doctor's life was saved by Himmler, however. But Brandt did not escape the Allies.

Trial of the Doctors

The case of the *United States* v. *Karl Brandt et al.* (and others) came to trial in Nuremberg, Germany, on December 9, 1946, and continued until August 20, 1947. Twenty-three doctors and scientists were charged with war crimes and crimes against humanity (see box). The hideous details of human experiments, some involving the drinking of seawater, deliberately infecting patients with diseases, immersion in icy water, and the use of mustard gas, came out at the trial. Brandt was asked whether he thought an order to experiment on human beings was reasonable when death would probably result. He replied that under the Nazi form of government, "any personal code of ethics must give way to the total character of the war." As for his involvement in Operation T-4, writer Robert Lifton said, Brandt "made no apology for the program, and declared it to be justified—justified out of pity for the victim and out of a desire to free the family and loved ones from a lifetime of needless sacrifice."

The court was not impressed with the doctors' statements. Sixteen of the men, including Brandt, were found guilty. Of the sixteen, seven, including Brandt, were sentenced to hang. His sentence was carried out on June 2, 1948.

Because some of the Nazi doctors argued that there was no law against human experiments, the Nuremberg court issued a statement called the Nuremberg Code, which defined when medical experiments on human beings were justified. The first point made in the statement was this: "The voluntary consent of the human subject is absolutely essential."

Where to Learn More

Conot, Robert E. *Justice at Nuremberg.* Harper & Row, 1983.

Gallagher, Hugh Gregory. *By Trust Betrayed: Patients, Physicians, and the License to Kill in the Third Reich.* Holt, 1990.

Lifton, Robert Jay. *The Nazi Doctors: Medical Killing and the Psychology of Genocide.* Basic Books, 1986.

Lifton, Robert Jay and Amy Hackett. "Nazi Physicians." In *Encyclopedia of the Holocaust.* Macmillan, 1990.

Speer, Albert. *Inside the Third Reich: Memoirs by Albert Speer,* Translated from the German by Richard and Clara Winston. Macmillan, 1970.

Wilhelm, Hans-Heinrich. "Euthanasia Program." In *Encyclopedia of the Holocaust.* Macmillan, 1990.

Eva Braun

Born February 6, 1912
Munich, Germany

Died April 30, 1945
Berlin, Germany

*Mistress, then wife for one day, of
dictator Adolf Hitler*

*Committed suicide with Hitler when it
became obvious Germany had lost
World War II (1939–45)*

B y most accounts, Eva Braun was a rather
ordinary woman whose only distinction
was her connection to Adolf Hitler (see entry).
She was uninterested in politics and had little
to say about Hitler's work. She was completely
devoted to him.

Early Life in Munich

Eva Braun (pronounced brown) was born
in Munich, Germany, on February 6, 1912. She
was the second of three daughters born to Frei-
drich (Fritz) and Franciska Dronburger Braun.
Her father was a schoolteacher, which placed
the family in the German middle class.

Braun attended a convent school
founded by English nuns in the eighteenth
century. She was a lively and athletic girl who
had little aptitude or interest in her studies and
barely managed to earn a diploma. Her teachers thought her frivolous (silly). In 1929, at the

age of 17, she left the convent and took a job as a bookkeeper and assistant to photographer Heinrich Hoffmann, who was Hitler's personal photographer. Thus fate threw her in the path of the man who would soon become dictator (he ruled with absolute power) of Germany.

The First Suicide

At the time Braun met Hitler through her work, he was involved in a stormy relationship with Angela (Geli) Raubel, the daughter of his half sister. Hitler was then 39 years old, and Raubel was 20. For a time, Raubel enjoyed her connection to the man who was becoming famous throughout Germany, but soon she began to resent his control over her, and she yearned to go out with younger people. Finally, after a dreadful quarrel with Hitler, Raubel committed suicide in 1931.

Hitler was shattered at the death of the woman some people say was the only one he ever really loved. He became withdrawn and depressed and turned the room where she died into a shrine. He then turned to Braun, also a much younger woman, for consolation. According to author Robert Payne, Hitler was attracted to the fair-haired, blue-eyed girl because she resembled Raubel but was quieter and less moody. Payne wrote: "Her difficult task was to be his mistress while remaining invisible, and she succeeded so well that very few people outside Hitler's immediate circle knew of her existence."

Braun Becomes Hitler's Secret Mistress

At some point in the early 1930s, Braun became Hitler's mistress, and he gave her a suite of rooms in his home. However, because he was unwilling to have their relationship become a matter of public knowledge, the couple pretended even in front of Hitler's staff of servants to be only friends. When important guests came to visit, Braun was told to stay in her room. Although she would have liked to meet these visitors, she accepted Hitler's order because she had no choice.

Braun kept a diary, and after World War II, 22 pages of it were found. They cover a brief period in 1935, when she was 23 years old. In the pages, she complains of Hitler's casual treatment of her, of loneliness, and of her fear of becoming an "old maid" (an older woman who has never married). It is obvious from her diary pages that she had little to occupy her

"A Germany without Adolf Hitler would not be fit to live in."

Eva Braun's Diary

Below is an excerpt from Eva Braun's diary, dated February 18, 1935.

"Yesterday he [Hitler] came quite unexpectedly, and we had a delightful evening. The nicest thing is that he is thinking of taking me from the [photographer's studio where she worked] and—but I had better not get excited about it yet—he may give me a little house. I simply mustn't let myself think about it. It would be marvelous. I wouldn't have to open the door to our 'beloved customers,' and go on being a shop girl. Dear God, grant that this may really happen not in some far-off time, but soon. . . .

"I am so infinitely happy that he loves me so much, and I pray that it will always be like this. It won't be my fault if he stops loving me."

thoughts except Hitler, who was often away. On at least two occasions she attempted suicide.

Rather than giving her expensive gifts, Hitler occasionally embarrassed Braun by publicly handing her envelopes full of money. She became a wealthy woman in her own right when Hitler gave her and photographer Hoffmann the exclusive rights to his photographs.

The War Years

World War II began in 1939 when Hitler invaded Poland. With the start of the war, Hitler stayed closer to home. He and Braun now had more time to spend together, and the couple grew closer. Braun gained confidence in knowing that she no longer had to contend with rivalry from Hitler's other female admirers. The wives of Hitler's aides did not like her and tried to avoid her, but she did develop a friendship with Albert Speer, Hitler's architect and one of the most important members of his government.

In his book *Inside the Third Reich,* which he wrote after the war, Speer offered a portrait of Braun. He said she was a simple woman who "dressed quietly and wore the inexpensive jewelry that Hitler gave her. . . . She was sports-loving, a good skier with plenty of endurance with whom my wife and I frequently undertook mountain tours [Hitler did not like snow]. . . . " Speer also described her as "pleasant and fresh-faced rather than beautiful and [she] had a modest air." She put up with Hitler's hurtful remarks such as, "A highly intelligent man should take a primitive and stupid woman. Imagine if on top of everything else I had a woman who interfered with my work!"

Braun apparently suited Hitler well. She must have been a good listener, because Hitler has been described as a man whose conversations consisted of him doing all the talking. She occupied herself with swimming, mountain climbing, playing with her two black Scotch terriers, and watching movies, in addition to skiing. She was a kindhearted woman who occasionally pleaded with Hitler to spare Jewish acquaintances of hers. (Hitler hated the Jews. He and the Nazis were engaged in persecuting Jews, a persecution that first involved forcing them to leave Germany but later led to the murder of millions.) When Hitler became enraged with his aide Rudolf Hess (see entry) and cut off relations with him, Braun secretly saw to it that Hess's wife received a small allowance.

The Last Suicide

By 1945, it was obvious Germany was losing the war. Berlin was being bombed, and Hitler had ordered Braun to stay in Munich for her own safety. After only two weeks, she returned unexpectedly to Berlin, telling her friends her place was at Hitler's side no matter what happened. She found Hitler a sick and broken man who believed that everyone but Braun had betrayed him. He had decided he would kill himself, and Braun agreed to join him in the act. In return, Hitler granted Braun's wish that he make her his wife.

In the will Hitler then dictated, he said: "Since I did not feel that I could accept the responsibility of marriage during the years of struggle, I have decided now, before the end of my earthly career, to take as my wife the girl who, after many years of loyal friendship, came of her own free will to this city, already almost besieged, in order to share my fate. At her own request she goes to her death with me as my wife. . . .

My wife and I choose to die in order to escape the shame of overthrow. . . . It is our wish that our bodies be burned immediately . . . "

Hitler then joined a radiantly happy Braun, who was dressed in a long black silk gown. According to the marriage laws existing in Germany on April 29, 1945, Hitler and Braun swore that they were both of pure Aryan (white, non-Jewish) descent and that they suffered from no hereditary diseases that would prevent them from marrying. They exchanged rings that "had probably been torn off the fingers of dead

Jews in one of the concentration camps," according to Robert Payne. The ceremony over, the couple hosted a champagne wedding breakfast attended by eight guests.

The next day Braun, Hitler, and his two secretaries discussed methods of committing suicide. Braun proposed to take poison because "she wanted to be a beautiful corpse," according to one of the secretaries. Hitler readied his poison capsules. One version of the story is that he tested a poison capsule on his pet dog to be sure it worked; the dog died. Later, at about 3:30 in the afternoon of April 30, 1945, Hitler and Braun were found dead in their suite. Braun had taken poison. Hitler died from a pistol shot. The bodies were carried to the garden and burned as shells from the approaching the Soviet (now Russian) army exploded all around. The bodies were then buried in shallow graves, where they were discovered by the Soviets four days later.

Where to Learn More

Payne, Robert. *The Life and Death of Adolf Hitler.* Praeger, 1973.

Sereny, Gitta. *Albert Speer: His Battle with Truth.* Knopf, 1995.

Shirer, William. *The Rise and Fall of the Third Reich.* Simon and Schuster, 1960.

Speer, Albert. *Inside the Third Reich.* Translated from the German by Richard and Clara Winston. Macmillan, 1970.

Toland, John. *Adolf Hitler.* Doubleday, 1976.

Charles E. Coughlin

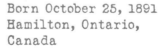

Born October 25, 1891
Hamilton, Ontario,
Canada

Died October 27, 1979
Bloomfield Hills, Michigan

Roman Catholic priest, radio personality, and controversial political figure in the period leading up to World War II (1939–45)

Anti-Jewish priest who strongly opposed U.S. involvement in World War II

Father Charles E. Coughlin (pronounced Caw-glin) rose from being the unknown pastor of a small-town church to being one of the most well-known radio voices in America. He offered hope to millions of Americans who were suffering during the Great Depression (1929–41), a period when the economy was at a standstill and unemployment was high. As the anti-Jewish Adolf Hitler (see entry) was coming into power in Germany, Coughlin began to spout anti-Jewish notions, and he became the most loved and most hated American of his time.

Early Life

Charles Edward Coughlin was the first-born child of Thomas and Amelia Mahoney Coughlin, who were both devout Catholics of Irish descent. Thomas was an American citizen who worked as a laborer on Great Lakes steamboats until he was forced to seek lighter work because of poor health. He settled in Hamilton, a small town in Canada, and first took a job as a maintenance man in the Catholic church there. Later he became a supervisor at a bakery. Amelia came from a family of Canadian farmers but later moved to Hamilton and worked as a seamstress. She married Thomas in 1890 and about a year later gave birth to Charles.

Amelia was a strong-willed woman; one of her dearest wishes was that her son would become a priest. When her second and last child was born in 1892 and died in infancy, Amelia devoted herself to raising her only child to fulfill the role she envisioned for him. At age 12, Coughlin was sent to Toronto, Canada, to begin his studies in preparation for the priesthood.

Coughlin excelled in school, developing a reputation as a star rugby (a type of football) player and public speaker. While studying to become a priest, he was exposed to new ideas that were sweeping through the Catholic Church. Traditionally the Church concerned itself only with religious matters; then in the early 1900s, it began to concern itself with justice for the working classes, who were often poorly treated by business owners. This was becoming an important issue in the United States, where hundreds of thousands of European Catholic immigrants (people from other countries who came to live in the United States) were flooding the country looking for work in the new factories opening there. Coughlin developed a lifelong commitment to the poor and a belief that the leaders of industry should give workers a fair share of the country's wealth.

Becomes Pastor of Obscure Michigan Parish

In 1916, Coughlin was ordained a Catholic priest. For seven years he taught English, Greek, and history, coached the football team, and enjoyed great popularity with the students at a small college near Windsor, Ontario, just across the river from Detroit, Michigan. Not content with simply his duties as a teacher, he also volunteered to give speeches to whatever groups would extend an invitation. His reputation as an electrifying speaker grew, and he came to the attention of Church leaders in Detroit. In 1926, Coughlin was chosen to oversee a new parish in a suburb of Detroit called Royal Oak.

Detroit in the 1920s

At the time Coughlin arrived in Detroit, the city had emerged from the boom days of high employment during World War I (1914–18) and was in the middle of a severe depression. Many small businesses had failed, unemployment was high, and there was a strong movement against labor unions, whose members were considered un-American. Detroit's economy was dependent on the automobile, but no one could afford to buy one. As the demand for automobiles declined, more and more Detroiters lost their jobs. Coughlin believed that America's capitalistic system, in which a few large companies controlled the production of goods, was responsible for the Great Depression that the whole country fell into in 1929.

Detroit was also experiencing a housing shortage as well as racial and ethnic problems. The Ku Klux Klan, a secret society that had developed in the South after the Civil War (1861–65) to terrorize newly freed blacks, was experiencing a resurgence in northern cities. This time the Klan directed its terrorist activities not only against blacks but also against Jews and Catholics. One of the Klan's scare tactics was to burn crosses on church lawns.

Claims He Will Fight Ku Klux Klan

Royal Oak, the location of Coughlin's new church, was just a small, rural area whose residents were surprised and not entirely happy to see Detroit's excess population headed their way. Whether or not there was actually Ku Klux Klan activity surrounding the new Royal Oak church (as Coughlin claimed) is, however, not entirely clear.

According to a story circulated by Coughlin, he came up against the Klan only two weeks after the completion of his small, wooden church, named the Shrine of the Little Flower in honor of Saint Thérèse. Coughlin claimed that the Ku Klux Klan set fire to a cross on the church lawn to indicate its displeasure with the Catholic presence there. Coughlin vowed not to give in to fear but instead to build a huge church on the site, with "a cross so high . . . that neither man nor beast can burn it down," wrote Alan Brinkley.

A Hollywood movie about the priest's life, filmed in the 1930s, showed a dramatic scene in which Coughlin was awakened from sleep and told to come quickly to his new church. There he was confronted with a great fiery cross burning fiercely next to his small church. The actor portraying Coughlin cried out that he would "construct a church that will stand as a monument in defiance of hatred!" The story has been repeated by Coughlin biographers. Writer Donald Warren asserted that the story was a complete fabrication, invented by Coughlin to make himself appear heroic and a fighter against prejudice.

Begins Broadcasting on Radio

At first his following was too small for Coughlin to obtain this dream of building a great church. In an effort to fight the anti-Catholic prejudice of his neighbors and to attract followers for his church, Coughlin decided he would take to the airwaves. At the time, commercial radio was only six years old but was already a major form of entertainment; about two-thirds of American homes had at least one radio. Coughlin delivered his first radio sermon on October 17, 1926, and received five favorable letters in response. It was not long, however, before he was receiving thousands of letters, from throughout Michigan and then from nearby states. Many listeners sent small donations to add to the contributions of those who began to crowd the church to hear him speak on Sunday. By 1928, construction had begun on the huge tower that would be the centerpiece of Coughlin's magnificent new church (it still stands at a major intersection in Royal Oak). So many Catholics moved into Royal Oak that they became a dominant force there, rather than the Klan.

Success Is His

Coughlin's commanding, athletic presence, his engaging voice, and his message continued to attract audiences, whose numbers eventually reached as high as 40 million (the total U.S. population in 1930 was 123 million). In the early days, he focused on religious and moral issues, but after the stock-market crash of 1929 ushered in the Great Depression, he began to speak about current topics and their moral implications. In 1930, he entered into a contract with the Columbia Broadcasting System (CBS) radio network, which was linked to 16 stations in the Northeast, and his talks became increasingly political. When questions were raised about whether a radio priest should be involved in politics, CBS dropped his contract. As a result, Coughlin established an independent network of stations to carry his broadcasts.

Throughout his radio career, Coughlin's primary audience consisted of Roman Catholics living in eastern industrial cities. However, he also attracted a significant audience of Protestants in the Midwest who appreciated his views on political subjects, if not his religion. By 1932, his office was receiving as many as 80,000 letters a week, his parish was thriving, and he built a modern radio office for his broadcasts.

Coughlin and President Roosevelt

The radio priest became sharply critical of President Herbert Hoover's inability or unwillingness to deal with the depression. In the 1932 election, he spoke out in favor of Franklin D. Roosevelt (see entry) for president, using the slogan "Roosevelt or Ruin." Coughlin always believed he was responsible for Roosevelt's 1932 victory and at first assumed he would be an important adviser to the new president. He endorsed Roosevelt's early ideas, and Roosevelt did consult Coughlin from time to time. However, Roosevelt followed little of the priest's advice.

By 1934, however, Coughlin had begun to criticize Roosevelt's programs and even occasionally the president himself, but he did not openly break with Roosevelt. The open break happened after a radio sermon on January 25, 1935, in which Coughlin accused Roosevelt of "selling out the American people to the international bankers" (by which he meant Jews, who were being blamed by many people for the economic problems of the depression). Coughlin began using the new slogan "Roosevelt and Ruin."

Also in 1934, Coughlin organized the National Union for Social Justice to assemble his millions of followers into an effective force for political change. The purpose of the organization, according to Coughlin, was "To learn social justice; to organize against sit-down legislatures and Congressmen [lazy lawmakers]; to battle . . . anti-Christianity wherever and whenever it is possible; to cure democracy before it withers and perishes; to protect our Supreme Court; to oppose the evils of modern capitalism without joining in the radical labor organizers and to secure an honest dollar and an hon-

Coughlin delivering one of his electrifying radio addresses.

est living for all Americans." The organization grew quickly, and although Coughlin claimed to have millions of members, more careful estimates suggest that about one million people belonged to the group at its peak.

Antisemitic Ranting

In 1938, Coughlin stunned the U.S. public when he suddenly began to voice antisemitic sentiments in his radio addresses. Antisemitism is the hatred of Jews, who are sometimes called Semites. (This was the same year that Hitler and his Nazi Party began implementing anti-Jewish regulations in Germany.) Although he never openly admitted to being an antisemite, Coughlin spoke in code words, blaming Jews for the Great Depression and other problems. He published in his newspaper *Social Justice* a false story about a Jewish conspiracy to seize control of the world. He lashed out against evil "international bankers," blaming them for the country's problems. He played to the age-old stereotypes that many people believe about Jews. (A stereotype is a distorted, one-sided image of a person or idea; stereotypes about Jews include the belief that they are secretly trying to take control of the world's money supply.) While there were others who were more forceful in their charges against Jews, none had Coughlin's huge audience.

Coughlin was a strong believer in the isolationist (non-involvement in other countries' affairs) movement of the 1920s and 1930s, which opposed involvement in European wars, and a large percentage of Americans shared his belief. He was an admirer of Benito Mussolini (see entry), and spoke out in favor of Adolf Hitler. Coughlin called Hitler's persecution of the Jews "a defense mechanism against Communism," because, he said, the Jews were responsible for the Russian Revolution that established the Communist Party in Russia, and they were trying to do the same thing in Germany. (Communism is an economic system that promotes the ownership of all property by the community as a whole.) Coughlin's influence was so great that as World War II began in Europe with Hitler's attack on Poland in 1939, violent fights broke out on the streets of New York between Coughlin's supporters and his enemies. Coughlin's critics pleaded with him to try to control his followers. These same critics denounced him in newspapers, calling him "thoroughly Hitlerish in outlook," "an enemy of democracy," "a fascist" (which was the "scare word" of the 1930s), and "a Nazi."

Coughlin's radio broadcasts ended in 1940 because he could no longer pay for radio time. He continued to work quietly at the Shrine of the Little Flower. He reportedly made a small fortune investing in the stock market, and lived a comfortable life in a wealthy suburb of Detroit. He announced his retirement in 1966, possibly forced out by his superior, who had received complaints from parents and students at the Shrine of the Little Flower School that Coughlin was a racist. In an interview a few years later, Coughlin remarked to writer Sheldon Marcus: "If I had to do it all over again, I would do it the same way."

Coughlin died of heart failure on October 27, 1979, two days after his eighty-eighth birthday. The *Detroit Free Press,* which had often been critical of him, wrote: "God is a giver and a forgiver, so why should we hold anything against one

Epilogue

After the world became aware of the horrors of the Holocaust, efforts were made to bridge the gap that existed between Christians and Jews. (The Holocaust refers to the systematic persecution and murder of approximately six million Jews as well as hundreds of thousands of Roma [often called Gypsies], homosexuals, and prisoners of war by the Nazis during World War II.) One such effort is described in *Radio Priest*. The "lone man" is representative of the mistrust and even hatred that some people still feel for the Jews.

In May 1992, a special effort was made in Detroit's Catholic and Jewish communities to exorcize (set free from) the ghost of Charles Coughlin. The event was a joint fund-raising reception held at the Shrine of the Little Flower . . . . The occurrence was newsworthy enough to receive an item in *The New York Times*. The article quoted the pastor of Coughlin's [former] church: "I would change history if I could." In his remarks on the special occasion, the Catholic official included an apology [to Jews] in the name of the [Catholic] church: "We need to find forgiveness in our lives whenever possible."

Not everyone, however, was ready to disagree with Coughlin.

Across the street from the Shrine, it was reported that "a lone man stood . . . holding a sign that read: 'Father Coughlin was on target concerning the Jewish Communist Conspiracy.'"

of our brothers? We remember not so much what Father Coughlin said, but what he believed. In his priesthood he had a deep loyalty to the Church he served. He never set himself above it. His joy was to be a faithful priest."

Where to Learn More

Alexander, Charles. "Coughlin." In *McGraw-Hill Encyclopedia of World Biography*. McGraw-Hill, 1973.

Brinkley, Alan. *Voices of Protest: Huey Long, Father Coughlin, & the Great Depression*. Alfred A. Knopf, 1982.

Glatzer, Nahum Norbert. "Anti-Semitism." In *Encarta*. Microsoft, 1994.

Marcus, Sheldon. *Father Coughlin: The Tumultuous Life of the Priest of the Little Flower.* Little, Brown, 1973.

Tull, Charles J. *Father Coughlin and the New Deal.* Syracuse University Press, 1965.

Warren, Donald. *Radio Priest: Charles Coughlin, the Father of Hate Radio.* Simon and Schuster, 1996.

Adam Czerniaków

Born November 30, 1880
Warsaw, Poland

Died July 23, 1942
Warsaw ghetto, Poland

*Civil engineer, teacher, writer, head of
Warsaw Jewish Council, diarist*

*Served in a capacity similar to mayor in
the Warsaw ghetto; committed suicide
rather than cooperate with the Nazis in
sending Jewish children to death camps*

Adam Czerniaków served for nearly three years as the leader of the half-million Jews who were forcibly confined in a ghetto (crowded, walled sections of cities were Jews were made to live in inferior conditions) in Poland's capital city of Warsaw during World War II (1939–45). He has been praised by many as a decent, honorable, and dignified man who represented his people with courage during a fearsome period in world history. He also has been condemned by others as a man who contributed to the deaths of millions of European Jews by cooperating with their murderers.

Born and Studied in Warsaw

Adam Czerniaków was born in 1880 in Warsaw, which was a center of political, social, and cultural life for Poland's Jews. His background was middle class. Not much is known about Czerniaków's childhood, although it was apparently not happy. In a diary entry dated July 8, 1940, he noted that his self-control and calm were "the product of my difficult childhood and the conditions of my parents' home. That is where I learned to suffer."

His family were assimilationist Jews, which means they were members of a minority that blended in with the culture of the Polish majority. As a young man he rejected his family's assimilation and began to study the Jewish religion.

Czerniaków studied chemistry at Warsaw Polytechnic (a school that specialized in the teaching of industrial arts and applied sciences). He then went on to study industrial engineering in Dresden, Germany. Afterwards he returned to Warsaw. He soon married a teacher by the name of Felicia. They had one son, Jan.

His career after graduation was varied. He taught in Jewish vocational schools, worked for the government, went into business for himself, and wrote educational and technical articles and even some poetry. His special interest was Jewish craftsmen.

Because Jews in Poland, as elsewhere, had long been discriminated against career-wise, they tended to be heavily concentrated in certain professions, such as law, medicine, and skilled crafts like tailoring and leather working. Half of all craftsmen in Poland were Jewish. In Warsaw the figure approached 80 percent. Czerniaków was active in protecting the interests of Jewish craftsmen, who faced constant efforts by Gentiles (non-Jews) to deprive them of their livelihoods. He became interested in public life and served as a representative of Jewish craftsmen on various government bodies.

"We do our daily work and weeping will not help us."

War in Poland

Discrimination against European Jews gradually turned into widespread hatred. The flames of that hatred were fanned by Adolf Hitler (see entry), who was living in Germany, Poland's next-door neighbor. Hitler blamed Jews for Germany's humiliating defeat in World War I (1914–18). When Hitler rose to the position of dictator (he ruled with absolute power) in 1933 as the head of the National Socialist German Workers' Party (Nazi for short), he was finally able to act on his antisemitic or anti-Jewish beliefs. He began to persecute German Jews, forcing many to leave the country and confining others in special places reserved for people regarded as "enemies of the state." These places were called concentration camps. He also began to build up the German army, which was a violation of the terms of the Treaty of Versailles that ended World War I. His plans were to regain, by force, the territory lost at the end of the war (including Poland). From there he would branch out into the rest of Europe, seizing the territory he would need for a vast new German Empire, filled with "pure" Germans and empty of all Jews.

In September 1939, Hitler was ready to fulfill his dream. Germany invaded Poland, and, as a result, World War II had begun. The Polish Jew who was chairman of the Jewish Community Council in Warsaw fled the city, and the mayor of Poland asked Czerniaków to take over. Although he had a visa (travel documents) that would have allowed him to leave for Palestine (now the Jewish state of Israel) and save himself, Czerniaków agreed to stay and assume the position of chairman. He was then 59 years old, a somewhat advanced age to be taking such a dangerous job.

When the German army marched into Warsaw, one of their first orders was that Czerniaków establish a Jewish Council to replace the earlier council. It would be called a *Judenrat*. The new Jewish Council would consist of 24 prominent Jews with Czerniaków as chairman. Czerniaków did as he was ordered. He also placed in his desk drawer a bottle of lethal poison tablets. He told the council members that if the Germans ever ordered them to do anything against their consciences, the poison tablets were available to all of them. He also began to keep his now-famous diary, in which he recorded his impressions and experiences every day until his death.

Czerniaków's first task as chairman of the *Judenrat* was to take a census of Jews and formulate a plan for their eventual placement in ghettos. In the early days of Poland's occupation by the Nazis, the true extent of their murderous plans was not apparent. The Nazis pretended they only wanted to keep peace among Polish Jews and use their labor to assist in the war effort. Czerniaków hoped to secure the safety of Poland's Jews by making the Nazis see that skilled Jewish craftsmen were indispensable to the war effort.

Oversees Life in the Ghetto
Persecution of Warsaw's Jews soon began. Their stores and homes were looted, their businesses were taken over, and

A Judenrat *official (possibly Czerniaków) at work in his office in the Warsaw ghetto.*

fines were levied against them for breaking various rules. Food was in short supply because the Germans were diverting most of it to their army. Before long famine and malnutrition were common.

In the spring of 1940, Czerniaków received the order to build a walled ghetto, for the confinement of Warsaw's Jews. Every Jew between the ages of 16 and 60 was ordered to bring several bricks to use in building their own prison. By October 1940, the job was done.

For nearly the next two years, Czerniaków was in almost daily contact with Nazi authorities over the affairs of the Warsaw ghetto, although he tried to run the ghetto with as little direct Nazi involvement as possible. He was required to submit reports to the Nazi authorities. In them, he complained bitterly about the terrible conditions in the ghetto, where people were sick and starving. Through his efforts, thousands of poor people were declared exempt (free from) from taxes on bread. Nevertheless, between January 1941 and July 1942, nearly 61,000 people died in the ghetto, mostly from starvation and diseases related to malnutrition.

Czerniaków also convinced the Nazis to permit him to provide Jewish labor in an orderly fashion so that Jews would not be roughly grabbed off the streets to be used for unpaid labor. On several occasions he was arrested and imprisoned for his harsh comments, but Czerniaków never softened his complaints to suit the Nazis.

Under Czerniaków's direction, the *Judenrat* dealt with health care, welfare, food distribution, sanitation, and police matters. Eventually, 6,000 Jews were working for the "city." Like his good friend Janusz Korczak (see entry), Czerniaków was especially concerned with children. He succeeded in setting up secret schools for children and secret classes in mechanics and chemistry for adults.

Czerniaków's leadership was often challenged. Other, wealthier Jews in positions of power did not like him badgering them for charity on behalf of the less fortunate. Citizens were sometimes unhappy when they asked him to go to the Nazis to get them special favors, and he was unsuccessful. These favors might include asking for the release of relatives who were in prison for "crimes" such as leaving the ghetto or failing to wear the armbands that identified them as Jews.

Throughout these years, Czerniaków often complained in his diary of feeling ill with headaches and "liver pain"; he suffered from frequent dizziness and nosebleeds. Yet he continued to work seven days a week. According to Josef Kermisz, writing in the introduction to *The Warsaw Diary of Adam Czerniaków:* "Only in work, he believed, lay salvation; he could not believe that the Germans would deprive themselves of the Jews' usefulness and destroy them because of some lunatic [crazy] theory." The "lunatic theory" refers to the Nazi belief that the entire Jewish race had to be eliminated.

The Order for Deportation

In the summer of 1942, rumors began to circulate through the ghetto of an impending mass deportation (forcibly removing people from their country or city) of Warsaw's Jews to the death camps, places where the Nazis murdered people they regarded as "enemies of the state." Nazi

From Czerniaków's Diary

Czerniaków sometimes complained about the Jews in the ghetto, who expected him to secure favors for them from the Nazis. In this diary passage he described his thoughts while sitting in the Nazi waiting room:

"I sit in a stuffy room resembling a jail. The Jews are constantly grumbling. They don't want to pay for the community [the services he set up to deal with health care, welfare, food distribution, sanitation, and police matters], but demand intervention [with the Nazis] on private affairs or catastrophes. And if the intervention does not succeed or goes on too long, there is no end to their dissatisfaction, as if the matter depended on me. And frequently these are very loud complaints." (July 1940)

By July 1941, though, the extreme suffering imposed on the Jews by the Nazis had taken its toll, muting their complaints. Czerniaków wrote:

"The Jewish masses are quiet and balanced in the face of the intense suffering. In general, the Jews only shout when things are going well for them."

authorities assured Czerniaków that this was not true. Still the rumors persisted and ghetto residents grew terrified. Czerniaków tried to encourage them to take heart, that there must be a misunderstanding.

On July 20, 1942, Czerniaków was once again told that there was no truth to the rumors, that they were "utter nonsense." The next day, several members of the *Judenrat* were arrested and Czerniaków's wife was taken hostage. On July 22, a representative of the Gestapo (Secret State Police) came to Czerniaków's office. That same day Czerniaków wrote in his diary: "We were told that all the Jews irrespective of sex and age, with certain exceptions, will be deported to the East [it was common knowledge that this meant to the death camps]. By 4 P.M. today a [group] of 6,000 people must be provided." On the afternoon of July 23, Czerniaków wrote: "It is 3 o'clock. So far 4,000 are ready to go. The orders are that there must be 9,000 by 4 o'clock." This was his last diary entry.

According to author Kazimierz Iranek-Osmecki: "He was faced with a tremendous decision. He returned home and wrote these words to his wife [who was still being held hostage]: 'They want me to kill the children of my people with my own hands. There is nothing left for me but to die.'" He asked her forgiveness for leaving her. He then consumed one of the poison tablets hidden in his desk and died.

The Aftermath

Czerniaków's wife was one of the few mourners at his hastily arranged funeral; his friend Janusz Korczak delivered the eulogy. Korczak praised him for completing "the important task of protecting the dignity of the Jews." Many people in the Warsaw ghetto did not know what to make of Czerniaków's suicide. They felt that he had failed them by not clearly warning them of German intentions. Because of this lack of warning, 300,000 Jews were deported without a chance to defend themselves. Others saw him as a hero, who took no salary and defended his people at great risk to his own safety.

Czerniaków left behind a diary. Although a few people knew it existed, its location remained a mystery until 1959. A survivor of the Warsaw ghetto bought it from a source she would not reveal and sent it to Yad Vashem, the Martyrs' and Heroes' Remembrance Authority in Jerusalem. With the help of several experts, it was painstakingly translated from the Polish and published in English in 1979. The diary, which is more than a thousand pages long, has been called by Raul Hilberg, a Holocaust expert and writer, "the most important Jewish record of that time."

Where to Learn More

Hilberg, Raul, Stanislaw Staron, and Josef Kermisz, eds. *The Warsaw Diary of Adam Czerniaków: Prelude to Doom.* Stein and Day, 1979.

Iranek-Osmecki, Kazimierz. *He Who Saves One Life.* Crown Publishers, 1971.

Lewin, Abraham. *A Cup of Tears: A Diary of the Warsaw Ghetto.* Edited by Antony Polonsky. Basil Blackwell, 1989.

Lifton, Betty Jean.*The King of Children: A Biography of Janusz Korczak.* Farrar, Straus and Giroux, 1988.

John Demjanjuk

```
Born April 3, 1920
Dub Makarenzi, Ukraine
```

Factory worker, farmer, soldier

*Tried and acquitted (found not guilty)
of being the notorious "Ivan the Terrible,"
a mass murderer of Jews at Treblinka
death camp*

Cases of mistaken identity are more commonly found in fictional accounts of trials than in the real world. But possible mistaken identity was the reason John Demjanjuk's (Dem-yahn-yook) death sentence was overturned by the Israeli Supreme Court in 1993. Demjanjuk had been put on trial for his cruel treatment of Jewish prisoners during World War II (1939–45). The story of Demjanjuk's life, including his trial as a mass murderer, reads like something a novelist might have made up.

A Poverty-stricken Childhood

Ivan Demjanjuk (he changed his first name to John when he became a U.S. citizen) was born on April 3, 1920, in a small Ukrainian village (Ukraine was once part of the former Soviet Union). Both of his parents were disabled. His father had lost several fingers in World War I (1914–18), and his mother had

> "... never
> in my life
> was I in
> Treblinka ...
> please do not
> put the noose
> around my
> neck for the
> deeds of
> others."

lost the use of one of her legs. Young Demjanjuk attended school off and on for nine years, but only completed four grades. It was said that he missed so much school because his father had to use the family's one pair of men's shoes when jobs became available.

A famine killed seven to ten million Ukrainians between 1932 and 1933. Starvation greatly affected the boy's village, too. Demjanjuk's family ate dogs and rats, as well as their pet cat and bird, in order to survive. About these times he once stated: "People were lying dead in their homes, in the yards, on the roads, exposed to sunlight. . . . Nobody collected them." To find some relief the senior Demjanjuk sold the family's home for the equivalent of eight loaves of bread and they moved to a farm near Moscow, Russia. When the situation there proved no better, the family returned to the village in the Ukraine.

Joins Army

The National Socialist Workers' Party (Nazi for short) under its leader Adolf Hitler (see entry) rose to power in Germany during the 1930s. In 1939, the Nazis took over Poland and started World War II. When they followed with an attack on the Soviet Union, they met fierce resistance. The Nazis rounded up Jews, homosexuals, and other people they considered "undesirables" or "enemies of the state" and sent them to forced labor camps, where eventually many were killed in huge gas chambers. (Gas chambers were sealed rooms that were filled with poisonous gas in order to kill the people locked inside.)

Meanwhile, Demjanjuk found a job driving a tractor. He received his draft notice (a notice requiring him to report for service) from the Soviet army in 1940, but he was not accepted until the following year because he did not have any underwear, an army requirement.

After completing his military training in 1941, Demjanjuk was sent to fight against the German army. He was injured by fragments from an exploding shell and still bears the scar. In early 1942, Demjanjuk and his unit were taken prisoner by the Germans. The events of Demjanjuk's life from then until the war's end in 1945 remain controversial and will be covered in the discussion of his trial in Israel, below.

Immigrates to the United States

When World War II ended, Demjanjuk found his way to a German camp for displaced persons (people living in a foreign country who have been driven there by war). There he met Vera Kowlowa, who would later become his wife. The couple spent several years at displaced-persons camps throughout Germany. In 1950 their daughter, Lydia, was born at one of them. The following year, Demjanjuk applied to relocate to the United States. Demjanjuk has said that because he feared being sent back to the Soviet Union (where he may have been killed for working for the Germans), he lied on immigration documents and claimed to be Polish.

Demjanjuk's application to immigrate to the United States was granted. In 1952, his family of three arrived in Indiana, where Demjanjuk found work on a farm. Through the help of friends, they later resettled in Cleveland, Ohio, where Demjanjuk secured work as an engine mechanic, and Vera was employed by a factory. They remained in these jobs for the rest of their working lives. The couple had two more children, a son, John Jr., and a daughter, Irene. The Demjanjuks first bought a house in Parma, Ohio, and in 1973 moved to the Cleveland suburb of Seven Hills.

Named a War Criminal

During the 1970s, a pro-Soviet journalist in New York accused Demjanjuk of having been a guard at the Sobibór death camp and at a German concentration camp, a place where Nazis confined people they regarded as "enemies of the state," in the town of Flossenburg. (No mention was then made of Demjanjuk's ever having worked at the Treblinka death camp in Poland, an accusation that evolved later.)

In response to a request, the U.S. Immigration and Naturalization Service (INS) sent Demjanjuk's immigration photo and information about him to the Israeli police, who were still looking for war criminals, people accused of violating the laws and customs of war. It was then that the investigation of Demjanjuk may have taken a wrong turn. Advertisements were placed by the Israeli police in the newspaper. They requested that survivors of Sobibór and Treblinka death camps report to Israeli police headquarters regarding an investigation against Ukrainian Ivan Demjanjuk. As a result, survivors may have arrived at the police station believing that they were supposed to identify Demjanjuk.

In addition, the police showed these potential witnesses a number of pictures, asking them to point out if any showed the notoriously cruel prison guard "Ivan the Terrible" of Treblinka. Among the smaller and fuzzier pictures was an exceptionally large and clear photo of Demjanjuk. According to writer Frederic Dannen, the way this picture was presented was "suggestive," in the language of police work—witnesses were inclined to pay more attention to this large, clear picture and to think it was more important. While no Sobibór camp survivors pointed out Demjanjuk's picture, five Treblinka camp survivors identified Demjanjuk as "Ivan the Terrible."

Israeli authorities sent the results of their investigation to the INS, mentioning that they must have been mistaken about Demjanjuk. Apparently he worked at Treblinka, they said, not Sobibór.

Loses U.S. Citizenship

In 1981, Demjanjuk underwent a trial in Ohio to determine if his U.S. citizenship should be revoked because he had lied on his application. As a result of this trial, he was stripped of his U.S. citizenship.

Jailed

In October 1983, the Israeli police sent out a warrant for the arrest of John Demjanjuk. He was flown to Israel in February 1986, and held at Ayalon Prison for one year, awaiting his trial.

Three Israeli judges were appointed to decide the case that charged him with serving as a death camp guard. He was also charged with (1) crimes against the Jewish people; (2) crimes against humanity (which included murder, extermination [total destruction], enslavement, deportation [forcibly removing people from their city or country], and other cruel acts committed against any civilian population); (3) war crimes; (4) crimes against persecuted individuals; and (5) murder.

The Israeli trial of Demjanjuk began on September 6, 1986. The survivors of Treblinka, who had identified Demjanjuk as "Ivan the Terrible" in the 1970s, testified to the same at the trial. Through his trial the whole world learned about the atrocities that had taken place at Treblinka death camp, where in one year alone 850,000 people had been murdered.

Daily Events at Treblinka

Based on the testimony of survivors, a picture of a typical day at Treblinka emerged. A train would arrive with about 100 Jews packed closely together in each car. The Jews would have arrived there after one- to three-day journeys with no food or water, and a few buckets to use for toilet facilities. After leaving the train, men and women were separated and ordered to remove their clothing. Female prisoners had their heads shaved.

The naked prisoners were then herded by whips down a narrow path and forced into gas chambers; the doors were bolted behind them. Crying out in terror, they were gassed to death with carbon monoxide (a poisonous gas) fumes generated by a powerful engine. After 30 minutes their bodies were removed and thrown into a burial pit. In the early days of the camp the pits were covered with chloride to dissolve the bodies, but later the corpses were burned in special ovens called crematoriums.

The only Jews to survive the process were those kept behind to perform work for the Nazis. These included clothing sorters, barbers, people whose job was to pry gold out of victims' teeth, and corpse carriers. The Nazis recruited about 100 Soviet army soldiers from prisoner-of-war (POW) camps to help the camp guards. One of the Soviets who operated the gas chambers was the man known as "Ivan the Terrible."

During Demjanjuk's trial, witnesses described how "Ivan the Terrible" often greeted those about to be gassed with beatings or cut off their ears or noses with the sword he carried. He also was reported to have broken prisoners' arms and legs with a steel pipe. Often appearing drunk, he struck and berated those who worked for him, insisting that they abuse the prisoners, too. One ex-prisoner remarked: "What pleasure he took in his tasks."

Prosecutors Name Demjanjuk "Ivan the Terrible"

The job of the prosecutors who argued their case before the Israeli court was to show that Demjanjuk was indeed "Ivan the Terrible" of Treblinka. They claimed that in 1942 the captured Demjanjuk volunteered to work for the Nazis at the POW camp where he was being held. They said he was taken to the Nazi training camp for Soviet collaborators at

Trawniki, Poland (collaborators are people who assist an enemy occupying their country). There he was trained to guard Nazi death camp victims, and was given a uniform, a rifle, and an identification card bearing his photograph. Prosecutors said that Demjanjuk once had a tattoo, later removed, that had identified him as working for the SS (an abbreviation for the *Shutzstaffeln* or Security Squad who acted as Hitler's personal bodyguards and guards at the various camps). They said that from September 1942 until August 1943 Demjanjuk served as a guard at Treblinka, where prisoners named him "Ivan the Terrible."

Prosecutors' Proof

The Israeli prosecutors based their argument that Demjanjuk was "Ivan the Terrible," in part, on an identification card said to be from Trawniki training camp, that featured his picture. The card correctly listed his date of birth, his father's first name, and his blond hair color. It also mentioned that he had a scar.

One problem with the identification card was that the picture on it had staple holes, indicating that it may have been removed from some other document. In addition, Demjanjuk's height, which is nearly six feet, was listed as five-feet-nine. Demjanjuk's lawyers said that the card was forged by Soviet officials (enemies of the Ukrainians) who wanted to injure the reputation of the Ukrainian community in the United States by incriminating Demjanjuk.

During the trial, weeks were spent examining the card in great detail, although the card has never been proven to be an actual training camp identification card. The biggest problem with the card was that it showed that Demjanjuk was sent to a work camp near Chelmno, Poland, and later, in 1943, to the Polish death camp at Sobibór—not Treblinka, where "Ivan the Terrible" performed his evil deeds.

Problems with the Survivors' Identification

The identification of Demjanjuk by concentration camp survivors, whose last contact with "Ivan the Terrible" had been four decades earlier, was also a problem. Demjanjuk is a large, somewhat oafish man, whose bulky wrists required specially made handcuffs. Certainly Demjanjuk and the "Ivan the Terrible" described by the survivors shared a strong

resemblance. They had round faces, ears that stuck out, slanted eyes, and thin lips. The survivors who came forward to identify Demjanjuk in court, however, already believed they "knew who he was supposed to be," said writer Tom Segev, because "they'd seen him testify in America." In other words, Demjanjuk's case was so widely covered by Israeli news reports that witnesses believed Demjanjuk must be the criminal he was accused of being.

Demjanjuk examines a document presented as evidence during his trial in Israel.

Demjanjuk's Testimony

At the completion of the prosecution's case, Demjanjuk's lawyer, John Gill, placed him on the stand to testify in his own defense. The testimony lasted for about one week. According to Demjanjuk, after his capture by the Germans in 1942, he was eventually taken to a Nazi prisoner-of-war camp in Chelmno, Poland. He claims he stayed there for 18 months until the spring of 1944. Demjanjuk has described the camp as having terrible conditions, with people dying in great numbers from disease and starvation. According to his story, he dug peat (a mossy material used for fuel) at the camp, and was then sent to another camp in Austria where he was tattooed to show his blood type. He stated that after the war the tattoo was removed; indeed there is a scar on his arm where the tattoo would have been.

Demjanjuk said that in 1945 he was permitted to join the Russian Liberation Army, a military unit that was funded by the Nazis and opposed the Soviet leader Josef Stalin. Later that year he surrendered to the Allies (the United States, Great Britain, the Soviet Union, and France).

Sentenced to Death

In February 1988, three Israeli judges began their private discussions to decide Demjanjuk's fate. Two months later they declared him guilty of being "Ivan the Terrible" and sentenced him to death by hanging. According to Israeli law, all death sentences automatically come under review by the Supreme Court of Israel.

Five judges from among the twelve who make up the Israeli Supreme Court were chosen to hear Demjanjuk's appeal in August 1993. Meanwhile, Demjanjuk had spent the previous six years in solitary confinement in an Israeli jail.

Sometime in 1991, the written statement of 32 former guards and 5 forced laborers at Treblinka death camp (most of whom were executed by the Soviets as Nazi collaborators) had come into the possession of the Israeli court. The statements all said that "Ivan the Terrible" was a man named Ivan Marchenko. Marchenko, a Ukrainian like Demjanjuk, was last seen in 1944 in Yugoslavia (and there is no evidence if and when he died).

Some U.S. officials came to believe that Ivan Marchenko and Ivan Demjanjuk were the same person. One reason was because Demjanjuk had listed "Marchenko" as his mother's maiden name on his application for a U.S. visa. Demjanjuk later said that he had forgotten his mother's maiden name and just used the name of Marchenko, which is common in Ukraine, to fill in the blank.

Demjanjuk Acquitted

Nevertheless the Israeli Supreme Court ruled in 1993 that the case against John Demjanjuk had not been proved

Demjanjuk's Life after His Acquittal

Evidence seems to support the idea that John Demjanjuk was probably a guard at the Sobibór death camp (not Treblinka), but what he may have done there remains a mystery. Some people feel that Demjanjuk should have been tried for the offenses he may have committed at Sobibór, but Israel has never put on trial such a low-level Nazi collaborator and did not pursue the matter.

Following his acquittal by the Israeli Supreme Court, John Demjanjuk regained his U.S. citizenship and returned home to Cleveland, Ohio. Demjanjuk issued a news release in 1996 on the third anniversary of his release from Ayalon prison. He extended his thanks and greetings to all the people who had supported him over the more than 20 years he was under investigation. Demjanjuk was reported to be readjusting to life within the Ukrainian community in the United States.

beyond a reasonable doubt. The judgment has been referred to by some as "careful and courageous" because Israel is a Jewish state and the atrocities committed against Jews in the Nazi death camps have particular meaning in Israel. Apparently the written statements taken from the Soviet soldiers played an important role in their decision. "We don't know how these statements came into the world and who gave birth to them," the court wrote. "But . . . when they came before us, doubt began to gnaw away at our judicial conscience; perhaps the appellant [Demjanjuk] was not Ivan the Terrible."

After the Supreme Court had presented its verdict, chief judge Meir Shamgar said: "The matter is closed, but not complete. The complete truth [cannot be known by] the human judge."

Where to Learn More

Beyer, L. "Ivan the Not-So-Terrible." *Time,* 142 (August 2, 1993): p. 42.

Dannen, Frederic. "How Terrible Is Ivan?" *Vanity Fair,* 55 (June 1992): p. 133.

Kozinski, A. "Sanhedrin II." *New Republic,* 209 (September 13, 1993): pp. 16-18.

Seibert, S. "Maybe He Wasn't the Nazis' Ivan the Terrible—But What Was He?" *Newsweek* 122 (August 9, 1993): p. 49.

Sereny, Gitta. "The Two Faces of Ivan of Treblinka." *The Sunday Times Magazine,* March 20, 1988, pp. 20-38.

Teicholz, Tom. *The Trial of Ivan the Terrible.* St. Martin's Press, 1990.

Wagenmaan, W. A. *Identifying Ivan: A Case Study in Legal Psychology.* Harvard University Press, 1989.

Shimson and Tova Draenger

Shimson Draenger

Born 1917
Krakow, Poland

Died 1943?
Somewhere in Poland

Writer, editor

Polish-Jewish resistance leader

Tova Draenger

Born 1917
Krakow, Poland

Died 1943?
Somewhere in Poland

Writer, Polish-Jewish resistance worker

Wrote a memoir of young Jewish resisters (against German domination) titled Justyna's Narrative

Shimson and Tova Draenger, a young Jewish couple living in Krakow, Poland, before and during World War II (1939–45), repeatedly put their lives at risk opposing the rule of the National Socialist German Workers' Party (Nazi for short) that had taken over their country. They realized the value of the printed word, using the journals and newspapers they published to encourage the rebellion of their fellow Jews. More than 50 years after the war, their tale of courageous and persistent resistance remains an inspiration.

Shimson Becomes Underground Leader

Shimson Draenger, often called Simek, was born in Krakow, Poland, in 1917. When he was 13, Shimson joined Akiba, a Jewish youth organization. Its members met on Friday evenings to celebrate the beginning of the Jewish Sabbath (the holy day of rest and reflection

"I swear by ... the memory and honor of dying Polish Jewry, that I will fight with all the weapons available to me until the last moment of my life to resist ... the [German invaders], and those in league with them, the mighty enemies of the Jewish people and of all humanity."

—*Tova Draenger*

observed each Saturday) through songs and poetry. Eventually Shimson became a leader of the group.

Shimson earned a college degree in liberal arts and became the editor of Akiba's weekly newspaper as well as its journal, *The Sayings of Akiba*. During the 1930s, the Nazis gained power in Germany through the use of force and as a result of the hypnotic speaking skills of their leader, Adolf Hitler (see entry). Hitler and the Nazis were antisemitic, meaning that they hated the Jewish people and continuously persecuted them. World War II began when the Nazis took over Poland in 1939, and Great Britain came to Poland's defense. At that time, Shimson's journal spoke out against the Nazis. On September 22, 1939, shortly after the Nazis occupied the city of Krakow, Poland, they arrested Shimson because of the anti-Nazi material he was publishing. His wife, Tova, was arrested along with him. He was taken to a prison camp in the nearby country of Czechoslovakia, but released in December of that year.

Shimson, a tough and somewhat humorless young man, soon brought his followers back together, under the pretense of carrying out educational activities. In fact, he was building a branch of Akiba in Warsaw, Poland, to continue resistance activities against the Nazis. He continued to publish his journal as well as his weekly newspaper.

From December 1941 through August 1942, Shimson was in charge of a farm set up by the Akiba Youth Organization in the Polish town of Kopaliny. He and the other young people in charge managed to convince the local people that they were Gentiles (non-Jews.) The farm served as a cover for Akiba's training of Jewish resistance workers. A colleague of the Draengers stated that the young people were never quite certain how they should proceed in their resistance efforts: "We were constantly debating ways and means, short-range versus ultimate goals, and were always dickering about what we could and could not hope to achieve."

While working at the farm, Shimson and Tova Draenger took care of their five-year-old nephew, Witek, who became a kind of mascot for the group. The farm was abandoned in August 1942 because activities there were starting to arouse suspicion among the locals and the Nazis. Shimson and his colleagues moved Akiba's operations to the Krakow ghetto (crowded, walled sections of cities where Jews were forced to live in inferior conditions). Shimson and his followers went voluntarily to the ghetto because they thought they could be of more help to Krakow's Jews if they were inside the ghetto. In the ghetto, Akiba continued its resistance work.

Urges Rebellion

The Nazis considered the Jews members of a separate, evil race who plotted against German society. During the middle part of World War II, it became known that the Nazis intended to murder all the Jews of Europe, in an effort they referred to as the Final Solution. Previously the Nazis had a policy of deporting (forcing people to leave their city or country) Jews from Europe for what they called "resettlement" elsewhere. The Nazis built hundreds of concentration camps throughout Germany and Eastern Europe, intending to clear out the ghettos in the cities and send their inhabitants to the camps. The camps were to house people the Nazis considered "enemies of the state." There prisoners would be forced to work long hours with very little food, and many would be killed in gas chambers, sealed rooms that were filled with poisonous gas in order to kill the prisoners locked inside.

The Nazis lied to Jews of the ghettos, promising them that they were to be resettled in labor camps with good conditions. When Shimson learned about what the Nazis' true intentions were, he declared that the Jews must make all possible efforts to disrupt the Nazi order. In September and October 1942, along with other groups of Jewish young people, Akiba formed the Jewish Fighting Organization to work against the Nazis' aims.

Shimson wrote: "We ought to go from town to town and explain to the people that there are no resettlements; that there is only death! They must have no illusions. They must flee. . . . They must not try to escape singly but do so in one great mass, so as to flood the trains, roads, the entire countryside. . . . It is true that [the Nazis'] round-ups would become gigantic massacres, but this is of no importance to us, while to them this would be an open rebellion. For every rebellion undermines the power and upsets their order."

According to a Polish man who knew Shimson well: "Sentiment, personal matters, even his relationship to

[Tova]—everything—all were replaced by the cause, which he regarded as sacred."

Arrested

By 1942, Jews were not permitted to leave or enter the Krakow ghetto without special permits checked by German guards. The Jewish Fighting Organization operated an office that forged permits allowing its members free access in and out of the ghetto. They also sold the permits to obtain firearms. Shimson was so skilled at doing the forgeries that German officials often thought his forged signatures were their own signatures.

During late 1942 and early 1943, the Jewish Fighting Organization conducted a series of raids against the Nazis and sabotaged tracks at the railroad station in Krakow. Several German hangouts were attacked by the group, with the most severe damage being done to a popular restaurant, where seven Nazi officers were killed and seven were wounded.

In the same period, Shimson and his Tova began producing an underground journal called *The Fighting Pioneer.* The ten-page publication, written in Polish, urged the readers to never give up their struggles against the Nazis. Beginning in September 1942 Shimson's group also published *The Voice of the Democrat,* which was distributed in the streets of Krakow.

Shimson was captured by the Nazis in January 1943 and taken to Poland's Montelupich prison. Upon learning that Shimson had been arrested, Tova surrendered to the Nazis and was also sent to Montelupich. Most of Shimson's fellow resistance leaders had already been captured and killed. Conditions in the prison were terrible, with inmates forced to submit to such brutalities as having their heads immersed in buckets of human waste. Always interested in the power of ideas, and hoping to bring inspiration to his fellow prisoners, Shimson established study groups focusing on the Bible and other topics.

Shimson escaped from prison in April 1943, and he and Tova, who had also escaped from prison, were reunited. They hid in a forest and engaged in resistance activities with other Jews.

Shimson resumed his writing and publishing. He encouraged the Jews in the forest to continue their fight and urged those still living in the ghettos to get out at all costs. He also appealed to the people of Poland not to divulge to the Nazis the whereabouts of Jews who were in hiding.

Shimson was recaptured by the Nazis on November 8, 1943, and was most likely executed by them.

Tova Cofounds Resistance Movement

Tova Draenger, who married Shimson Draenger in 1938, was born Gusta Davidson in Krakow, Poland, in 1917. Along with Shimson, she worked on a weekly newspaper for young people and also cofounded and participated in an underground (secret and illegal) resistance movement in Krakow.

Tova has been described as attractive, intelligent, charming, and eager to express her feelings. Along with her husband, she was arrested on September 22, 1939, for being part of the Jewish resistance. She was released from prison camp in December 1939. Soon she and Shimson reorganized the Akiba movement in the cities of Warsaw and Krakow.

Tova Surrenders to the Nazis

In 1941 and 1942, Tova was part of the resistance group her husband operated on a farm. Coconspirator Jozef Wulf described her main activities there: "She did technical work, sought out hiding places for the inexperienced revolutionaries, accompanied the first fighting groups to the forest, took part in numerous consultations among the leaders, brought guns, and suffered in silence because her husband . . . did not have time for her."

In 1942 and 1943, Tova was involved in planning the anti-Nazi raids conducted by the Jewish Fighting Organization. Tova and Shimson had already agreed that if one were captured, the other would surrender. When she learned that Shimson had been arrested on January 18, 1943, Tova surrendered to the Nazis.

Reuben Ainsztein referred to Tova's behavior as noble and generous, although he also called it "a romantic gesture typical of the Akiba group, who never ceased to be romantic amateurs in their underground work." However, Ainsztein commended Tova for refusing to reveal any information despite repeated beatings and torture. He told how the Nazis brought her in contact with her husband expecting that she

Excerpt from *Justyna's Narrative*

A 1996 edition of Tova Draenger's memoir, called *Justyna's Narrative,* recounts the history of the Akiba Movement from April 1941 to March 1943. Tova described the diary as "the true story of the last and most daring revolt of the young fighters."

In this passage, the character Justyna, who represents Tova herself, talks about the difference between the attitudes held by young and older Jewish people in the face of Nazi torture and extermination:

"In general, the older folks lacked the fighting spirit needed to resist the enemy. But why should that come as a surprise. Anyone who has not lived through three years of degradation, humiliation and baiting, who has not clung desperately to a life hanging by a thread in the midst of a [raging] storm, will not be able to understand the despair of these people. Only someone who has had the luxury of an unruffled existence could condemn them for having resigned themselves to their fate. If you could just see into the murkiness of their bruised, despairing souls and live a single hour in that black hopelessness, knowing that all struggle is meaningless and to no avail, knowing that there is nothing at the end of the tunnel but the ugly letters that spell out 'death,' then you would know what they felt, and you would say to yourself, as they said, 'Let come what may'—and wait for it to happen.

"It was different with the young. They clutched at life, and refused to accept their fate passively. Their powerful desire to live drove them to active resistance, which was not without its ironies, since it was this irresistible lust for life that drove them to engage an overwhelmingly superior enemy, thereby exposing themselves to certain death.... The force demanding their survival was the very force pushing them to their deaths."

would then break down in tears and tell them what she knew. Instead, she said, "Yes, we have organized Jewish fighting groups and we promise you that if we succeed in escaping from your hands, we shall organize even stronger . . . groups."

Tova Writes Memoirs

While a prisoner in Montelupich prison, Tova helped to organize a series of activities for the prisoners to help keep up their spirits. These included intellectual discussions, Bible reading, singing, and writing and reciting poetry.

At Montelupich, Tova also produced a diary, later published as *Justyna's Narrative,* about the successful raids her group had led against the Nazis. Fearing that these stories would die along with the group's young heroes, Tova wanted to preserve them for future generations. Since what she wrote might have been found by guards, Tova used made-up names for the characters; the name she chose for herself was Justyna. She wrote her thoughts on pieces of toilet paper. With the help of cellmates, several copies of the diary were produced and hidden on the prison grounds.

Writers Eli Pfefferkorn and David H. Hirsch described Tova's efforts: "In [Tova's] relatively spacious cell . . . a handful of women huddled together in a circle, and in the center of the circle sat [Tova], inscribing tiny letters on scraps of paper. When her fingers became numb from exertion, another woman would take over the writing while she dictated. Every single note was checked by [Tova] before being stashed away. . . . 'This is history and it must be accurate,' she insisted." Fortunately, 15 of the book's 20 chapters have survived.

On April 29, 1943, Tova and other women prisoners were lined up two-by-two on a forced march outside Montelupich prison. Tova and another woman attacked the nearest guards when they saw a chance. The other prisoners followed, while several women ran away. Most of the women were killed by machine-gun fire, but Tova managed to escape. She rejoined Shimson, who had also escaped. They hid in a forest, where they continued their publishing and other underground activities.

Surrender and Probable Murder

After Shimson was arrested a second time on November 8, 1943, Tova again surrendered to the Nazis. Her fate following the surrender is unknown; she was probably executed. The disappearance of the Draengers brought an end to the Jewish Fighting Organization of Krakow.

Jozef Wulf wrote in 1945: "They were both fighters, and both fought passionately to preserve the honor of the Jewish people; they still dreamed of continuing the struggle against the Germans . . . they both died at the hands of the German executioners."

Where to Learn More

Ainsztein, R. *Jewish Resistance in Nazi-occupied Europe*. Harper & Row, 1974.

Draenger, Gusta Davidson. *Justyna's Narrative*. Edited by Eli Pfefferkorn. University of Massachusetts, 1996.

Adolf Eichmann

Born March 16, 1906
Solingen, Germany

Died May 31, 1962
Ramle, near Tel Aviv, Israel

*Lieutenant colonel in the SS,
a unit of the German military*

*Planned and directed the rail system that
took millions of men, women, and children
to the death camps during World War II;
helped develop the gas chamber*

One of the most sinister figures of World War II (1939–45), Adolf Eichmann claimed responsibility for the murder of millions of people in eighteen countries before he escaped to South America. Eichmann was kidnaped by Israeli secret agents in 1960, taken to Israel, tried for crimes against humanity and the Jewish people, and hanged. Crimes against humanity include murder, extermination (total destruction), enslavement, deportation (forcibly removing people from their city or country), and other acts committed against the nonmilitary population of a country. In his defense, he claimed he was only a junior official with no authority to issue orders and that as a good soldier he was simply following orders.

Childhood in Germany, Austria

Otto Adolf Eichmann (pronounced Eyek-muhn; called Adolf) was born in 1906 in Solingen, Germany, the first of five children born to Karl Adolf and Maria Schefferling Eichmann. His father was an accountant, a stern and devoutly religious man who ran an orderly household and apparently instilled in his son a dislike for religion. Eichmann was about ten years old when his mother died. His father remarried shortly thereafter and moved the family to Linz, a picturesque town in Austria.

Eichmann was a solitary boy and a poor student who dropped out of high school at the age of 16 to begin an apprenticeship in his father's electrical construction company. It is interesting to note that he dropped out of the very same high school that Adolf Hitler (see entry) had dropped out of nearly 20 years before. Easily bored, he was unable to finish the apprenticeship program. Eichmann spent the early 1920s doing odd jobs and drifting about. He was working as a traveling salesman when he first heard Hitler speak. It may have been out of boredom that he joined the National Socialist German Workers' Party (Nazi for short) in 1932, but the party soon became the center of his life.

"It was a job I had. It wasn't anything I'd planned, nor anything I'd have chosen."

Origins of the Nazi Party

The Nazi Party grew out of a small, anti-Jewish group that began in 1918. Hitler became its leader in 1921, and built it up so that by the time of the 1933 elections, he was able to take control of Germany. The party had more than two dozen objectives, mainly revolving around repression of the Jews, who were considered "enemies of the state." The Nazi Party declared that Jews could not be citizens; they were to be treated as foreigners; they were prohibited from publishing and from holding public office; and they were to be expelled from Germany under certain conditions.

Moves Up in Nazi Party

When he was fired from his job as a traveling salesman, Eichmann made his way to Germany and joined the military branch of the Nazi Party, the SS, in 1934. Although the training was brutal, he excelled, and discovered within himself a capacity for enduring great pain and a love for precision and order. Not long after, he volunteered to work in the SD, the German Security Office (an intelligence or spy operation) and he moved to Berlin, the capital of Germany.

According to author Hannah Arendt, Eichmann's new boss in the SD told him to read two books about Zionism, which may have been among the few serious books he would ever read. Zionism is the belief that Jews should have their own nation, an opinion that Eichmann immediately adopted. For the rest of his life he would claim that he always favored sending Europe's Jews away to their own nation rather than exterminating them.

When Eichmann next acquired a little knowledge of Hebrew and Yiddish (a language spoken by eastern European Jews), he became the SD's "expert" on Jews. He visited Palestine, parts of which later became the modern State of Israel, homeland to the Jews, to learn about the Jewish community already established there. He was named director of the "Jewish Emigration Office," an organization that kept track of Jews. Thus began his career as a mastermind behind the solution to the "Jewish question." Between 1937 and 1941 Eichmann was promoted four times. He was often complimented by his superiors for his thorough knowledge of the party's "enemies," the Jews. He became so powerful that he was assigned his own four-story building to carry out his work.

During this period, Jews were not yet being exterminated but were being forced by Eichmann to leave Europe. One of the tactics he used to "persuade" Jews to emigrate (move to another country) was to have the Gestapo (the German Secret State Police) terrorize them. He then arranged that departing Jews would be stripped of their property. So many Jews left Europe that it became difficult to find countries willing to accept them. As a result, millions of Jews were left behind in Germany.

Eichmann had become a master at moving large numbers of people. He grew more confident in his own abilities. At some point during this time he married Veronika (Vera) Lieble, had two children, and embarked on a string of romances. He discovered a fondness for gourmet food, fine wines, and luxury cars. All the while he told himself that he was actually helping the Jews by sending them to a place where they would have "soil of their own."

Wartime Activities

Eichmann's duties were expanded as a result of the Wannsee Conference (January 20, 1942). There he and other top Nazi officials laid down the details for the Final Solution (the complete elimination of European Jews). Eichmann later claimed that he had objected to extermination of the Jews (preferring to force them out of Europe), but since this was now his superiors' policy, he did his best to carry it out with efficiency.

Eichmann oversaw a vast and complicated operation involving organizing transportation, providing supplies and equipment to German soldiers, and rounding up victims for the concentration camps (places where the Nazis confined people they regarded as "enemies of the state"). At first he had special SS units follow directly behind Hitler's army as it marched through Europe. In each country that was conquered, Jews would be rounded up and some would be lined up in front of trenches and told to kneel. Then soldiers moved along the line and, according to Peter Malkin, "fired point-blank into the backs of their heads and, in a move they had practiced, sent each victim pitching forward with a sharp thrust of a boot."

But Eichmann saw problems with this method of murdering Jews. For one thing, bullets were scarce and expensive. And some German soldiers felt sympathy for the victims, a feeling Eichmann could understand because he too was sickened by the sight of blood. So he began to investigate new ways to kill. After discarding several other possibilities, he ordered the building of new concentration camps containing large gas chambers disguised as showers where large numbers of people could be disposed of in a short period of time. Gas chambers were sealed rooms that were filled with poisonous gas in order to kill the people locked inside. When a new type of gas, called Zyklon B, became available, Eichmann's gas chambers became even more efficient. (Much later, as part of their training in chemical warfare, German soldiers were required to stand in gas chambers. They called the chambers "Eichmann Hobby Shops.")

Eichmann continued the killing even when it became obvious that Germany was losing the war. He later told Peter Malkin, one of the Israeli secret service agents who captured him in South America: "Near the end, [Heinrich] Himmler [see entry] himself wanted me to stop. He thought we could save our skins. But I pressed on. If a man has an assignment to perform, he does not stop until it is done." A witness at the Nuremberg Trials held immediately after the war testified that he heard Eichmann say: "I will leap into my grave laughing, because the feeling I have five million human beings on my conscience is for me a source of extraordinary satisfaction."

Keeps a Low Profile

For his part in the horrors of the Holocaust (the name given to the systematic persecution and murder of millions of Jews and other innocent people by the Nazis), Eichmann became a legend among Jews. Knowing that there was a chance Germany might lose the war and he would someday be held accountable for his actions, he deliberately aimed to keep a low profile. Michael A. Musmanno, a judge who later appeared as a witness at Eichmann's trial, writes that he asked an Eichmann associate why Eichmann's military rank was so low, considering how much power he had. The reply was that Eichmann preferred this arrangement. He felt that if he had a high rank, he would be more conspicuous, and more people would be aware of his activities. As it was, "Eichmann could operate like a weasel on a chicken farm . . . and then cunningly disappear before the victims could defend themselves."

Even some high-ranking Nazi officers did not know the extent of his power. Whenever Nazi officers posed for photographs, Eichmann arranged to be standing in the last row, with his face hidden by another person. Therefore, few knew what he looked like. When he was captured by the Americans in 1946, he passed himself off as a clerk of no importance and eventually escaped.

Escape and Capture

In 1950, Eichmann made his way to Argentina; his wife and two sons followed in 1952. Under the name Richard Klement, he took a job on the assembly line of the Argentine branch of a German automobile company in Buenos Aires. A conscientious employee, he soon had worked his way up to a management position. Eventually a third son was born. Eichmann developed friendships among the community of former Nazis in Argentina, all of whom knew who he really was. He even gave an anonymous interview to a Dutch Nazi

Eichmann at his 1961 trial in Israel.

journalist, in which he stated: "I have to conclude in my own defense that I was neither a murderer nor a mass murderer. . . . I carried out with a clear conscience and faithful heart the duty imposed upon me."

Although it seemed that most of the world had forgotten about him, there were some who could not get Eichmann out of their thoughts. Simon Wiesenthal (see entry) is a dedicated Nazi-hunter who made the capture of Eichmann a top priority. Evidence collected by Wiesenthal helped bring Eichmann to justice.

Finally, in a daring, carefully plotted, top-secret mission, Israeli secret agents kidnapped Eichmann near his home in 1960. In his account of the capture, *Eichmann in My Hands,* Israeli agent Peter Malkin spoke of standing guard over Eichmann in the bedroom of the house where he was held captive and interrogated before being taken to Israel. Malkin, who had lost relatives because of Eichmann's actions, described Eichmann talking about his love for children. He recalled how Eichmann's sense of military discipline reached absurd proportions during his captivity—Eichmann would not eat or use the toilet unless ordered to do so. And throughout his captivity, Eichmann continued to insist that what he did was right because he was following orders.

Eichmann's kidnapping caused a worldwide uproar. Argentina charged Israel with violating its rights by abducting Eichmann out of that country. Critics all over the world condemned Israel, flinging accusations of "illegal practices and violence." The kidnapping was only the beginning of the outrage, though. It continued as more than 100 witnesses came forward at trial to present the full details of the Holocaust.

The Trial of Eichmann

Eichmann was accused by an Israeli court of crimes against humanity and against the Jewish people. He was also accused of membership in hostile organizations—the SS, SD, and Gestapo. Eichmann's answer to every charge presented against him was "not guilty."

A witness at the trial described Eichmann's demeanor.

> I study him as he sits in a bullet-proof glass enclosure, so he may be safe from any possible act of vengeance attempted by some grief-crazed survivor of the crimes attributed to him. . . . His beady, snakelike eyes sink into a startling skull, over which the yellowish parchment of his skin crinkles and almost crackles. . . . His thin lips curl, twitch, and bunch at either side of a mouth which any fox could call its own. . . .

> Throughout the trial Eichmann remained as rigid and aloof as a slab of stone. Even when a man

Hannah Arendt (1906–1975) Covers Eichmann Trial

Hannah Arendt, the only child of a Jewish engineer, was born in Hanover, Germany, in 1906. She earned a Ph.D. in political theory at the University of Heidelberg (Germany) in 1928. Five years later she fled to France to escape the Nazis and, in 1941, with the assistance of Varian Fry, she fled to the United States. There she became a citizen and taught at several universities, becoming the first woman ever to be named a full professor at Princeton University in New Jersey. When her first book, *Origins of Totalitarianism,* was published in 1951, she established a reputation as a major political thinker.

In 1961, she was asked by *The New Yorker* magazine to cover the Adolf Eichmann trial. She wrote a series of magazine articles about the trial, and out of them grew the book *Eichmann in Jerusalem: A Report on the Banality of Evil.* The views she expressed about the character of Eichmann created a considerable controversy.

Banality means "something that is trite, obvious, or predictable; a commonplace."

Arendt believed that Eichmann was a very ordinary man who was not motivated by hatred of the Jews. She believed that he was simply carrying out orders, as he himself claimed ("he left no doubt that he would have killed his own father if he had received an order to that effect"). Many other people believed that Eichmann was an evil man, fully responsible for the actions he performed. Justice Michael Musmanno called him "this colossal figure of evil." Peter Malkin, one of the Israeli secret service agents who captured Eichmann in Argentina, called him "a monster." Still, he said: "[H]e was not an obviously cruel or thoughtless man. Were he living among us today and, say, running a shoe factory, he would probably be regarded with quiet respect, a steady husband and father, producing excellent shoes at a fair price, a pride to his community." In other words, a "predictable, commonplace" man. Whatever one's point of view, though, writer Leni Yahil concluded: "What cannot be doubted is that Eichmann served the Nazi program for exterminating the Jewish people with zeal and efficiency."

in the balcony hurled insults at him he did not react. He could not be bothered with people who came to look at him and ask themselves why this man, with the protruding ears, could not have heard the cries of screaming mankind and heeded its plea to cease the mad slaughter.

Eichmann was found guilty on all counts and sentenced to death. He was executed by hanging on May 31, 1962. His last words to the court were: "I had to obey the rules of war and my flag. I am ready."

Where to Learn More

Arendt, Hannah. *Eichmann in Jerusalem: A Report on the Banality of Evil.* Penguin, 1977.

Harel, Israel. *The House on Garibaldi Street: The First Full Account of the Capture of Adolph Eichmann, Told by the Former Head of Israel's Secret Service.* Viking, 1975.

Malkin, Peter Z., and Harry Stein. *Eichmann in My Hands.* Warner Books, 1990.

Musmanno, Michael A., Justice. "Witness Against Eichmann." In *The Verdicts Were Just: Eight Famous Lawyers Present Their Most Memorable Cases.* Edited by Albert Alverbach. Lawyers Co-Operative Publishing. 1966.

Yahil, Leni. "Eichmann, Adolf." In *Encyclopedia of the Holocaust.* Macmillan, 1990.

Zentner, Christian, and Friedemann Bedurftig, eds. *The Encyclopedia of the Third Reich.* Macmillan, 1991.

Anne Frank

Born June 12, 1929
Frankfurt, Germany

Died March 1945
Bergen-Belsen concentration camp

German Holocaust victim and diarist

Wrote a diary depicting life as a Jew during World War II

Although hundreds of thousands of children perished during the Holocaust because of the faith they were born into, Anne Frank has become the most famous. The Holocaust refers to the period between 1933 and 1945 when Nazi Germany systematically persecuted and murdered millions of European Jews and other innocent people. Frank and her diary, which chronicles her experience hiding from the National Socialist Germany Workers' Party (Nazi for short) and records the anxieties of an adolescent girl, have become symbols to the world of all the hope and innocence that was lost during the Nazis' anti-Jewish campaign.

The Rise of Hitler

Anne Frank was born in Germany on June 12, 1929, about a decade after the close of World War I (1914–18). The war had left Germany in a shambles. According to the terms of the Treaty of Versailles, which ended the war, Germany was forced to greatly reduce its army and it had to make large payments, known as reparations, to the victorious countries. These terms left the German citizens resentful. When Nazi leader Adolf Hitler (see entry) began rising to power, he promised the German people that he would make Germany a great nation again, as it had been before the war. Once he became dictator (he ruled with absolute power), Hitler began rebuilding the German army. He convinced Germans that many of their troubles were caused by minority groups, especially the Jews. Hitler was paving the way for another terrible world war.

Anne Frank's Early Life

Frank was the second daughter of Otto and Edith Hollander Frank. The family had a comfortable, prosperous life in Frankfurt, Germany, where Otto Frank headed the banking business that had been in his family for generations. But in 1933 the bank failed and closed its doors forever. That same year, Hitler came to power in Germany and began promoting his plan to control the Jews and other minorities. His antisemitic or anti-Jewish policies—which included denying Jews the privileges of German citizenship and forbidding them to vote or hold public office—convinced Otto Frank to move his family to Amsterdam, Holland, where he opened a company to manufacture products used in making jam. For a while the Franks again lived a happy life. Anne Frank, who was only four years old at the time of the move, loved Amsterdam and made many friends. She was described by people who knew her at the time as a bubbly, chatty girl, very curious about everything. Her sister Margot was quiet and studious.

The family's life was disrupted once again when, in 1940, when Hitler invaded Holland and established the same antisemitic policies that were in place in German. Up to this time, Frank had been attending a private school, but Hitler's new laws did not allow Jewish children to attend non-Jewish schools. Because the new laws also prohibited Jews from owning businesses, Otto Frank had to turn his company over to one of his employees.

Goes into Hiding

On July 5, 1942—less than one month after Anne Frank's thirteenth birthday—her older sister, Margot,

"I still believe people are really good at heart."

SEPT 11 1934

Jhr ↓ Gewicht

kg · · · · kg

24 25 2

PHOTOWAAGE
BAD AACHEN

A photo of Anne Frank at age five, just one year after her family had moved to Holland.

received orders to report to a concentration camp. Concentration camps were places where the Nazis confined people they regarded as "enemies of the state," such as Jews. Otto Frank had been preparing for this moment and had set up a hiding place in the attic of his office building. Immediately after Margot received the summons, the family went into hiding in the attic, or the "Secret Annex" as Anne called it. During the next two years, Frank recorded in her diary—which she addressed as "Kitty"—her impressions of her time in hiding.

Writes Diary

In the annex the Franks were soon joined by another family, a Jewish couple Frank called Hermann and Petronella van Daan and their teenage son Peter, and a Jewish dentist named Albert Dussel (these were not their real names). Everyone had to be absolutely silent during business hours and had to go to bed early in the evening so they would not attract the attention of anyone on the outside. Frank occupied herself by reading, taking lessons given by her father, listening to the radio, performing household chores, and writing in her diary.

At first Frank wrote the diary for herself. Then one day she heard a radio broadcast announcing that after the war, eyewitness stories about life in Holland during the Nazi occupation would be collected so everyone could read them and know how the people had suffered. Frank decided that a book based on her diary would make a fine contribution to the collection, so she began to edit and rewrite it.

From her hiding place, Frank could see the daily deportation of Jews to either death (extermination) camps or concentration camps. Frank knew what would happen to her and her family if the Nazis discovered their hiding place. In one diary entry she wrote: "Our many Jewish friends are being taken away by the dozen. The people are treated by the Gestapo [the Nazi secret police under the control of Heinrich Himmler; see entry] without a shred of decency, being loaded into cattle trucks. . . . We assume most of them are being murdered. The English radio speaks of their being gassed [the Nazi process of filling a sealed room with poisonous gas in order to kill the people locked inside]."

In her diary entry dated July 15, 1944, Frank wrote: "I feel the sufferings of millions. And yet, when I look up at the sky, I somehow feel that everything will change for the better, that this cruelty too shall end, that peace and tranquility will return once more."

Sent to Concentration Camp

Frank did not live to see the end of the cruelty or the publication of her book. On August 4, 1944, after the Franks had lived undetected for 25 months, someone informed the police of their hiding place. As the war had dragged on and on, many Dutch citizens who helped the Jews were having second thoughts. They were afraid of being punished if they

Life in Close Quarters

Getting along with others for a long time in a small space can be hard under normal circumstances. When you fear all the time that you might be discovered and shot, it is even harder. Anne Frank had strong opinions about the people she lived with in the annex, and she described them in her diary.

> [My family are] always saying how nice it is with the four of us, and that we get along so well, without giving a moment's thought to the fact that I don't feel that way.

Later she had this to say about Peter van Daan:

> . . . no one takes Peter seriously anymore, since he's hypersensitive [extra sensitive] and lazy. Yesterday he was beside himself with worry because his tongue was blue instead of pink . . . His Highness has been complaining of lumbago [muscle pain] too. . . . He's an absolute hypochondriac [he is not really ill but thinks he is]!

Frank especially resented Petronella van Daan's comments about Frank's manners and upbringing. Frank had these comments to make:

> Mrs. van Daan is unbearable. I'm continually being scolded for my incessant chatter . . . Some people, like the van Daans, seem to take special delight not only in raising their own children but in helping others raise theirs . . . . More than once the air has been filled with the van Daans' admonitions [warnings] and my saucy replies . . . .This is always how her tirades begin and end: "If Anne were my daughter . . . " Thank goodness I'm not.

Frank had the mixed feelings about her own mother that teenagers often have. She also had mixed feelings about her sister Margot. About the two of them she wrote:

> At moments like these I can't stand Mother. It's obvious that I'm a stranger to her; she doesn't even know what I think about the most ordinary things . . . . Margot's and Mother's personalities are so alien to me. I understand my girlfriends better than my own mother. Isn't that a shame? . . . Is it just a coincidence that Father and Mother never scold Margot and always blame me for everything?

Later, Frank had to share a bedroom with Albert Dussel, the dentist. Although she accepted this arrangement with good grace, she did not find Dussel an agreeable companion:

> Mr. Dussel . . . has turned out to be an old-fashioned disciplinarian and preacher of unbearably long sermons on manners. . . . since I'm generally considered to be the worst behaved of the three young people, it's all I can do to avoid having the same old scoldings and admonitions repeatedly flung at my head and to pretend not to hear . . . . Really, it's not easy being the badly brought-up center of attention of a family of nitpickers.

were found out. Food was becoming scarce, and the Nazis were offering rewards for the betrayal of Jews in hiding.

The Franks, the van Daans, and Albert Dussel were sent to the Auschwitz-Birkenau concentration camp in Poland. There Otto Frank was separated from his family and sent to the men's camp, while Hermann van Daan was immediately sent to the gas chambers and killed. Peter van Daan and Albert Dussel were sent to other camps in Germany where they died of illness. Edith Frank died at Auschwitz-Birkenau on January 6, 1945. Petronella van Daan, Margot, and Anne were sent to the Bergen-Belsen concentration camp, where conditions were even worse than at Auschwitz. From there Petronella van Daan was sent to an unknown destination and did not survive. At Bergen-Belsen Margot and Anne developed typhoid fever, an infectious disease spread under crowded, unsanitary conditions. In late February or early March 1945, Margot died; a few days later, Anne died too. It is likely that the bodies of both girls were placed in one of the camp's mass graves. If the eight residents of the Secret Annex had managed to remain hidden for only a few weeks more, they probably would have survived, for the camps were liberated in the spring of 1945.

Diary Published

Otto Frank was the only one of the Secret Annex refugees to survive his concentration camp imprisonment. When he returned to Amsterdam, Miep Gies (see entry), his former employee who had helped the family while they were hiding, gave Otto Frank Anne's diary, which Gies had saved. Otto Frank was urged to publish the diary, and the first edition was released in 1947. Since that time, the diary has become immensely popular because of its power as both a document of the suffering endured during Hitler's regime and a testimony of a girl becoming a young woman.

Lives on after Her Death

"I want to go on living after my death," Frank had once written. Her wish has been granted through her diary, which has sold 18 million copies in 52 editions, and has been translated into more than 50 languages. In an introduction to an early edition of Frank's diary, Eleanor Roosevelt, wife of President Franklin D. Roosevelt (see entry), wrote: "This is a remarkable book. Written by a young girl—and the young are not afraid of telling the truth—it is one of the wisest and most moving commentaries on war and its impact on human beings that I have ever read."

A Broadway play based on Frank's life called *The Diary of Anne Frank* opened in New York in 1955. New York theater critics described the play as "a lovely, tender drama," made from "what must have been one of the most heartbreaking documents of the. . .war." When the play was performed in Germany, audiences were so moved that they could not even applaud and left the theater in stunned silence.

A movie version of the play was released in 1959, and a made-for-television version was broadcast in 1967. An Academy Award-winning documentary film called *Anne Frank Remembered* was released in 1995. The documentary contained previously unknown information about the Frank family, including the fact that Anne and her mother rediscovered their love for one another while imprisoned at Auschwitz-Birkenau, and that Margot and Edith Frank gave up a possible chance at survival by choosing to remain with Anne, who was too sick to travel.

Where to Learn More

Bachrach, Susan D. *Tell Them We Remember: The Story of the Holocaust.* Little, Brown and Company, 1994.

Berenbaum, Michael. *The World Must Know: The History of the Holocaust as Told in the United States Holocaust Memorial Museum.* Little, Brown and Company, 1993.

Brown, Gene. *Anne Frank: Child of the Holocaust.* Rosen Publishing Group, 1991.

Frank, Anne. *The Diary of a Young Girl.* Doubleday, 1967.

Frank, Anne. *The Diary of a Young Girl: The Definitive Edition.* Doubleday, 1991.

Hurwitz, Johanna. *Anne Frank: Life in Hiding.* Jewish Publishing Society, 1988.

Leonard, William T. *Theatre: Stage-to-Screen-to-Television.* William Torbert Leonard, 1981.

Tames, Richard. *Anne Frank.* Franklin Watts, 1989.

Tridenti, Lina. *Anne Frank.* Silver Burdett, 1985.

Hans Frank

Born May 23, 1900
Karlsruhe, Germany
Died October 16, 1946
Nuremberg, Germany

Lawyer, government official

*Served as German-appointed
governor general of Poland, 1939–45*

Hans Frank was appointed the governor general of Poland during World War II (1939–45) by the conquering Germans. He has been described as weak, unstable, and full of strange contradictions. Frank made flowery speeches about furthering justice and honor while treating both the Poles and Jews in Poland with great cruelty and injustice. Frank worshiped National Socialist German Workers' Party (Nazi for short) leader Adolf Hitler (see entry), almost to the end of Frank's own life on the gallows. This devotion blinded Frank to the fact that any standards of common decency were totally abandoned by Hitler and his followers.

A Childhood of Neglect

Hans Frank (pronounced Hahnz Frahnk) was born in Karlsruhe, Germany, in 1900, the son of Karl Frank, a lawyer who had been disbarred (forbidden to practice law for improper conduct). Hans Frank's father was a man who wined and dined women, promising to marry them, and then swindled them out of their money. Hans Frank's mother left her husband and child, running off to Czechoslovakia, a nearby country, with another man. Growing up motherless, young Frank often had to go to a neighborhood tavern for free leftovers if he wanted to have any supper. The lack of parental concern for him was thought to contribute to his insecurity and led to his desire to please Hitler at all costs.

Earns Degree

Frank graduated from high school in Munich, Germany, in 1918. He became part of a military-style organization while studying law at the University of Munich. In 1923, he joined the Nazi Party. He became part of the Storm Troopers (a Nazi group, also called the SA, that used terror tactics to help Hitler gain power in Germany). Frank was among Hitler's Nazi supporters during Hitler's unsuccessful attempt in 1923 to take over the German government. Fearing arrest, Frank then fled to Austria.

Frank returned to Germany to complete his college studies in 1924. In 1926, he began working as a lawyer in Munich. He was also hired as an assistant professor of commercial and business law at the Munich Institute of Technology.

Defends Nazis in Court

One day, Frank responded to an ad in a Nazi paper that said "lawyer sought to take over the defense of poor, unemployed [Nazi] party members in court trial. No [pay]." Frank took the case and got the Nazi defendants off with minimal sentences. Eventually Hitler asked him to be in charge of some major cases for the Nazis, including cases against Hitler himself. Frank was also put in charge of searching Hitler's family tree to find out if he had any Jewish ancestry. (Apparently he didn't.) The anti-Jewish Nazis did not permit anyone who had Jewish blood to become part of their organization, as they wanted to keep it "pure." The Nazis considered the Jews an evil, separate race who were inferior to Aryans (white, non-Jews). The Nazis believed intermarriage of Germans and Jews would taint German bloodlines.

"It is as though I am two people—me, myself . . . and the other Frank, the Nazi leader. And sometimes . . . this Frank looks at the other Frank and says, 'Hmm, what a louse you are, Frank!—How could you do such things?'"

Frank quit the Nazi Party in 1926 over a minor dispute, but rejoined the following year. In 1929, he expressed his intention to start a career as a legal scholar, but Hitler persuaded him to remain working for the Nazis.

Heads Nazi Legal Department

In 1930, Frank was made head of the legal affairs department for the Nazi Party. Until 1933, he represented the Nazis in thousands of legal actions brought against party members. However, once Hitler seized power in Germany in 1933, and no longer had to face his opponents in court, Frank's usefulness as a lawyer rapidly diminished.

Leads Academy

Frank rose through the ranks of the Nazi Party. In 1934, he became president of the Academy for German Justice (popularly called the Academy for German Injustice), which he founded. He was supposed to reformulate German law on the basis of Nazi principles. But "the various drafts of a new legal code . . . never went beyond the first stages. . . . This was because of the regime's continued practice of intervening by force in the legal system, whenever it wished . . . ," wrote Joachim C. Fest. In other words, Hitler preferred to govern not by principle, but by brute force.

Angers Hitler

On June 30, 1934, Hitler had Ernst Röhm, head of the SA, and the other high-ranking SA men arrested and put into Munich's jail. (This event has come to be called the "Night of the Long Knives.") Hitler supposedly feared that Röhm and his henchmen were conspiring to take over the government and place themselves as the new rulers. Two of Hitler's personal bodyguards told Frank they had orders from Hitler to shoot all the SA leaders—110 men—immediately. Frank refused, saying they were "standing on territory that belonged to Justice." The bodyguards called Hitler, who shouted at Frank over the telephone: "You hesitate to carry out one of my orders?" The incident made Hitler furious, and Frank said about himself that he was "after 1934 a slowly but steadily declining political force."

Hitler considered lawyers weaklings and fools. For Hitler, the law was merely a tool useful in defeating his polit-

ical opponents. He once said to Frank: "Here I stand with my bayonets. There you stand with your law! We'll see which counts for more!"

Reversal of Fortune

In 1939, Germany successfully invaded Poland, which began World War II and then divided the country between itself and the Soviet Union (now Russia). Frank's position greatly improved when Hitler appointed him governor general of Poland. He headed the central section of the country.

"Brigitte, you are going to be the Queen of Poland,"
Frank told his wife, a former secretary he had married in
1924. The Franks went to live in Krakow Castle, the former
home of Polish royalty, with their young son, Niklas. Brigitte
called the castle "fabulous"; Frank filled it with art work and
furniture looted from the Jews and Poles. Although Frank had
a grand vision of himself as the head of Germany's eastern
kingdom, Hitler considered Poland "a racial dumping
ground, the slave-labor reservoir, and . . . the slaughter yard
of the Third Reich (meaning 'Third Empire,' the name Hitler
gave to his term as Germany's leader)," in the words of writer
Christopher Browning.

Although Frank was the governor general of Poland, he
was not in charge of the concentration camps (where Jews and
other "enemies" of the Nazis were imprisoned) located in the
region. The SS (an abbreviation for *Shutzstaffeln* or Security
Squad; this unit served as Hitler's personal bodyguards and
camp guards) and the police were in charge of the camps.
Frank objected to this, not because he was against the murder
of Jews that took place there, but because he resented others
having control over a major operation occurring in "his" area.

Begins Anti-Jewish Measures

Shortly after his being appointed governor general,
Frank published a regulation requiring that all Jews ten years
of age or older had to wear on the right sleeves of their clothing an arm band with a Jewish symbol, the six-pointed Star
of David, on it. This emblem served to bring about the isolation of the Jews from the rest of the population. He also
issued an order requiring forced labor for Jews. They had to
live at work camps and engage in such tasks as road paving,
swamp draining, and building structures. Although they
were required to do strenuous jobs, they received very little
food, and the death rate among them was quite high.

By November 1940, the Jews of Warsaw and other Polish cities were forced to live in ghettos (crowded, walled sections of cities where Jews were force to live in inferior conditions). The population of the Warsaw ghetto finally reached
nearly 400,000. It was fully operational from November 1940
to July 1942, when the Jews began to be deported (forced to
leave the city) to concentration camps in large numbers. In
August 1942, Frank stated: "It is not necessary to dwell on the

fact that we are sentencing 1.2 million Jews to death. That much is clear. And if the Jews do not die of starvation, it will be necessary to step up anti-Jewish measures, and let us hope that too will come to pass."

Deterioration of Polish Life

Before Frank became head of Poland, the Poles were conducting fairly normal lives. But after Frank took over, the mayor of Warsaw was arrested and shot, and nearly 200 professors of some of Poland's major universities were seized and taken to concentration camps. Universities, schools, libraries, publishing houses, and museums were closed. Polish monuments and works of art were looted, and music by Polish composers was banned. The purpose of these moves was to break the spirit of the Poles. Frank himself had declared that Poland would be treated like a colony of the Nazis, and its citizens would be "slaves of the Greater German Empire." There was even talk of completely doing away with Poland as a nation.

Under Frank's rule, the amount of food for each Polish citizen was gradually reduced. "The daily food rations in Warsaw [for non-Jews] provided . . . 669 calories per day, compared to the Germans' 2,613 calories," according to historian Keith Sword. Jews were allotted only 184 calories. Disease flourished, as did the black market (an illegal underground market with high prices), which many Poles were forced to use to obtain food. The Polish birth rate was reduced when Frank set a higher minimum age for marriage and sent millions of people to work in Germany.

Frank frequently changed his mind about what position to take on various matters. One time he would support keeping the Jews healthy so they were strong enough to work; at another time he supported the mass murder and starvation of the Jewish workers. Even though he was quoted as saying: "You can depend on it that I would rather die than give up this idea of justice," unjust anti-Jewish laws were passed without the slightest protest on his part. Sometimes he encouraged the inclusion of Polish culture into Nazi life; at other times he carried out policies that greatly suppressed the Poles.

His Power Diminishes

The power Frank enjoyed in his position as governor general did not last very long. On March 5, 1942, he was brought before a court made up of top-level Nazis and had many of his powers taken away. This was partly because he had secretly enriched members of his family with goods looted from the Jews. (His wife Brigitte loved furs; on more than one occasion she pointed to a Polish woman walking down the street in a lovely fur coat, a signal for her body-guards to go and forcibly take the coat from the woman.) In a 1942 diary passage, Nazi official Joseph Goebbels (see entry) wrote: "Frank enjoys absolutely none of [Hitler's] esteem any more."

Soon after, Frank delivered four speeches at four differ-ent German universities protesting the takeover of "German justice" by the Nazi police. He also sent Hitler a letter criti-cizing various Nazi policies. As a result, Hitler stripped Frank of all his power. Although he forbade Frank to make public speeches, he refused to accept Frank's resignation, prefer-ring to keep him as a puppet governor general (one without real power).

Arrest, Prosecution, Execution

When the Soviet Union (now Russia) began the takeover of Poland from the Germans in 1945, Frank fled. He took with him a detailed daily account of activities and obser-vations of the Third Reich that he had written. When he was arrested by the victorious Americans, Frank surrendered these diaries, which also contained his speeches and notes about his trips, receptions, meetings, and conferences. Passages from his diaries were used as evidence in the trials of other Nazi criminals held in Nuremberg, Germany, after the war.

Frank himself was tried in Nuremberg in 1946 and found guilty of war crimes. War crimes include violations of the laws or customs of war, such as murder, ill-treatment, deportation, forced labor, or destruction not militarily neces-sary. During the trial, Frank spoke of the guilt Germany had brought upon itself by its activities. He claimed that he had rediscovered God and had returned to the Roman Catholic faith of his youth. The judges were unmoved, and Frank was executed by hanging on October 16, 1946.

Near the end of his life, Frank wrote: "I could weep when I think of all the things I have done in absolutely the wrong way during my life, I, the number-one pupil at the

Frank's Son Condemns Him

In 1991, Niklas Frank, the son of Hans Frank, published a remarkable book about his father. Niklas, who was seven when his father died in 1946, was raised by his mother to think of Hans Frank as a sensitive, cultivated intellectual. It took Niklas Frank years of research to uncover the true character of his father.

Niklas Frank's book, *In The Shadow of The Third Reich,* is written in the form of a letter to his father, condemning him for his evil life and deeds. At the beginning of the fourth chapter, Niklas Frank wrote: "The snapping of your neck [during hanging] spared me from having a totally screwed-up life. You certainly would have poisoned my brain with all your drivel, the fate of the silent majority of my generation [the children of other Nazis] who did not have the good fortune of having their fathers hanged."

"That's why I am happy to be your son. How poor by comparison are all the millions of other children whose fathers spouted the same garbage filled with deceit and cowardice, with bloodthirstiness and inhumanity, but who were not so prominent as you. Their tirades were not worth recording, their journals not worth preserving. I have it good. I can scrape together the festering scraps of your life in the archives of Europe and America. . . . No matter how often I try to get to the root of them, with scalpel or hammer, the same typical German monster emerges . . . ."

"There is no doubt about it: you will also lose the second Nuremberg Trial, this mini-trial with your son as prosecutor, judge, and hangman in one."

[high school], number-one student at the university, as Ph.D. [with highest honors, decorated] with medals and titles—and now, nothing left for me at all."

Where to Learn More

Browning, Christopher R. "Hans Frank." In *The Encyclopedia of the Holocaust.* Edited by Israel Gutman. Vol. 2. Macmillan, 1990.

Fest, Joachim C. *The Face of the Third Reich.* Translated by Michael Bullock. Pantheon Books, 1970.

Frank, Niklas. *In the Shadow of the Reich.* Translated by Arthur S. Wensinger with Carole Clew-Hoey. Alfred A. Knopf, 1991.

Gutman, Yisrael. *The Jews of Warsaw 1939–1943: Ghetto, Underground, Revolt.* Translated by Ina Friedman. Indiana University Press, 1982.

Snyder, Louis L., ed. "Hans Frank." In *Encyclopedia of the Third Reich.* McGraw-Hill, 1976.

Sword, Keith. "Poland." *The Oxford Companion to World War II.* Edited by I.C.B. Deer. Oxford University Press, 1995.

Zentner, Christian, and Friedemann Bedurftig. "Hans Frank." In *The Encyclopedia of the Third Reich.* Translated by Amy Hackett. Vol. 1. Macmillan, 1991.

Viktor E. Frankl

Born March 26, 1905
Vienna, Austria

Died September 2, 1997
Vienna, Austria

Psychotherapist, physician, university lecturer, concentration camp survivor, author

Founder of Logotherapy

Victims of torture who witnessed their innocent loved ones being taken off to their deaths during World War II (1939–45) might be expected to emerge bitter, even doubting that life has any meaning. Although these events happened to Viktor Frankl, his response was very different. Partly as a result of what he experienced during the war, he developed a way of looking at his experiences, called Logotherapy. Logotherapy is based on the belief that every human situation has meaning.

Childhood in Vienna

Viktor Frankl (pronounced Vick-ter Fronk-el) was born to a Jewish couple in Vienna, Austria, in 1904. As a young man, his father, Gabriel, wanted to become a doctor but money problems prevented it. Instead he became a civil servant in the Ministry of Social Service. Frankl's highly emotional mother was an educated and cultured woman. Frankl claimed that he took after both his mother and his father, who was very responsible and a perfectionist. A psychiatrist who once did some testing of Frankl said that he had "never seen such a range between rationality and deep emotions."

"The meaning of my life is to help others find the meaning of theirs."

As a child, Frankl showed interest in both medicine and philosophy (the pursuit of wisdom). At around age five, the thought came to him that some day he would die. "What troubled me then," wrote Frankl, "was not the fear of dying, but the question of whether the [briefness] of life might destroy its meaning." Once in a science class the teacher gave his opinion that people are nothing more than a mixture of chemicals. The young Frankl rose to his feet and demanded to know: "If that's really true, what meaning does life have?"

Frankl studied the Jewish religion as a youngster and had his bar mitzvah (a ceremony marking a young Jewish boy's becoming a man) at age 13. By then, he knew that he wanted to become a doctor. While in school, he wrote letters about his aspirations to Sigmund Freud (pronounced Sigmund Froyd), and Freud answered him with encouraging letters. Freud was a world-famous psychiatrist, a person who specializes in the treatment of mental illness. By age 15, Frankl was attending public lectures offered by socialist teachers (they supported socialism, a system in which the ownership of the means of producing and distributing goods are owned collectively and political power is exercised by the whole community). At 19, he published his first scholarly work, a paper that appeared in Freud's journal of psychology that was read around the world. At 20, he was president of an organization for socialist high school students throughout Austria.

University Career

During his college years, Frankl turned away from the theories of Freud, who taught that much of human behavior is based on a person's secret sexual impulses. Frankl found this view too simple. He embraced the theories of another Viennese doctor, Alfred Adler. Adler believed that human beings were motivated by a need to accomplish things. Frankl's second scientific paper appeared in Adler's professional journal in 1925. Frankl began to travel around Europe giving lectures about the need to treat all classes of people fairly. By this time, Frankl had given up the Jewish faith.

By 1927, Frankl's enthusiasm for Adler's work had dimmed. Frankl and others founded the Academic Society for Medical Psychology, and he was elected vice-president. By 1930, Frankl had developed the concept that there are three possible ways for finding meaning in life. They include: "1) a deed we do, a work we create; 2) an experience, a human encounter, a love; and 3) when confronted with an unchangeable fate (such as an incurable disease), a change of attitude towards that fate."

Work as a Doctor

Frankl graduated from the University of Vienna Medical School in 1930 and began practicing medicine. He continued his studies in psychiatry and neurology (the study of the nervous system). He worked with patients who, having lost their jobs because of a worldwide economic depression (downturn in the economy), now seemed to suffer from a lack of meaning in their lives. According to writer Edward Hoffman: "[I]f they . . . took up volunteer work and dwell[ed] less on their own woes, their depression often lifted considerably. [Frankl] became increasingly convinced that our underlying sense of purpose in daily life is a vital, and badly ignored, psychological factor."

In the early 1930s, Frankl organized counseling centers for young people in Vienna and in six other Austrian cities. Students could come to the clinic to talk about the problems that were troubling them. As a result of the success of these centers, he was invited to lecture in Germany, Czechoslovakia, and Hungary. He also spoke before groups of young socialists.

In 1937, Frankl went into private practice. A short time later, Adolph Hitler's (see entry) National Socialist German Workers' Party (Nazi for short) took over Austria. The Nazis were seeking revenge for Germany's loss of World War I (1914–18). They blamed the Jewish people for Germany's defeat by claiming that Jews were out to take over the world. Soon after their invasion of Austria, the Nazis were forcing Jews into concentration camps, places where the Nazis confined people they regarded as "enemies of the state." For his safety and that of his family, Frankl applied for, but was unable to obtain, a visa (travel papers) that would let them leave the country. Frankl then accepted a job as chief of neurology at Rothschild Hospital. As part of his work, Frankl performed brain surgery, which was to remain an interest for the rest of his life.

In 1938, Frankl began writing articles for medical journals that centered on a system he called Logotherapy. The system is based on the belief that people seek meaning, and that discovering the special significance in one's life is a healing process.

Family Affairs and Marriage

In 1941, Frankl was granted a visa that would allow him to move to the United States. However, no such visas were available to his parents, who were probably going to be sent to a concentration camp. Frankl gave a great deal of thought to the situation and decided to remain in Vienna with his family. He continued working, and the family remained safe for about one year.

While working at Rothschild Hospital, Frankl met a young nurse named Tilly Grosser, whom he described as looking "like a Spanish dancer." Admiring her kindness and good character, Frankl asked her to be his wife. Frankl and Tilly wed in 1941, the last of the Viennese Jews permitted to marry before the Nazis changed the laws as part of their ultimate plan to eliminate the Jewish race. Jews were from then on forbidden to marry, produce children, and become part of accepted society.

Sent to Concentration Camp

Any semblance of a normal life for the young couple was very short-lived. Jews from all over Europe were being taken from their homes and transported to massive concentration camps. At first these camps functioned as work camps to aid the German war effort. Eventually they turned into killing factories, where the so-called "enemies" of the Nazis met their deaths. At the camps, men and women lived in separate areas, so although they arrived together they were never able to see each other once they were settled.

Nine months after they wed, Viktor and Tilly were sent to Theresienstadt concentration camp merely because they were Jewish. From there, Viktor was ordered to Auschwitz death camp. Tilly had been assured that she would not be sent to Auschwitz for two years because of her job as a munitions worker. Viktor pleaded with Tilly not to volunteer to go with him, but she did not want to be separated from him. The couple were separated at Auschwitz and never saw each other again. Viktor later learned that she had died after the war.

Life in the Camps

Frankl later wrote about his contact at Auschwitz with the notorious Nazi doctor Josef Mengele (see entry). When prisoners first arrived Mengele separated them into two groups; this was known as selection. Those on the left went to their deaths in gas chambers (sealed rooms that were filled with poisonous gas in order to kill the people locked inside); those on the right went to work as laborers. Mengele indicated that Frankl should go in the left line. "Since I recognized no one in the left line," wrote Frankl, "behind Mengele's back I switched over to the right line where I saw a few of my young colleagues. Only God knows where I got that idea or found the courage."

Frankl was forced to give up his good coat, which contained the precious manuscript for his first book in the pocket. He took an old, torn coat from a pile. In its pocket he found a page from a prayer book that said, "Hear, oh Israel, the Lord our God is One." The prayer inspired Frankl to keep going despite all he was to experience.

At the camp, Frankl survived an attack of typhus (an infectious disease carried by fleas and spread in crowded, unsanitary conditions) and respiratory problems. He always believed that his strong desire to reconstruct his first book and eventually to have it published kept him alive. In that book he talked about a practice he used in the camps called self-distancing. One day when he was starving and in great pain from having frozen feet, Frankl imagined how he would describe his reactions to an audience in a lecture hall. Years later, he gave talks on this very topic.

In addition to Auschwitz, Frankl also spent time in the Theresienstadt, Kaufering II, and Turkheim camps. Frankl's parents and his brother, Walter, all died in the camps. His sister, Stella, avoided their fate by escaping to Australia.

Psychological Impact of Living in Concentration Camps

Viktor Frankl spent more than three years in Nazi concentration camps, places where the Nazis confined people they regarded as "enemies of the state." During this time, he observed that prisoners went through three phases of reaction in the camps. The first was the period just after being admitted, the second was when life settled into a daily routine, and the third was when the prisoner was freed from the camp.

Upon arrival at a concentration camp, people were stripped of their clothing, had all their body hair shaved off, and were forced to give up all of their possessions. The camp provided a ragged shirt and pants that were to be worn every day. At first, a number of people committed suicide. The most popular way was by touching an electrically charged barbed-wire fence that surrounded the camp. One eight-foot-wide wooden slab served as the bed for nine men, who had only two blankets to share among them. Frankl said that prisoners in the first few days did not fear death for it would "spare [them] the act of committing suicide." At first, most prisoners retained strong curiosity about what would happen next.

In the second phase a few days later, most prisoners became apathetic—that is, they began to feel or show little emotion. Prisoners had to deal with a number of difficult emotions, including a longing for home and family, and a disgust for the situation in which they were living. At first, prisoners looked away so that they would not have to see other prisoners punished by being struck by guards and forced to march for long hours. But within a few days or weeks they no longer averted their eyes, and began to grow unmoved by the cruel things were witnessed. Frankl said that prisoners were no longer capable of feeling "disgust, horror and pity," and that this inability to care about things helped to provide them with a protective shell.

Many inmates developed frostbite on their hands and feet but had to continue working anyway if they wanted to avoid being hit with a rifle butt. The daily rations provided to prisoners for their long days work were about ten and one-half ounces of bread and one and three-fourths pints of a very watery soup. Occasionally prisoners received a dab of butter, a slice of cheese, or a bit of sausage.

A major law of the camp was not to draw the attention of the guards. At the camp, one became merely a number, not an individual. For example, the skeleton-like bodies of sick people were placed on carts to be transported. If one of them died before the trip began, the corpse was still thrown on the cart to keep the numbers correct. The list mattered more than did human life.

Resumes Medical Career

By 1945, Hitler could no longer deny to himself that Germany had lost the war. In order not to be captured by the Allies (the United States, Great Britain, the Soviet Union, and France), Hitler committed suicide on April 30, 1945. Germany surrendered soon after under the authority of Admiral Karl

(Continued from previous page)

Prisoners frequently dreamed of warm baths, comfortable beds, and good food. Frankl observed that even among the large group of adult men there was very little sexual interest or activity, as so much energy had to be focused on survival. The prisoners who seemed to survive best were not necessarily the most hardy, but the ones who had sensitivity and a rich intellectual life. Sometimes the prisoners put together entertainment made up of singing, joking, and poetry. Occasional humor also helped people to rise above their circumstances.

Most of the prisoners suffered from an inferiority complex. People who had once been "somebody" now were treated as if they did not matter at all. Their tired state increased the level of irritability among the prisoners and fights frequently broke out. From witnessing the daily beatings of inmates, the "impulse to violence" also increased.

Frankl believed that even in the harshest of circumstances, like those he witnessed, people still have a choice of how to act. Throughout the camps there were people who went out of their way to comfort the suffering, and share their meager rations with others who were worse off than they were. Frankl believed that "any man can, even under such circumstances, decide what shall become of him—mentally and spiritually. He may retain his human dignity even in a concentration camp." Frankl held that "Life ultimately means taking the responsibility to find the right answer to its problems . . . . Our answers must consist, not in talk and meditation, but in right action and in right conduct."

Frankl described the third stage of a concentration camp prisoner's mental reaction, which occurred after being freed. When the Allies (United States, Great Britain, the Soviet Union, and France) liberated the prisoners, they were able to walk out of the camp into the countryside. But at first, still numb to emotion, most people could not even feel any pleasure in freedom. "Everything seemed unreal, as in a dream," he said. "The body ate and drank in great quantities." With the sudden release from the mental pressure of living in the camps, some people became bitter and cruel to others, behaving as their captors had. Others suffered severe disappointment when they found out that the loved one they had dreamed of seeing for so many years no longer existed.

Frankl pointed out that the best part for the person returning home was that, after all he had suffered, there was nothing he needed to fear any longer—"except his God."

Doenitz, Hitler's successor. With the end of the war, the concentration camps were liberated by the Allied forces one by one. Following his liberation, Frankl returned to his beloved city of Vienna. There he alienated some colleagues by speaking against the then-popular concept of "collective guilt." He denied the notion that all the non-Jewish people who lived

Frankl discussing the principles of Logotherapy in his office.

under the Nazi shadow shared in the guilt of the murder of the approximately six million Jews and hundreds of thousands of other innocent people who perished in the camps.

Frankl grieved over the death of his wife and other family members. He accepted a job as head of the neurology department at the Vienna Policlinic Hospital, where he stayed for 25 years. There he finally wrote and had his first book, *The Doctor and the Soul*, published. In 1948, Frankl married Eleonore Katharine Schwindt, who was a nurse at the hospital. The couple had a daughter, Gabriele.

About losing his entire family in the Holocaust, Viktor Frankl once said: "I lost all that could be taken away from a person except one thing—the last of the human freedoms—to choose one's attitude in any set of circumstances, to choose one's own way." The Holocaust is the term that refers to the period between 1933 and 1945 when Nazi Germany systematically persecuted and murdered millions of Jews and other innocent people.

Attains Worldwide Acclaim

Frankl developed a system of psychotherapy called the Third Viennese School. Psychotherapy is a method for treating mental and emotional disorders that involves establishing an interpersonal relationship between a psychotherapist (a person who practices psychotherapy) and his or her patient. Frankl's method was called the Third Viennese School because it came after the methods developed by Sigmund Freud and Alfred Adler. Frankl's second and most famous book, *Man's Search For Meaning,* was written in nine days and sold nine million copies. It outlined the principles of Logotherapy. He wrote 29 other books detailing his theories.

Worldwide interest in Frankl increased greatly with the establishment in 1977 of the Viktor Frankl Institute of Logotherapy in Berkeley, California. In 1985, Frankl was granted the prestigious Oskar Pfister Prize by the American Association of Psychiatrists, the first non-American to be so honored.

Viktor Frankl died in Vienna of heart failure on September 2, 1997, at the age of 92. He was a man of many talents and interests, which included mountain climbing, piloting airplanes, composing music, and product design. He lectured at more than 200 universities around the world, many of them in the United States. His books have been translated into 24 languages.

Where to Learn More

Frankl, Viktor E. *Man's Search For Meaning: An Introduction to Logotherapy.* Simon and Schuster, 1959.

Frankl, Viktor E. *The Doctor and the Soul: From Psychotherapy to Logotherapy* (second, expanded edition). Alfred A Knopf, 1965.

Frankl, Victor E. "The Search For Meaning," *Saturday Review.* September 13, 1958.

Frankl, Viktor E. *The Will To Meaning: Foundations and Applications of Logotherapy.* World Publishing, 1969.

Frankl, Viktor E. *Viktor Frankl: Recollections, An Autobiography.* Plenum Press, 1997.

Friedman, Maurice. "Viktor Frankl," In *The Worlds of Existentialism,* Random House, 1964.

Hoffman, Edward. "Viktor Frankl at 90: A Voice For Life." *America.* 172, no. 9 (March 18, 1995): p. 17.

Ungersma, Aaron J. *The Search for Meaning: A New Approach in Psychotherapy and Pastoral Psychology.* Westminster Press, 1961.

Varian M. Fry

Born October 15, 1907
New York, New York
Died September 13, 1967
Easton, Connecticut

Magazine editor, writer, teacher

Rescued an estimated 1,500 to 4,000 Jews, including famous artists and scientists, from German-occupied France

Varian Fry (pronounced Very-un Fry) has been referred to as "America's Schindler," a reference to Oskar Schindler (see entry), who rescued 1,200 Jews during World War II (1939–45). Fry volunteered for a dangerous mission to help artists and intellectuals (people who are involved in academic study, ideas, or issues) escape from German-occupied France during the war. At great personal risk, he operated an underground railroad that used false identity papers, disguises, and other means to get a number of very famous people out of France and to safety. In 1941, he was ordered by the French government to leave. His heroism went unrecognized by the American people for 50 years.

Born, Educated, and Worked In and Around New York

It was not until 1983, 16 years after his death, that extensive biographical information about the "forgotten hero" Varian Fry was made public. Writer Donald Carroll's article about Fry titled "Escape from Vichy" appeared in *American Heritage,* a magazine sponsored by the Society of American Historians. Thanks to Carroll, a little is known about the early life of Fry.

" . . . it took courage [to stay in France], and courage is a quality that I hadn't previously been sure I possessed."

Born in New York City in 1907, Fry, the son of a stockbroker, grew up in suburban Ridgewood, New Jersey. Carroll described the young Fry as "moody" and "introverted" and afflicted with a condition called hypochondria. An introvert is primarily interested in him or herself. A hypochondriac constantly thinks he or she is ill or about to become ill and sometimes experiences real pain caused by these "illnesses."

As a boy, Fry displayed no interest in either his school work or his schoolmates, so his parents sent him away to a private school for the elite in Connecticut when he was 14 years old. There he faced his first real social and school challenges—and became even more introverted. He displayed a flair for languages, especially Latin. He had no tolerance for people less gifted than he was. He developed some personal habits that set him apart from the other students, such as wearing fancy clothing, displaying an interest in fine food and wine, and smoking. His attitude, wrote Carroll, "attracted few friends and much ridicule," so he "resigned" from school. His parents sent him to another private Connecticut school, "which he found more to his liking."

Fry earned a bachelor's degree from Harvard College (now Harvard University) in 1931 (he later took graduate courses at Columbia University in New York City). His college career was marked by even odder behavior than he had shown in his youth—he became more arrogant and dressed in unusual clothing. He did attract some favorable attention when he founded a magazine when he was only a sophomore. He left the magazine in a fit of anger, however, after he and his partner disagreed about the correct use of English.

Upon his graduation, Fry married Eileen Hughes, a magazine editor who was seven years older than he was. The couple moved to New York City, and for the next four years Fry earned a living as an editor and writer.

Visits Prewar Germany

In 1935, Fry was offered a job as editor of a prominent magazine that published articles on international affairs. As a condition of employment, Fry was told that he should visit Germany, where Adolf Hitler (see entry), leader of the National Socialist German Workers' Party (Nazi for short), had recently come to power. Fry's job was to observe what was happening there. While he was in Berlin, the capital of Germany, Fry was stunned to observe the Nazis' anti-Jewish violence. He later described the scene this way: "[I] saw with my own eyes young Nazi toughs gather and smash up Jewish-owned cafés, watched with horror as they dragged Jewish patrons from their seats, drove hysterical, crying women down the street, knocked over an elderly man and kicked him in the face."

This violence had a tremendous impact on Fry. As a result, the solitary young man returned to the United States with a cause that he felt passionate about. He began to speak out and write about the terrible things that were happening in Germany to the Jews and other people the Nazis considered "undesirable." He believed Hitler was a dangerous threat to peace.

War in France

France had long been regarded as a safe place for Europeans seeking to escape repression in their own countries. Since the early 1930s, intellectuals, artists, and refugees from Germany had been moving into France in great numbers to escape the Nazis. In 1939, the Nazis invaded Poland and from there swept through Denmark, Norway, Belgium, and on into France. On June 17, 1940, the French government surrendered to Hitler.

Under the terms of the armistice (truce) between the French government and Hitler, German troops would occupy the northern half of France and the country's Atlantic Ocean coastline. The French government would be left in control of the southern half of the country, where the artists, intellectuals, and refugees immediately fled, but they could go no further without special travel papers. The part of the armistice agreement that concerned Fry was the requirement by the Germans that the French "surrender on demand" any person the Germans wanted. It was obvious that the Germans meant to demand the surrender of artists and intellectuals, who had been outspoken in condemning Nazi horrors. In the book Fry later wrote about his experiences in France, called *Surrender on Demand,* he declared that "the fall of France, in June, 1940, meant . . . the creation of the most gigantic man-trap in history. . . . I could not remain idle as long as I had any chance at all of saving even a few [of Hitler's] victims."

Emergency Rescue Committee Formed

Back in New York, a group of shocked U.S. citizens immediately formed the Emergency Rescue Committee, whose purpose, Fry wrote, "was to bring the political and intellectual refugees out of France before the [German police] . . . got them." A fund-raising luncheon raised $3,500 for the cause. Still to be decided was who would go to France to arrange the escapes. According to Fry: "After several weeks of fruitless searching for a suitable agent to send to France, the Committee selected me. I had had no experience in refugee work, and none in underground work. But I accepted the assignment because . . . I believed in the importance of democratic solidarity [that citizens of all democratic countries should work together]."

Fry spoke with Eleanor Roosevelt, wife of President Franklin D. Roosevelt (see entry). It was arranged that Fry would be issued 200 special visas for the 200 people on his list. Visas were needed along with passports to permit the people on his list to travel from one country to another.

Fry arrived in France in the summer of 1940, and it soon became obvious that far more than 200 visas were needed. Refugees began coming to his hotel the day after his arrival. "Many of them had been through hell," he wrote; "their nerves were shattered and their courage gone." While trying to find the people on his list—people who were in particular danger and thus hard to locate—Fry began trying to help everyone who arrived at his door.

Success . . . and an Order to Leave

Fry found a cartoonist who created counterfeit identity papers and travel documents for the refugees. He bribed government officials and made deals with criminals. For a little more than a year he and about ten other persons succeeded in arranging the escape of important people such as novelist Heinrich Mann and Golo Mann, brother and son of Nobel Prize-winning author Thomas Mann; artists Marc Chagall,

Fry at work in his office in France during his 1941 effort to rescue Jews from the Nazis.

Andre Masson, Wilfred Lam, and Max Ernst; sculptor Jacques Lipchitz; poet and dramatist Franz Werfel; Nobel Prize-winning physicist Otto Meyerhoff; historian Konrad Heiden; writer and political scientist Hannah Arendt; historical novelist Lion Feuchtwanger; mathematician Emil Gumbel; journalist Hans Natonek; novelists Leonhard Frank, Alfred Polgar, and Hertha Pauli; harpsichordist Wanda Landowska; and Jaques Hadamard, called the "[Albert] Einstein of France." Estimates of the number of people Fry saved range from 1,500 to 4,000.

Fry's work was complicated and made more dangerous by the fact that the new French government, based in the city of Vichy (pronounced vish-ee or vee-shee), was really just a puppet of the Germans. He might have expected sympathy and even help from the French. Instead, he found that many French officials eagerly carried out German orders. Fry was questioned by the French police several times but he always managed to turn their suspicions aside. Eventually, however,

An American Heroine in France with Varian Fry

A few daring souls were brave enough to assist Varian Fry in his rescue efforts. One of them was American heiress Mary Jayne Gold (1909–1997) of Evanston, Illinois. Gold attended a finishing school in Italy (a finishing school is a private school that prepares wealthy girls for life in polite society). Then, armed with a small fortune, a pilot's license, and her own airplane, she arrived in Paris, France, in 1930, prepared to live a life devoted to parties and vacations. Her goals changed when German troops invaded France in 1940. Gold than agreed to help Fry rescue Jews from France when he asked her.

Gold's money paid for false passports and travel documents. Long after the war had ended, she told a journalist: "Women weren't taken too seriously in those days." The journalist added: "But when someone had to charm the commander of a French prison camp into freeing four [prisoners], Gold was sent to do the job."

Gold finally left France in 1941, shortly before Fry was ordered to do so. She later published a book describing her adventures. Called *Crossroads Marseilles 1940,* it was published by Doubleday in 1980. (Marseilles, pronounced Mar-say, was the town in southern France where Fry set up his rescue committee.) After the war, Gold returned to France, where she lived until her death in October 1997. She never married, and she had no children.

A few years before her death, Gold's friend, French filmmaker Pierre Sauvage, announced plans to make a movie based on her book. (Sauvage's parents were among those who sought help from the Fry committee.) Sauvage said of his friend: "She was a very shrewd woman whose heart was on the right side of issues and who at a crucial turning point in history understood what was called for. . . . [She always] felt that only one year in her life really mattered and it was the year she spent in Marseilles."

the Vichy government ordered him to leave the country. The U.S. government refused to come to his aid. A U.S. official based in France told Fry: "We can't support an American citizen who is helping people evade French law." In September 1941 Fry found himself back in the United States.

Ignored in His Own Country

Fry began to write and give speeches about what he had seen and experienced in Europe. He warned of the impending massacre of Europe's Jews. But it seemed that few listened.

Fry wrote two books about his experiences in France, *Surrender on Demand* and *Assignment: Rescue,* which was a version of his experiences created for young readers. He did so with little help from the very people he had rescued. According to Donald Carroll: "[Some] wanted to forget about the whole business and just get on with their lives. Some, including people who had once begged on their knees for Fry to save them, were too busy to be bothered by his modest requests for help." Both books sold poorly.

Fry experienced many other setbacks. His marriage ended in divorce; he remained on good terms with Eileen, though, and was grief-stricken when she died of cancer in 1948. He had trouble finding jobs, and those he did find he couldn't hold on to. By some accounts, his trouble finding jobs was due to an investigation of his activities in France conducted by a suspicious Federal Bureau of Investigation (FBI). When possible employers learned there was an FBI file on him, they were unwilling to hire Fry. The army would not accept him because of his weak stomach.

Fry found some happiness with his second wife, Annette Riley, with whom he had three children: Sylvia, Thomas, and James. He took jobs teaching Latin and Greek and continued freelance writing. Mostly, he was depressed, in part about the way he had been forgotten, and he took out his frustrations on his wife and children.

Finally, in 1967, he was awarded a medal from the French Legion of Honor. To his sorrow, he remained unrecognized by his own country, and he died alone of a heart attack on September 13, 1967. He had been working on another book about his rescue mission. The policeman who discovered the body told a reporter that the book "appeared to be a work of fiction."

Honored Long After His Death

In 1991, 24 years after his death, Fry received his first official recognition in the United States in the form of the Eisenhower Liberation Medal. An exhibit titled "Assignment: Rescue, The Story of Varian Fry and the Emergency Rescue Committee" was held at the U.S. Holocaust Memorial Museum from 1993 to 1994. On February 4, 1996, U.S. Secretary of State Warren Christopher planted a tree at Yad Vashem, the Martyrs' and Heroes' Remembrance Authority in Jerusalem. It honors Varian Fry as one of the "Righteous

Among the Nations of the World," those "high-minded Gentiles [non-Jews] who risked their lives to save Jews." Fry is the only American-born person to be so honored.

A bill was introduced in the U.S. Congress in 1996 proposing a combined Varian Fry-Raoul Wallenberg medal (see Raoul Wallenberg entry). Both of Fry's books were reissued when it appeared there was interest in learning about his adventures. In 1996, the Varian Fry Foundation Project/IRC (International Rescue Committee) was formed. Its purpose is to make the Varian Fry story more widely known in the United States, especially to school children. In 1997, Barwood Films, established by actor/singer Barbra Streisand, announced plans to make a television movie based on the life of Fry. The man who rescued even more Jews than Oskar Schindler is finally being recognized for his heroism.

Where to Learn More

Carroll, Donald. "Escape from Vichy." *American Heritage,* 34, no. 4 (June/July 1983): pp. 82+.

Chesnoff, Richard Z. "The Other Schindlers." *U.S. News & World Report,* March 21, 1994, pp. 56+.

Fittko, Lisa. *Escape through the Pyrenees.* Northwestern University Press, 1991.

Fry, Varian. *Assignment: Rescue.* Scholastic, 1968.

Fry, Varian. *Surrender on Demand.* Johnson Books, 1967.

Varian Fry Foundation Project/IRC, 405 El Camino Real, #213, Menlo Park, CA 94025; telephone (650)323-0530; e-mail fe.wem@forsythe.stanford.edu.

"Varian Fry Website." http://www.almondseed.com/vfry

Miep Gies

Born February 15, 1909
Vienna, Austria

Resistance worker in Holland

*Provided food and friendship to
Anne Frank's family in hiding
during World War II*

Miep Gies (pronounced Meep Geze) was one of more than twenty thousand courageous Dutch people who helped to hide Jews and others from the Germans during World War II (1939–45). Nearly every day for more than two years this woman, who insists that she is "not a hero," brought food, companionship, and news of the outside world, at tremendous personal risk, to eight Jewish people concealed in an attic in Amsterdam, Holland. The eight people are remembered today because one—Anne Frank (see entry)—wrote a famous diary that was saved from destruction thanks to Gies.

A Sickly Austrian Child Rescued by the Dutch

Miep Gies was born Hermine Santrouschitz in 1909 in Vienna, Austria, to working-class parents. (Miep was a nickname she later received.)

"My story is a story of very ordinary people during extra- ordinarily terrible times."

When the child was only five years old, World War I (1914–18) began in Austria. The shortage of food caused by the war did not end when the war did. By the time she was ten years old, Gies was a scrawny, undernourished little girl. By 1920, with a new baby sister in the house, there was even less food to go around. Gies's parents were told that if something was not done for her, she would die.

Children throughout Austria were starving. In response, a program was set up by the generous people of the Netherlands (the Dutch) to help rescue the children of Austrian workers. So it came about that one day in 1920, the German-speaking Gies found herself taken in by a Dutch-speaking family in Leiden, Holland, headed by a father who worked for a coal company. The family, who had five children of their own, treated Gies with great kindness, fed her, and helped her regain her strength. She became like another child to them, and they were the ones who gave her the nickname "Miep," which is a term of affection in Dutch.

Gies attended a Dutch school in Leiden, where she quickly learned to speak the language. She developed a love for classical music, especially that of Mozart, and was encouraged to read the newspapers and discuss current events. She loved nearly everything about her new Dutch life except for ice skating.

When she was 13 years old, Gies moved with her new family to the city of Amsterdam in Holland. Three years later she returned for her first visit to her birth family. By then, however, she had become so thoroughly Dutch that she felt out of place in Vienna. Her mother noticed this, and believing that her daughter would be happier living in Amsterdam with the new family, she gave her consent for Gies to return to Holland. However, no thought was given to changing Gies's citizenship from Austrian to Dutch, and when another war broke out in 1939, this oversight was to prove a great mistake.

Carefree Prewar Days

At some point in her late teens or early twenties, Gies, by then an attractive blue-eyed blonde a little over five feet tall, took her first job as an office worker. She had a lively social life and spent her free time going to the movies and to dances at a local dance club. "I was one of the first girls in

Amsterdam to learn the Charleston, the two-step, the tango, and the slow fox," she later wrote. Gies was somewhat vain about her appearance and prided herself on dressing well.

Holland, like much of the rest of the world, had not recovered economically from the effects of World War I, and unemployment was high. Gies was fired from her office job in 1933, when she was 24. She was undaunted, however. "Being a young woman with an independent spirit," she later wrote, "I was longing to be working again."

Goes to Work for Otto Frank

One day she saw an advertisement in the newspaper for an office job only 20 minutes by bicycle from her home (everyone in Amsterdam bicycled to and from work and school in those days). The advertisement directed her to apply to Otto Frank at Travies and Company, a firm specializing in products for homemakers.

Gies was interviewed by Otto Frank himself. She found him to be a gentle, shy man, a Jew who had recently moved from Germany to escape the anti-Jewish rantings of Adolf Hitler (see entry). Hitler had just come to power as the head of the National Socialist German Workers' party (Nazi for short). Hitler hated Jews, blaming them for Germany's loss of World War I and for standing in the way of Germany's return to greatness. Even before Hitler assumed a position of power in Germany in 1933, his followers had been persecuting Jews. It was obvious to Otto Frank that these policies were not going to stop and would probably get worse, so he and his family moved to Amsterdam.

For her "job interview," Gies was required to make jam with a new product called pectin. Although she knew very little about cooking, Gies soon proved herself an expert at jam making. She got the job, which was as head of the Complaint and Information Desk. When homemakers tried making jam with pectin and failed, it was Gies's task to listen to their complaints and help them.

Whispers of War

Gies gradually developed a close relationship with the Frank family. She had met a special young man, Jan Gies, and the two were sometimes invited to dine with the Franks. The

situation with Hitler in Germany was a popular topic of conversation. More and more Jews had fled Hitler's Germany, as the Frank family had done, and settled in Amsterdam and other places. Finally, there was not enough room for them all. Many countries, including Holland, which had always had a reputation for being welcoming and tolerant, were refusing to allow any more refugees to enter.

One day in March 1938, the entire staff of Travies and Company heard on Otto Frank's radio that Hitler had marched into Vienna, Austria, the city where he had spent his boyhood and Gies had been born. Gies wrote: "All of us were soon stunned when the news came that Viennese Jews had been made to clean out public toilets and to scrub the streets in an orgy of Nazi depravity, and that these people's possessions had been seized by the Nazis."

Not long after the Germans took over Austria, Gies went to the police department to have her Austrian passport stamped, as she was required to do annually. This time her passport was taken from her and she was issued a new German passport. From then on she was to consider herself a German citizen, even though "in my heart I was Dutch through and through."

Several weeks later, Gies was visited by "a very blond young woman about my age wearing a sugary smile." The woman invited her to join one of the Nazi Girls' Clubs that were forming throughout Europe. Membership was a way of demonstrating loyalty to the Nazi Party. "How can I join such a club?" Gies asked. "Look at what the Germans are doing to the Jews in Germany." Gies did not know it then, but her refusal to join the club would be noted and remembered by Nazi officials.

War . . . and Marriage

The news from Germany about Hitler's torment of the Jews grew increasingly frightening. When she heard that an attempt had been made to assassinate Hitler, Gies was glad. "I wanted Hitler to be put down, murdered, anything. Then, as I reflected on my gnawing feelings, I realized how much I had changed. I had been brought up never to hate. . . . And here I was, full of hate and murderous thoughts."

In September 1939, Hitler invaded Poland, marking the beginning of World War II. One after another, the countries of Europe fell to the mighty German army until finally, on May 10, 1940, Germany invaded the Netherlands. Four days later Holland surrendered. "Now, suddenly, our world was no longer ours," Gies wrote.

As Dutch Jews experienced more and more pressure from Nazi restrictions placed on them, Gies, too, was having problems. One day she was summoned to appear before German officials in Amsterdam. When she said it was true she had refused to join a Nazi Girls' Club, her passport was marked with a black "X," which made it unusable, and she was ordered to return to Vienna within three months. The only way out of the dilemma was for her to marry a Dutch citizen. Overcoming many obstacles related to her citizenship status and her invalid passport, she finally was able to marry Jan Gies on July 16, 1941. Among those present at the simple ceremony were Otto Frank; his daughter Anne; and Mr. and Mrs. van Daan, who would soon join the Franks in hiding from the Germans.

Franks Go into Hiding

After her marriage, Miep Gies continued to work at Otto Frank's company. More and more restrictions were ordered against Jews; they were published in the local Jewish newspaper. "Perhaps the Germans thought that this way we Christians wouldn't know what was happening to the Jews. But word of every new measure spread like fire," Gies wrote. "At home, at night, the frustration and anger of the day left me drained dry." In the spring of 1942 Jews were ordered to sew a yellow star, a Jewish symbol, on their clothing to identify themselves as Jews. This order, "somehow so much more enraging than all the others, was bringing our fierce Dutch anger to a boil."

It was not long after this that Otto Frank informed Gies that he, his family, and the van Daans planned to go into hiding. He asked if she would care for the group. "Of course," she replied. In July 1942, Gies and her husband helped the Franks move their belongings into the hiding place they had prepared in the attic Otto Frank's office building.

Wartime Deprivations

For 25 months Gies helped the little group survive. Twice a day, except when she was sick, she visited the group, picking up their list in the morning, and returning in the evening with groceries. Her visits were eagerly looked forward to, because she also brought news of what was happening outside. The news grew more and more grim. "Every time [I entered the hiding place], I had to set a smile on my face, and disguise the bitter feeling that burned in my heart. I would take a breath . . . and put on an air of calm and good cheer that it was otherwise impossible to feel anywhere in Amsterdam anymore," she wrote.

What Qualities Do Holocaust Rescuers Share?

The Holocaust refers to the period between 1933 and 1945 when the Nazis systematically persecuted and murdered millions of European Jews and other innocent people. The Holocaust was part of the Nazi plan to establish a pure "master race." Millions of seemingly ordinary people stood by and did nothing while the Holocaust took place. Some, like Miep Gies, helped, and risked their own lives doing so.

Experts who have studied Holocaust rescuers have found that these people had some traits in common. Most came from warm, loving homes. Feelings of self-worth were encouraged and parents disciplined children through reasoning rather than punishment. As children, many Holocaust rescuers lost or were separated from a loved one but experienced caring from another. These experiences made future rescuers sensitive to others' suffering.

Gies, for example, lost her home and her family when she was sent to live in Holland. Yet she was welcomed by a warm and loving Dutch family, even though she was different from them. Thus she learned acceptance and tolerance for those who are "different." And she was able to take direct action when she saw that the lives of helpless victims were threatened.

Food became harder and harder to get as the war went on, because the Germans were sending it back home to "the Fatherland." Even soap grew scarce. Gies grew close to Anne Frank, who was growing into a young woman while in hiding. "I felt a particular kinship with Anne," she wrote. "I became determined to find something grown-up and pretty for Anne in the course of my searches [for food]." She found a pair of second-hand, red leather shoes, which she presented to the girl—the first and only pair of high-heeled shoes Anne would ever have. "Never have I seen anyone so happy as Anne was that day." It was Gies who supplied Anne with writing paper after the girl's diary pages were filled.

The war went on and on, and so did the scarcities. Winter was the worst time. Tempers flared, and illnesses struck. Sometimes the only food Gies was able to get made people sick. The group lived through two terrible winters in their hiding place. At home, Gies and her husband were concealing a young Jewish student, a boy named Karel. Gies wrote: "I'd cook the best dinner I could put together. [Jan], Karel, and I would sit down and eat. Often Karel would chatter away, hungry for company after another day of total isolation. [We] would listen silently."

Hopes Rise and Fall

On June 6, 1944, U.S. and British forces landed on the beaches of Normandy in France, a day known as D-Day, which marked the first step of victory in the war in Europe. All Amsterdam was filled with excitement, sure that their rescuers would soon be there. The American general Dwight D. Eisenhower spoke on the radio, assuring his listeners that "total victory over the Germans would be coming within this very year, 1944." Otto Frank hung a map of Europe on the wall, and on it the daily advance of their rescuers was marked with pins.

A little more than a month later, on July 20, 1944, everyone's hopes rose when it was learned that yet another attempt had been made on Hitler's life, one of several that occurred over the years he was in power. This attempt was made by Hitler's own military leaders, but it too failed. Life in Amsterdam got worse. Gies was in her office on August 4, 1944, when the Nazis came and took away the little group of people she had kept alive for so long. Someone had informed the police of their hiding place. Much later she wrote: "I could hear the sound of our friends' feet. I could tell from their footsteps that they were coming down like beaten dogs." After the war ended the following spring, only Otto Frank was still alive.

Finally Publishes Book

Otto Frank came to live with Gies and her family for a time after the war. Gies gave him Anne's diary, which she had saved but could not bring herself to read until long after it was published.

Gies retired from her job in 1947 to devote herself to homemaking. In 1950, at the age of 41, she gave birth to a son, Paul. She remained anonymous until the publication in 1987 of her book *Anne Frank Remembered*. She wrote the book after the death of Otto Frank in 1980, when she and Jan realized that they were the only witnesses left alive to speak of the Frank's tragedy. "It was very painful for us," she told an interviewer, "but we finally did it."

In the 1990s, following the publication of her book (which has also been made into a movie), Gies, then well into her eighties, toured the United States, giving lectures about her experience hiding her Jewish friends from the Nazis.

Where to Learn More

Beauregard, Sue-Ellen. "In Search of the Heroes: Forget Me Not—the Anne Frank Story." *Booklist* 93, no. 17 (May 1, 1997): p. 1509.

De Pres, Terrence. "Facing Down the Gestapo." *The New York Times Biographical Service,* May 1987, pp. 449-50.

Gies, Miep, with Alison Leslie Gold. *Anne Frank Remembered: The Story of the Woman Who Helped to Hide the Frank Family.* Simon and Schuster, 1987.

Kauffmann, Stanley. "Anne Frank Remembered" *The New Republic* 214, no. 10 (March 4, 1996): p. 30.

Small, Michael. "Miep Gies, Who Hid Anne Frank, Adds a Coda to the Famous Diary." *People Weekly* 29, no. 15 (April 18, 1988): p. 123.

Mildred Gillars
("Axis Sally")

Born November 29, 1900
Portland, Maine

Died June 25, 1988
Columbus, Ohio

*Radio personality, English
teacher, actress, model*

*Made radio broadcasts for the
Germans during World War II*

The morale of the soldiers (the state of their spirits) fighting a war is often vital in determining whether they will win or lose. During World War II (1939–45), U.S. citizen Mildred Gillars was hired by the Axis countries (Germany, Italy, and Japan) to try to hurt the morale of U.S. soldiers. The radio programs of "Axis Sally" (Gillars's radio name) actually entertained American troops and ironically had a far more negative effect on her own life than on that of the soldiers.

A Transient Youth

Mildred Elizabeth Sisk was born in 1900 in Portland, Maine, to Vincent and Mae Hewitson Sisk. The couple divorced when little Mildred was seven. Her mother remarried to a dentist, Robert Gillars, whose name both mother and daughter adopted. The Gillars' family moved constantly, and Mildred Gillars graduated from high school in Conneaut,

Ohio, in 1917. She attended Ohio Wesleyan University, in the town of Delaware, Ohio, from 1918 to 1922. Although Gillars did well in her study of speech and drama, she didn't accumulate enough credits to graduate.

Works In Europe

After she left college the young woman held a variety of low-paying jobs, including sales and waiting tables, as she struggled to become a professional actress. In 1919, she and her mother took a six-month trip to Europe, and she studied in France. After returning, Gillars got some minor acting and dancing jobs in New York City, and also worked as a nanny and in sales.

During the 1920s, Gillars traveled to Germany to pursue an acting career. She was said to have worked as a model and a dressmaker's assistant in Paris, France and studied music in Dresden, Germany. The prematurely gray-haired young woman arrived in Berlin, Germany, in 1934. Soon she got a job teaching English at the Berlitz School of Languages. She fell in love with a married man named Max Otto Kosichwitz, who had been a professor at New York City's Hunter College. At the start of World War II, Kosichwitz began to work for the German foreign office, and served as Radio Berlin's program director.

During the 1920s and 1930s, the National Socialist German Workers' Party (Nazi for short) grew in numbers and political power in Germany. The German economy was in shambles after World War I (1914–18), and the German people began blaming the Jewish people for their humiliating loss during the war. The Germans started following Nazi leader Adolf Hitler (see entry), who claimed the Jew were a poisonous race that must be eliminated.

In 1938, the Nazis marched into Austria and took over the country. The takeover of other nearby countries soon followed. The Nazis wanted to establish an empire in Europe and beyond without any Jews. World War II began in 1939 when Great Britain declared war on Germany, after Germany had taken over the country of Poland.

Kosichwitz convinced Gillars, who had already been working in German radio as an actor and a radio announcer, to do radio propaganda (official government communica-

"Hello, Gang. Throw down those little old guns and toddle off home. There's no getting the Germans down."

"Tokyo Rose"

"Tokyo Rose" was a name applied to a number of female propagandists who broadcast radio programs on behalf of Japan that were aimed at harming the morale among Allied troops serving in the Pacific. A number of different nationalities were represented by the women: Japanese, American, Australian, and Filipino.

The best-known "Tokyo Rose" was an American citizen named Iva Toguri Ikoku, who was born in 1916 to Japanese parents. After the war she was returned to the United States, and in 1948 she was tried and found guilty of treason. She was fined $10,000, and ordered to serve ten years in prison. She was released after six years and received a presidential pardon in 1977.

tions to the public that are designed to influence public opinion). Her broadcasts for the Nazis were aimed at U.S. soldiers.

"Axis Sally" Broadcasts

Gillars broadcast a radio program, called "Home Sweet Home," from late in the evening until early in the morning. Most of her shows were broadcast from Berlin, but sometimes they came from France or the Netherlands. After the Allies (United States, Great Britain, the Soviet Union, and France) landed in North Africa, she broadcast her program from there. Although she referred to herself as "Midge at the mike," U.S. soldiers named her "Axis Sally."

GIs (American soldiers) from all over Europe, North Africa, and the United States listened to Gillars's sexy voice as she played their favorite jazz recordings. Before starting the music, she sympathized with them about their loneliness and desire to return home. She also teased them about the possibility that their wives and girlfriends were dating back home while they were thousands of miles away. In addition, "Axis Sally" would comment on information that was supposed to be secret, welcoming new arriving units by name, and bidding farewell to units on their way from North Africa to fight in Italy. She constantly liked to remind the Allied soldiers that they were fighting a losing battle.

Another of Gillars's technique was to read the serial numbers of American GIs who had been captured or killed. It has been said she may have done more good than harm, though, because the Allied troops so enjoyed listening to the American jazz music she played and were able to disregard most of her propaganda messages. One of the songs she liked to play, "Lilli Marlene," became an international hit.

Postwar Capture

Gillars's program ran from December 11, 1941, through May 6, 1945. During the Soviet (now Russian) capture of Berlin in 1945, Gillars's lover, Max Kosichwitz was killed. At the war's end, Gillars was found, near starvation, in the cellar of a bombed-out building. Her identity was not immediately discovered, and she received the help of charitable agencies in getting food and shelter. She was treated at an American hospital in Germany for three weeks, and spent some time living at a camp for homeless people.

In late 1946, Gillars obtained a pass allowing her to live in Berlin's French Zone (the city had been divided up into sections run by various Allied countries.) When she later traveled to Frankfurt, Germany, to renew her pass, U.S. agents took her into custody. About a year later Gillars was sent to Washington, D.C., where she was put in jail.

Goes On Trial

Gillars was one of only twelve Americans charged with treason (betraying their country) after World War II. Her trial began in January 1949. The chief prosecutor began by pointing out that while working for Radio Berlin, Gillars had signed an oath of loyalty to Hitler and his Nazi Party.

During the war, all of Gillars's programs had been recorded by representatives of the Federal Communications Commission (an American agency responsible for monitoring American radio). Prosecutors said that the broadcasts were "sugarcoated propaganda pills," whose purpose was to get GIs to defect to the side of the Nazis. The broadcasts failed miserably in that purpose.

Mildred Gillars ("Axis Sally")

"Axis Sally" entertaining reporters before her trial for treason.

Evidence Presented

The program that caused Gillars to be prosecuted was one she broadcast on May 11, 1944, that was titled "Vision of Invasion." It was aimed at the soldiers stationed in England awaiting the D-Day invasion (the Allied invasion of Europe) that occurred on June 6 of that year. Americans also heard the program, which went over U.S. airways. On it, Gillars assumed the role of the mother of an American soldier who dreamed that her son died while crossing the English Channel in a ship that went up in flames. Gillars did an effective acting job, and the background sounds of soldiers portrayed as groaning in agony as they were shot at from the beaches had quite a dramatic impact. The voice of an announcer was heard to say, "the D of D-Day stands for doom . . . disaster . . . death . . . defeat . . . ." Testimony at the trial by a German radio official stated that the purpose of the broadcast was to scare American soldiers out of taking part in the planned invasion.

Gillars had sometimes pretended to be a worker for the International Red Cross, and in that disguise often persuaded young soldiers to make recordings for the people back home. She later added propaganda material to their messages, designed to undermine morale. In one message she was quoted as saying: "It's a disgrace to the American public that they don't wake up to the fact of what [President] Franklin D. Roosevelt (see entry) is doing to the [non-Jewish people] of your country and my country."

At Gillars's trial, several ex-GI witnesses testified that she had tried to get them to answer questions for recordings. One pointed at her, saying: "She threatened us as she left—that woman right there, that American citizen. She told us we were the most ungrateful Americans she had ever met and that we would regret this."

Defense of Gillars

Gillars's defense attorney pointed out that treason, which she was accused of, must be something more than the words one utters. He said: "Things have come to a pretty pass if you cannot make an anti-[Jewish] speech without being charged with treason. Being against President Roosevelt could not be treason. There are two schools of thought about [him]. One holds he was a patriot and martyr. The other holds that he was the greatest [rascal] in all history, the greatest fraud, and the greatest impostor that ever lived."

Gillars's lawyer also defended his client by saying that she was heavily influenced to begin the propaganda broadcasts by Kosichwitz, the older man with whom she was in love. Gillars took the stand three times, breaking down in tears on all three occasions. She said she had lived with Kosichwitz in Berlin and was heartbroken when she heard reports that he had died. According to *The New York Times:* "Gillars fascinated the public and the press with her flamboyance and cool self-possession. She cut a theatrical figure in tight-fitting black dresses, long silver hair, and a deep tan. She had scarlet lips and nails."

Trial Ends In Conviction

In his closing statement, the prosecutor said that Gillars had taken great pleasure in doing the broadcasts, especially when reporting the agonies suffered by wounded soldiers before they died. "She thought she was on the winning side," he said, "and all she cared about was her own selfish fame."

Gillars's six-week trial ended in March 1949. A jury of seven men and five women decided her fate. (The jury purposely had been made up of individuals who were neither Jewish nor could speak German.) After deliberating (consulting with each other to reach a decision) for more than one hundred hours, they were unable to agree on a verdict. The judge then had them sequestered (they were required to stay together with no outside contact) in a hotel. After seventeen hours of further deliberation, Gillars was acquitted of seven of the eight counts, and convicted on the count that involved the broadcast of the program "Vision of Invasion."

Gillars received her sentence on March 26, 1949. She was sentenced to ten to thirty years in prison and a fine of $10,000. She was declared ineligible for parole until ten years had passed. (Paroled prisoners are given early release from prison on conditions of continued good behavior.) "Axis Sally" was jailed in the Alderson, West Virginia, federal prison. She was eligible for parole in 1959, but fearing the response of people outside the prison to her Nazi past, she waived the right to ask for freedom. Two years later she did apply, her parole was granted, and she was released from prison.

Life After Prison

In 1961, Gillars went to live at the Sisters of the Poor Child Jesus Convent in Columbus, Ohio. At the convent's school she taught German, French, and music. She lived her life very much out of the public eye.

Gillars returned to Ohio Wesleyan University when she was seventy-two—fifty years after dropping out—and earned her B.A. degree in speech. She died of colon cancer at the age of eighty-seven in Columbus, Ohio.

Where to Learn More

Boatner, Mark M., III. *Biographical Dictionary of World War II.* Presidio Press, 1996.

Burgess, Patricia, ed. *The Annual Obituary,* 1988. St. James Press, 1990.

http://www.thehistorynet.com/World War II/articles/1195 cover.htm

Massakyo, Duus. *Tokyo Rose: Orphan of the Pacific.* Kodansha International, Ltd., 1979.

Snyder, Louis Leo. *Encyclopedia of the Third Reich.* McGraw-Hill, 1976.

Joseph Goebbels

Born October 29, 1897
Rheydt, Germany

Died May 1, 1945
Berlin, Germany

*Minister of Culture and Minister
of Propaganda for Nazi Germany*

*Known as "the little doctor"
and "the father of lies"*

T he life of Joseph Goebbels is an example of the fact that morality does not necessarily go along with high intelligence. This very well educated man, who influenced the minds of millions of Germans, used his talents to spread hate and violence. Having no respect for people whose ideas differed from his own, he ordered the large-scale burning of books and the murder of political opponents of German leader Adolf Hitler (see entry) before and during World War II (1939–45).

A Difficult Childhood

Joseph Goebbels (pronounced Yo-seff Goor-bulz), the son of working-class German Catholic parents, was born on October 29, 1897, in Rheydt, Germany. His hard-working family of seven managed to budget carefully and buy a small house. To maintain their middle-class status, the whole family made wicks for oil lamps. Despite efforts to correct the problem, the boy grew up with a club foot, a deformity that prevented him from walking properly.

As a result, Goebbels developed an inferiority complex and spent a great deal of time alone in his room, often reading. Goebbels was an excellent student, and his affectionate parents encouraged him to develop his intellectual gifts. He was not popular at school, where he kept aloof from the other students, but showed a talent for acting. According to writer Ralf Reuth: "Powerful displays of emotion, dramatic facial expressions and gestures were his [specialty]." A favorite teacher helped him to develop his language skills.

"It is almost immaterial what we believe in, so long as we believe in something."

College Years

In 1917, Goebbels enrolled at the University of Bonn in Germany to study literature. When he developed money problems, a Catholic organization provided him with loans for several semesters. Later, the group found it very difficult to get the loans repaid.

In 1914, at the beginning of World War I (1914–18), Goebbels had eagerly volunteered to fight for Germany. He had been disappointed when he was rejected because of his severe limp, and the fact that he was only five feet tall and weighed barely one hundred pounds. These physical conditions were to remain for the rest of his life. In 1917, with the war raging, the military was less selective, and Goebbels was called, but merely to do paperwork. He interrupted his college studies to serve.

After the war, Goebbels returned to college and wrote several plays and an autobiographical novel, titled *Michael Voorman's Youth*. In this book, he wrote about his own self-hatred, how he had worked so hard at school to try to make up for his physical disabilities, and his tendency to become "arrogant and tyrannical." In 1922, Goebbels received his Ph.D. in literature from the University of Heidelberg in Germany. His attempts to become a playwright and a novelist proved to be a failure, however.

Early Days with the Nazis

In 1924, Goebbels began to write and edit political journals, and in 1925 he joined the National Socialist German Workers' Party (Nazi for short), led by Adolf Hitler. Goebbels was at first a follower of Gregor Strasser, a Nazi who believed Hitler was not extreme enough in his ideas for social and economic change. After meeting Hitler on several occasions, however, Goebbels became enchanted with him. Hitler, realizing this, flattered Goebbels and cultivated his loyalty. Goebbels became the Nazi's district leader for the Berlin-Brandenberg area in 1926. His task was to reorganize the Nazi Party there. "I recognize [Hitler] as my leader quite unconditionally," he wrote. "He is the creative instrument of Fate and Deity [God] . . . good and kind, but also clever and shrewd."

"Yes-man" is a perfect description of Goebbels, at least in his relationship to Hitler. A story is told about the Nazis leaders viewing a film that Goebbels referred to as magnificent. A short time later, when Hitler entered the room and stated his opinion that it was absolutely no good, Goebbels was heard to exclaim, "Yes, my Führer [pronounced Fyoor-uhr]. It was feeble, very feeble." Führer was a popular name for Hitler, meaning "my leader."

Rises in the Nazi Party

By 1928, Goebbels had become one of twelve Nazi deputies. The most intellectual of the Nazis, Goebbels was charming and witty and possessed a deep, musical voice. He had black hair, dark eyes, and high cheekbones, as well as a long nose and wide mouth. Hitler appointed the gifted communicator head of party propaganda and public information in 1930. Propaganda is official government communications to the public that are designed to influence opinion. The information may be true or false. Goebbels was also in charge of the Nazis' chaotic election campaigns from 1930 through 1933.

Goebbels's public speaking abilities earned him the office of Reichsminister of Propaganda following Hitler's rise to dictator (he held absolute rule) in 1933. Goebbels was responsible for the impressive torchlight parades and well-orchestrated Nazi rallies. According to author Peter Neville: "Goebbels' most important task was to reinforce the iron grip of the Nazi Party on the lives of ordinary German people." He controlled the media, and in 1933 organized a burning of books disliked by the Nazis. He also imposed Nazifica-

tion (the promotion of only Nazi values) on the artistic and cultural branches of German life. Goebbels helped fashion what writer Thomas Fuchs refers to as the "Führer myth." This myth held that Hitler was superior to all other human beings, lived a simple life with no luxuries, and was infallible (he couldn't make a mistake). Fuchs says that the Führer myth "insured that Hitler remained unsullied, uncriticized, and perfectly free to undertake whatever course of action he chose." It was Goebbels's idea to have thousands of small record players produced so that supporters could listen to Hitler's speeches.

Nazi Party Symbols

The swastika, a bent-arm cross, was an ancient symbol that first appeared in India, signifying good luck. In more recent times it was used by very conservative German political groups, including the Nazis. The Nazi swastika always appeared in black within a white circle and set on a red background. Hitler explained that red always captured people's attention.

Old movies about the Nazis are full of people raising their arms in a stiff fashion and declaring "Heil Hitler!" or "Seig Heil!" After Hitler's ascent to power, "Heil (meaning hail) Hitler" became the official greeting when Nazis met one another. The repetition of these two phrases at huge Nazi rallies came from the suggestion of a friend of Hitler. When Hitler's friend was in the United States attending Harvard University, he saw how cheerleaders whipped up enthusiasm among the crowd at Harvard football games by getting the spectators to clap and repeat cheers.

Hitler copied the rigid outstretched arm salute used by the Nazis from Italian dictator Benito Mussolini. Hitler was known for being able to keep his own arm extended in the salute for very long periods. Some insiders attributed this to his wearing a collapsible spring under his sleeve.

Anti-Jewish Hatred

Goebbels grew to be extremely anti-Jewish or antisemitic, although he was raised in a home with no particular anti-Jewish feelings. His strong Jewish beliefs developed during the mid-1920s when he began to see Jews as the perpetrators of economic ideas that he opposed.

As the Nazis were growing more powerful in the mid-1930s, Goebbels played a large role in fighting the Nazis' political opponents within Germany. By the time World War II (1939–45) began, Hitler was Germany's dictator and no longer had those enemies to fight. That is, with one exception—the Jews. By then, Goebbels was known to be an extreme antisemite (hater of the Jews, who are sometimes called Semites). He was responsible for an infamous event that took place on November 9, 1938. That night, several thousand Jews were brutally rounded up and sent to concentration camps, and all their worldly goods taken from them. Concentration camps are places where the Nazis confined people they regarded as "enemies of the state." As an added injury, the Jews were made to pay an enormous fine. This event, which came to be called *Kristallnacht* (meaning "Crystal Night" or "The Night of Broken Glass"), was also something for which Goebbels took credit. The name *Kristallnacht* refers to the tons of windows from Jewish-owned stores that lay shattered in the streets. *Kristallnacht* resulted in the death of more than 90 Jews and the destruction of nearly 300 synagogues (Jewish places of worship).

The historian Robert Hirzstein wrote: "Goebbels had all along been the one high Nazi leader who had insisted upon the necessity of actually exterminating the Jews." Like Hitler, Goebbels was very fond of the movies. He produced films that glorified Nazi heroes, and portrayed Jews as ugly and sinister. Goebbels reveled in violence and did not hesitate to use the SA or storm troopers (Hitler's private army) to attack and murder people. Once the war began, he did his best to worsen the living conditions of the Jews in Berlin. The first transport of Jews from Berlin to a ghetto in the city of Lódz, Poland, was in fulfillment of his promise to the Führer to make Berlin "cleansed of Jews." (Ghettos were crowded, walled parts of a city where Jews were forced to live in inferior conditions.) The Nazis enjoyed being especially brutal to the Jews on Jewish holidays, and these days became known as "Goebbels's calendar."

Master of Propaganda

During World War II, Goebbels played a key role in influencing the minds of the German people. Sometimes called the "father of lies," he believed that people would only believe lies if they were repeated often enough. He also said that the bigger the lie, the more likely people were to believe it. Goebbels's campaigns were always built around causing the German people to hate some particular person or group. Germans were kept from knowing the truth of how the war was progressing, saw defeats portrayed as victories, and heard an endless stream of official lies—for example, that Winston Churchill, Great Britain's prime minister, was a drunk or that U.S. president Franklin D. Roosevelt (see entry) was Jewish.

Goebbels's last big lie was that Hitler died near the end of the war, leading his troops in battle, rather than committing suicide as he actually did in his underground bunker.

Helps Hitler Overcome Plot

Goebbels played a very important role as Hitler's savior in a situation that occurred in 1944. A group of Nazi officers, realizing that the Nazis were losing the war, attempted to assassinate Hitler. They hoped to spark an overthrow of the Nazi government. They might have succeeded in their plans had Goebbels not stepped in and taken charge. He brought together troops for support, and soon had most of the plotters jailed or murdered.

Relationships with Women

Goebbels was married and the father of six children. Despite that, he was known for having many romances with women—especially the young actresses under his control as head of the Nazi movie industry. At one point his adulterous behavior was so bold, Hitler told him to stop it. Hitler said Goebbels was harming the image of wholesomeness that the Nazis liked to portray. Goebbels did as he was ordered for a short time, then secretly resumed his former behavior.

Murder and Death

Hitler's suicide took place in the spring of 1945, once it was obvious that the Nazis were going to lose the war. Goebbels intended to commit suicide right after Hitler, but could not bring himself to do so. Goebbels refused to accept the position of Reich chancellor, an appointment that Hitler had specified for him in his will. With the approach of the Soviets (now Russians), he sent a Nazi general to talk with the Soviet troop commander and attempt to negotiate a peace treaty. The Soviets were not interested.

Many historians believe that, as the war ended, the lives of Goebbels's six children could have been saved. There is no doubt that the children, ages four to twelve, would have suffered some difficult times, though. Before his death, Hitler had advised Goebbels's wife, Magda, to leave Germany by plane. Ever loyal to the Führer, however, this was not what Joseph and Magda Goebbels wanted. On May 1, 1945, Goebbels and his wife sedated their children, and then killed each of them with injections of poison, finally killing themselves. As Goebbels had instructed before his death, his own body and that of his wife were then burned.

Where to Learn More

Heiber, Helmut. *Goebbels.* Da Capo, 1972.

Manvell, Robert, and Heinrich Fraenkel. *Dr. Goebbels.* Simon and Schuster, 1960.

Reimann, Viktor. *Goebbels.* Doubleday, 1976.

Reuth, Ralf Georg. *Goebbels.* Harcourt Brace, 1990.

Riess, Curt. *Joseph Goebbels.* Hollis and Carter, 1949.

Semmler, Rudolf. *Goebbels: The Man Next to Hitler.* Westhouse, 1947.

Trevor-Roper, H. R. *The Last Days of Hitler.* 3rd ed. Macmillan, 1962.

Hermann Göring

Born January 12, 1893
Rosenheim, Germany

Died October 15, 1946
Nuremburg, Germany

*Field marshal and commander in chief
of the German Air Force*

Known as der Dicke ("the fat one")

More than any other of the major German officials who worked for the anti-Jewish dictator Adolf Hitler (see entry), Hermann Göring is an example of a decent man who became corrupted by power. During Göring's boyhood, at the end of the nineteenth century, Germany was vigorous and full of promise. As a young man, he saw his country, which was defeated in World War I (1914–18), grow frightened and desperate. The people finally turned to Hitler to save them. Instead, Hitler involved Germany in a bloody and barbaric series of events that ended in shame and defeat. Hermann Göring's fate was no better.

Unhappy Beginnings

Hermann Wilhelm Göring (pronounced Hair-mon Vil-helm Ger-ring) was born in a little town south of Munich, Germany, in January 1893. His father, Heinrich Ernst Göring, represented Germany's business interests in various foreign countries. When she was nineteen, Göring's mother, Franziska "Fanny" Tiefenbrun, married Heinrich Göring, a forty-five-year-old widower with five children. Besides serving as stepmother to these children, she also gave birth to four children of her own. Hermann was the last.

When Göring was three months old, his mother went to join her husband in the country of Haiti, where he was stationed. Göring was left behind for three years to be raised by a family in the town of Furth. Without his family, Göring was a lonely, unhappy child. When they were finally reunited he struck at his mother in rage.

Back in Germany, the career of Göring's father reached a dead end because he advocated that black people be treated as human beings. This was a highly unpopular idea among the Germans at that time. He soon retired and died from alcoholism in 1913.

Childhood and Schooling

After his father's retirement, Göring went to live at the castle of his godfather, an Austrian physician named Hermann von Epenstein. One day at the private school he attended, the teachers criticized Göring for writing an admiring essay about his godfather. The teachers said that von Epenstein was Jewish and that students were not expected to write essays in praise of Jews. That night the 11-year-old Göring packed his bags and returned home.

Göring then attended two different military academies, where he excelled at mountain climbing and horseback riding. A loyal, self-confident boy, he dreamed of becoming a hero that all of Germany would respect. He graduated in 1912 with highest honors. After graduation, Göring served as a junior officer in the Prinz Wilhelm Regiment. He was popular with young women, in part because of his striking blue-green eyes and blond good looks.

During World War I, Göring proved to be a brave pilot. He was awarded Germany's highest honor for an aviator, the Blue Max. On July 7, 1918, he was appointed the last commander of the famed Richthofen Squadron and began to develop his excellent management skills.

"I pledge my destiny to you [Adolf Hitler] for better or for worse. . . ."

After the war, Göring worked as a stunt pilot and as a commercial pilot for a Swedish airline. In Stockholm, Sweden, he met 32-year-old Swedish baroness Carin von Fock-Kantzoa, a married woman with an 8-year-old son. The baroness divorced her husband, a Swedish soldier, and she and Göring were married in 1923.

Göring and many other young German soldiers during the postwar period felt betrayed by their government. Their political leaders never led them to suspect that they might be forced to surrender to the enemy. When the war ended in 1918, Germany's enemies saw to it that the country was punished. The victorious countries demanded huge sums of money, known as reparations, to make up for the damages Germany had caused during the war. The payment of these reparations resulted in economic hardships for the German people. The lack of jobs was also a serious problem. Poor and stripped of illusions, Göring, like many young men, was looking for something in which to believe.

Joins the Nazi Party

Adolf Hitler now marched into the life of Göring and all of Germany. Anti-Jewish feeling and talk of German racial purity were rampant. As head of the National Socialist German Workers' Party (Nazi for short), Hitler preached that Germans were a superior race and should rule the world. He believed that Jews were a "poisonous" race that had caused Germany's defeat in the war. Hitler also said that the terms of the Treaty of Versailles that ended World War I must be done away with. Göring agreed and joined the Nazi Party. At first Göring resisted Hitler's strong anti-Jewish or antisemitic beliefs. However, Göring totally worshiped Hitler and soon abandoned his own tolerant views and went along with the Nazi leader's anti-Jewish speeches and writings.

By 1923, the Görings' house had become the hub of Nazi social activities. It was at this house that the Nazis planned their first failed attempt to take over the German government. This would later be called the Munich Beer Hall Putsch. In the aftermath, Göring was severely wounded. He fled to Austria and then Switzerland. During Göring's slow recovery, he was in great pain and became a morphine (a highly addictive pain medication) addict, a problem that was to plague him on and off for the rest of his life.

Göring was free of drugs and had healed from his wounds by 1926, but the ordeal had disturbed his glandular system. From then on he remained very fat, and future enemies enjoyed making fun of this condition. The next year Germany excused all political prisoners and Göring returned to his native land.

A Change of Fortune

By 1927, the Nazi Party had grown large and enjoyed a great deal of support among the German people. Göring, who had not been invited to rejoin Hitler's staff, got a job selling BMW automobiles. Within a year, he became very successful and visible in Berlin's (Germany's capital) social scene. Hitler, now aware of how he could use Göring, selected him to head the ticket of the Nazi Party in the 1928 elections. Although the party lost, Göring was able to prove his popularity. Hitler rewarded him with a handsome salary, and the Görings bought a large house in a desirable district of Berlin.

Over the next four years the Nazi Party grew in political strength, and so did Göring. On January 29, 1933, Germany's president, Paul von Hindenberg, appointed Hitler chancellor. Göring persuaded von Hindenberg that Hitler was the only man who could lead Germany out of its difficult problems caused by the worldwide depression (economic downturn). Göring became the most important minister in Hitler's cabinet.

A political crisis required that a new election be held on March 5, 1933. The Nazis did well, but failed to earn a winning majority. On March 23, through political maneuvering, Göring had many of the Nazis' opponents arrested on questionable grounds. Their absence allowed the Nazis to drum up more than the two-thirds majority vote they needed to have Hitler placed in charge of the government. In June a new law was decreed: "The [Nazi] Party constitutes the only political party in Germany."

That same year, the former political police force was replaced by the Secret State Police, better known as the Gestapo. Thousands of Germans were arrested for being Jews or Catholics, or because their opinions differed from the Nazis', who put them in concentration camps. The camps were places where the Nazis confined people they regarded as "enemies of the state." Göring was held in contempt by the more brutish Nazis for his "squeamishness" about inflicting pain and suffering on others. He tried unsuccessfully to keep brutality out of the camps where the prisoners were sent. Nevertheless, Göring learned to turn a blind eye to the growing terroristic tactics practiced by the Nazis throughout German society.

With his love of flying, Göring particularly enjoyed being Reichminister of Aviation. As head of the *Luftwaffe,* the German Air Force, he spent the years 1934 through 1936 strengthening the country's air power.

By 1933, the Nazis maintained ultimate power over Germany. Hitler combined the office of president with that of chancellor, making himself head of state as well as commander in chief of the armed forces. He was now dictator (he ruled with absolute authority) of Germany. Göring gathered his senior officers later that day, and all swore allegiance to Hitler.

Loss and Remarriage

Göring's wife, Carin, died in 1931 after a long illness, leaving him heartbroken. Northeast of Berlin he built himself a grand mansion named Carin Hall in her honor. Göring, now a collector of fine art, furnished the home with priceless tapestries and paintings. By this time, Göring had begun sporting elaborate costumes, and wearing rouge and expensive colognes.

Beginning in 1933, Göring had a new companion, the German actress Emmy Sonnemann. She became his second wife in 1935 at an elaborate wedding attended by Hitler and other Nazi dignitaries. Emmy gave birth to Göring's daughter, Edda, three years later.

In 1936, Hitler began planning for war, a secret that soon leaked out. His aim was to place all German-speaking peoples outside of Germany's borders under the Nazi flag. Göring, now second in command only to Hitler, was made head of all economic matters. At the height of his powers in 1938 and 1939, Göring presided over the passage of laws reducing the freedom of German citizens and destroying that of the Jews.

Start of the War

Germany's attack on Poland in 1939 marked the beginning of World War II. After Germany's quick victory over Poland, Göring was treated as a hero. Germany's war against the West made great gains with the fall of Holland, Belgium, and France in 1940. Hitler granted Göring the title of Reich Marshal and, in a speech, even referred to Göring as his successor.

Loss of Favor

Göring was not to remain Hitler's right-hand man for long. During the course of World War II he fell into disfavor with the Führer (meaning "my leader"), the title Hitler gave to himself, over a variety of issues. As Hitler became unreasonable and increasingly bad tempered, Göring grew disillusioned. When the Nazis started to lose ground in the Soviet Union (now Russia), Hitler denied all responsibility. "[As head of the air force] I certainly got the blame," Göring was

Göring receiving reports from plane crews during the war.

quoted as saying. "From that time on the relationship between the Führer and myself steadily deteriorated." Göring was also held responsible for the declining protection afforded by the *Luftwaffe* during the massive Allied bombing campaigns against German cities and industries. (The Allies consisted of the United States, Great Britain, the Soviet Union, and France.) Hitler began to berate Göring and refer to him scornfully. Eventually, Göring assigned most of his duties regarding concentration camps and the Gestapo to various underlings.

By this time, Göring was pessimistic about the war and frightened about his family's fate if Germany lost. He continued to obey the orders of the Führer, but avoided contact with the Nazi leadership as much as possible. Göring now spent most of his time at Carin Hall. When Hitler found out that Carin Hall was being protected by German paratroops, he ordered them to leave. Göring had his most precious possessions packed and taken to Bavaria. In February 1945, he and his aides left in a staff car, and he had Carin Hall destroyed by dynamite.

Arrest and Imprisonment

Göring arrived in Obersalzberg, Bavaria, where he set up military headquarters. Hitler was wrongly informed by Göring's enemies that he had launched a coup d'etat (a sudden overthrow of the government by force). Hitler then stripped him of all his titles, and had SS troops arrest Göring and his family at the castle where they were staying. (The SS, an abbreviation for *Shutzstaffeln* or Security Squad, was Hitler's protection unit.) In April 1945, Hitler committed suicide in order to avoid falling into the hands of Soviet troops who were closing in on his underground bunker. Göring, who by now had been freed, expressed regret that he would never have the chance to convince Hitler of his loyalty.

In May 1945, near the end of the war, Göring was arrested by the Allies. He still believed, however, that he would be able to charm his way back into a comfortable civilian life. At first he received special treatment, including fine food and wine, to encourage him to talk. He condemned Hitler, discussed Nazi policies and procedures at length, and did his best to make his own actions appear favorable to his Allied captors. But he was soon placed in solitary confinement and treated as just another prisoner of war.

Göring's Testimony at Nuremberg

The courtroom was packed on March 13, 1946, the day Hermann Göring testified in his own behalf at the Nuremberg Trials. Having lost much of the extra weight that made him almost a comic figure, he appeared handsome and even noble. During his testimony he was initially very nervous, which was betrayed by his shaking hands. But his voice gained strength and confidence with each question he answered.

"He embellished his replies with [witty answers], attracting gales of laughter from the public in the courtroom, then subtly hushed the listeners with some throwaway self-incrimination of apparent sincerity," according to his biographer David Irving. Newspapermen in the courtroom were amazed by his brilliant performance on the stand. One prosecutor commented: "Now you see why he was so popular." One Nazi lawyer commented about him admiringly: "That Göring is quite a guy. . . . "

Although arrogant, Göring handled himself very effectively against the U.S. prosecutor, smirking and making clever, sarcastic comments. The bullying British prosecutor did cause Göring to break out into a sweat, however, when he asked why Göring had executed escaped British pilots, and questioned his loyalty to Hitler in the light of the atrocities ordered by Hitler.

Proud of his own performance on the stand, Göring told his fellow defendants: "If you handle yourselves half as well as I did, you'll be doing all right." An attorney for one of the other defendants remarked: "Göring had nothing to lose. That's why he played the part to the very end—with [vigor] and shrewdness . . . . He won round after round against [the American] . . . but he's as self-centered, vain, and pompous as ever."

In his final address to the Nuremberg court, Göring declared: "The German people trusted the Führer. Given his authoritarian direction of the state, [the people] had no influence on events. Ignorant of the crimes of which we know today, the people have fought with loyalty, self-sacrifice, and courage, and they have suffered too in this life-and-death struggle into which they were arbitrarily thrust. The German people are free from blame."

In 1946, the Allies put the Nazi criminals publicly on trial in Nuremberg, Germany. According to author Leonard Mosley, the Nuremberg Trials were meant "to draw a picture of Hitler's Germany in the fullest detail possible so that the German people themselves, and the rest of the world, could at least see what a horrendous spectacle it had been."

Testifying at the trials, Göring tried to justify the rule of the Nazis, and surprised everyone with his intelligence and his masterful speaking skills. Nevertheless, the tribunal found "his guilt . . . unique in its enormity" and sentenced him to death by hanging. Göring listened to the verdict stonefaced, but after returning to his cell he fought an emotional breakdown and asked to be left alone. Göring's written request to be executed by a firing squad, in the military tradition, was refused.

At around 11:00 P.M. on October 15, 1946, just a few hours before he was to be hanged, Göring swallowed a dose of poison. He was found dead in his bed within minutes. How he procured the vial of poison remains a mystery. The next day, his body and those of the Nazi criminals who had been hanged the night before were burned in a crematorium. Their ashes were later poured into a muddy gutter.

Göring thought that he would be remembered as a hero in Germany. This never happened. Despite his many outstanding qualities, and his successful efforts to save a number of Jews who were family friends, he was guilty of moral cowardice. "All through his association with Adolf Hitler," author Leonard Mosley points out, "there were moments when he might have changed the course of National Socialism and Germany's race to [hell]—by arguing with and persuading the Führer to begin with, [and] by [seizing power from] him when that was no longer possible."

Where to Learn More

Butler, Ewan, and Gordon Young. *The Life and Death of Hermann Göring.* Borgo Press, 1990.

Hoyt, Edwin P. *Angels of Death: Göring's Luftwaffe.* Tom Doherty Associates, 1994.

Irving, David. *Göring: A Biography.* William Morrow, 1989.

Lee, Asher. *Göring: Air Leader.* Ballantine Books, 1972.

Mosley, Leonard. *The Reich Marshal: A Biography of Hermann Göring.* Doubleday, 1974.

Shirer, William. *The Rise and Fall of the Third Reich: A History of Nazi Germany.* Secker and Warburg, 1960.

Skipper, G. C. *Göring and the Luftwaffe.* Children's Press, 1980.

Mendel Grossman

Born 1917
Poland

Died 1945
Germany (somewhere outside the
Konigs Wusterhausen work camp)

Photographer

*Recorded 10,000 photographs of life
in Poland's Lódz ghetto, where Jews
were forcibly confined*

Since the birth of photography in the 1800s, some of the most haunting pictures ever taken have been Mendel Grossman's photographs of life in Poland's Lódz ghetto. Ghettos were crowded, walled sections of cities where members of the National Socialist German Workers' Party (Nazis for short) forced Jews to live in inferior conditions. The pain-filled faces of children, mothers and fathers, and old people testify to the horrors imposed on their lives, and the hope that sometimes remained in their hearts. The work of Grossman eloquently defies those who deny that the Holocaust ever took place. The Holocaust refers to the period between 1933 and 1945 when the Nazis systematically persecuted and murdered millions of Jews and other innocent people.

Youth in Lódz

Mendel Grossman was born into a family of Hassidic Jews (members of a strict Jewish sect) in 1917. He was a short, slender young man who often wore an oversized topcoat. He walked slowly and carefully, and was frequently seen carrying a briefcase brimming over with papers.

Young Grossman loved the theater, literature, and the arts. He was a painter, a sculptor, and a photographer. He took pictures of a wide variety of subjects from flowers and animals, to landscapes, street scenes, and portraits. He often did paintings of these same types of subjects.

During the 1930s, Grossman became especially interested in photographing humans on the move. His interest in this subject developed on the occasion when he was photographing members of a theatrical troupe who were performing in his home town of Lódz, Poland. He recorded compelling behind-the-scenes images of the expressive faces and bodies of the actors and dancers. When he saw these fine pictures, he realized that he had a special gift for capturing people in motion.

"Such despair was never seen in the ghetto."

Photographs Poor People

Grossman then began to photograph people he encountered in the poorer sections of Lódz. He photographed men at labor, children playing, and women preparing the family meals. His work became well known and respected. In 1939, a Jewish organization dedicated to promoting children's health hired him to take photographs of poor but healthy children in the neighborhoods of Lódz. That same year, Germany invaded Poland. Germany was ruled by Adolf Hitler (see entry),who hated Jews. He and members of his Nazi Party believed that the Jews were a poisonous race that needed to be eliminated in order not to "infect" German blood. After the invasion, the Nazis immediately began the persecution (and eventual murder) of Poland's Jewish people.

As the persecution of the Jews gathered momentum, Grossman's photographs were lost in the chaos. With the worsening of conditions, Grossman realized his ultimate calling—to photograph his people in their time of darkness.

Begins Recording Ghetto Life

The Lódz ghetto was a place where the Nazis forced Jews and other so-called "undesirables" to live. Grossman brought his camera along as he moved into the ghetto. He captured

Why Were the Ghettos and Death Camps in Eastern Europe?

From their beginnings, the Nazis displayed an inner core of hostility toward the Jews. They blamed German Jewish industrialists for undermining German efforts to win World War I (1914–18) for their own gain. Adolf Hitler preached that the Jews were "parasites" on German society and that intermarriage with them poisoned the purity of German blood. Exactly when Adolf Hitler arrived at the "Final Solution"—the extermination of all European Jews—remains unclear. The first Polish ghetto was begun in 1939 in the town of Piotrkow. Next came the Lódz ghetto, wherein lived the second largest Jewish community in Poland. By the end of 1940, ghettos were set up in almost all Polish towns that had significant Jewish populations. The Warsaw ghetto alone housed more than 400,000 people.

The ghettos were eventually emptied and their prisoners were sent to concentration camps, where the Nazis confined people they regarded as "enemies of the state." While concentration camps were spread throughout Europe, the major Nazi camps, whose primary purpose was the killing of all their inhabitants, were located in Eastern Europe.

According to writer Barbara Rogasky, the three major reasons the Nazis set up ghettos and death camps in Eastern Europe were: (1) because almost all of the Jews of Europe lived there; (2) the enormous land area and miles of forests separating communities allowed the Nazis to operate in secret; and (3) the Nazis, hoping that they would not meet much resistance among the local populations, wanted to take advantage of the long-standing anti-Jewish sentiment in Eastern Europe.

on film images of the fear, suffering, and sickness of the ghetto inhabitants.

In order to hide what he was doing, for he knew it was forbidden by the Nazi authorities, Grossman took a job in the photographic laboratory of the Lódz ghetto's department of statistics. He became aware of the vast store of information about the ghetto that passed through the statistics office (the Nazis kept track of all sorts of major and minor details about ghetto inhabitants). Grossman used this information to guide him to places and events especially worthy of being captured in pictures. Photography paper and chemicals were easily available at the laboratory, allowing Grossman to do his own developing. He took full advantage of the opportunity to photograph life in the ghetto.

Mendel Grossman

Writer Arieh Ben-Menahem described the subjects of these photos. "There were children bloated with hunger . . . convoys of men and women condemned to death in the ovens of Chelmno [death camp] . . . public executions . . . ." He shot one photo of a whole family wheeling a wagon of excrement through the streets. They responded this way to his request to photograph them: "Let it [the photo] remain for the future, let others know how humiliated we were." Ben-Menahem wrote: "He gave in to that urge which motivated so many of the best of our [Jewish] people: to leave a record, to write down the events, to collect documents, to scratch a name on the wall of the prison cell, to write next to the name of the condemned the word vengeance."

Photographs Middle-Class Jews

Grossman was able to carry out his work partly because he had a bad heart, which prevented him from doing heavy physical labor. To avoid being observed and captured by the police, he hid his camera in his overcoat. To use it, he manipulated the camera through holes cut into the sleeves.

At one point, prosperous Jews from other parts of Europe were brought to the Lódz ghetto. These people wore handsome coats and quality shoes, and carried suitcases stuffed with their personal possessions. They spoke an educated dialect and tried to bring to the ghetto, as much as possible, a higher quality of life. They also tried to avoid contact with other ghetto inhabitants.

Grossman kept a pictorial record of the deterioration of these middle-class Jews. He recorded how they grew dirty and ill with ghetto diseases, and experienced physical and mental destruction. By the time they were forcefully loaded on the trains for the Chelmno death camp, their sad and painful story was etched on their faces.

Decides to Proceed Despite Risks

After several unsuccessful attempts to photograph executions by the Nazis, Grossman succeeded in capturing the image of a young man who was hanged for trying to escape on a railroad train. When Grossman saw the excellence of this picture, he decided to abandon his more timid approach and risk all to take pictures that could most powerfully and painfully record the human suffering inflicted by the Nazis.

DER AELTESTE DER JUDEN
IN LITZMANNSTADT
STATISTISCHE-ABTEILUNG
KIRCHPLATZ 4, TELEFON 22

E H Nr. 46 den 21.1. 194 4

Betrifft:

B E S C H E I N I G U N G

Der Fotograf Herr G r o s m a n Mordka, wohnhaft

Kelmstr.55 ist berechtigt für die Statistische Abteilung

Strassenaufnahmen zu machen.

S.Erlich
Leiter der Statistischen Abt.

As Ben-Menahem described: " . . . he climbed electric power posts to photograph a convoy of deportees on their way to the trains, he walked roofs, [and] climbed the steeple of a church that remained within the confines of the ghetto in order to photograph a change of guard at the barbed-wire fence."

Even though Grossman's own physical condition was becoming worse, he insisted on continuing his efforts. He photographed the Institute for Feather Cleaning. There, feathers from the stolen bedding of Jews on their way to the death camps were sorted and shipped to Germany for reuse by the Nazis. He photographed carts hauling off the corpses of Roma (more commonly called Gypsies) who had developed typhus (an intestinal disorder caused by living in unsanitary conditions) in their quarter of the ghetto. Gypsies are dark-haired, dark-skinned people who are believed to have originated in India. They were considered inferior by the Nazis.

The permit issued to Mendel Grossman by the Statistical Division of the Lódz ghetto, which allowed him to take photos.

Grossman hid his negatives in circular tin cans, which grew in number daily. It was Grossman's desire, and that of almost all of the Jews in the ghetto, to record the horror of their daily lives for future generations to see.

Documents Those Exiled to Death Camps

The cruelty of the Nazis escalated in 1942 when the decision was made to send ever-increasing numbers of people to Poland's death camps. Nazi authorities imposed a strict curfew, and, over a five-day period, thousands of people were taken from their ghetto dwellings.

In a diary written when he lived in the Lódz ghetto, Josef Zelkowicz describes the powerlessness of the ghetto-dwellers in trying to keep their loved ones from being carted off. He wrote:

> "It is to no avail that a child clutches its mother's neck with its two small hands. It is to no avail that the father throws himself in front of the doorway like a slaughtered ox (saying only over my dead body will you take my child). It is to no avail that the old man clings to the cold walls with his gnarled [crooked] hands and begs, 'Let me die here in peace.' It is to no avail that the old woman falls on her knees, kissing the [policeman's] boots, and begs, 'I have grown-up grandchildren who are like you.' To no avail does the sick man bury his feverish head in the sweat-covered pillow and sob away his last tears . . . ."

These are the types of images that Mendel Grossman captured with his camera.

Photographs the Dead

In 1943, the Nazis forced a large number of the people living in the Lódz ghetto to leave the country. Those who tried to escape were shot, and soon the odor of rotting human flesh was overwhelming. Despite the peril, Grossman accompanied a group of gravediggers who were given permission to bury the bodies. He used his camera to photograph the mass grave. He took photos of corpses stored in a cemetery hall, marking each body with a number, so that their relatives could later determine where their loved ones were buried. (The numbers would show up on their grave markers.) Gravediggers lifted the head of each corpse so that Grossman could snap the image of the dead. They were people of all ages, with a variety of expressions frozen on their faces.

Uses Telescopic Lens

Grossman continued his photographic work until the great purge of the ghetto was completed. Then he returned to shooting the more placid images of daily life there. When another mass deportation (the forcible removal of people from their city or country) of Jews started later in the year, friends warned him against taking pictures of the prisoners because there were many observant Nazi guards. It would take only one mistake for him to be found out. Despite the danger, Grossman persisted. He began to use a heavy, telescopic lens, made for him in a ghetto workshop, to photograph the large number of people being hauled away. Telescopic lenses have sections that slide one inside another and can be used to take long-distance photos.

Grossman was particularly interested in capturing the young people of the ghetto, with their youthful, hopeful faces. Whenever possible he photographed the comfortable life of the Nazis running the ghetto, contrasting it with the horrible conditions of the people they ruled over.

Grossman was very generous in distributing his photographs to all in the ghetto who requested them. It was his hope that some would survive the war. He made many friends, and they did their best to help him accomplish his work, sometimes carrying his heavy satchel. He looked out for his friends, often taking them along if it were to a place where a little bit of food or warmth might be made available.

Hides Negatives in Wall of Building

After four-and-one-half years of work, Grossman had amassed more than ten thousand negatives. In late 1944, when the Germans were about to go down in defeat, Nazi headquarters issued an order to totally destroy the Lódz ghetto. Grossman knew that he must find somewhere to hide his negatives. He removed a portion of the window frame in his apartment, took out some bricks, and deposited a crate full of negatives inside the brick wall, then replaced the window frame. He could only hope that his vital negatives would be safe.

Ordered to German Work Camp

Grossman continued to take his photographs as the liquidation (elimination) of the ghetto proceeded. He worked endlessly, taking pictures as the trains carried the prisoners off to unknown places. Grossman had already left the ghetto by the time Nazi officials realized what he had been doing. One of the last to leave the ghetto, he was sent to Konigs Wusterhausen work camp in Germany, camera still intact and hidden under his coat. He continued to take pictures there, even though he could not develop and print them.

Shortly before the surrender of the Nazis in 1945, all the people being confined in the German work camp where Grossman was ordered on a death march. On a death march, people were forced to walk great distances without the proper food or clothing. Exhausted by years of toil, his weak heart could not bear the strain of the march out. He died on the road at age 32.

Negatives Retrieved, Then Destroyed

After the end of World War II, Grossman's sister went to the ghetto and retrieved his photographs that were hidden in the wall. She sent them to Israel, where they were stored on a farm. During Israel's War of Independence in the late 1940s they came into the possession of the Jews' Egyptian enemies. Tragically, they were destroyed.

Most of the Grossman photos that remain today are those he had freely distributed to friends during their time in the Lódz ghetto. Nahman Sonnabend, a friend of Grossman's, was able to save some of the photographs, along with other documents, at the bottom of a well in the ghetto. This precious memorabilia can be seen at the Museum of the Holocaust in Israel and at the Ghetto Fighter's House in Israel.

Where to Learn More

Adelson, Alan and Robert Lapides, eds. *Lódz Ghetto: Inside A Community Under Siege.* Viking, 1989.

Plank, Karl A. *Mother of the Wire Fence: Inside and Outside the Holocaust.* Westminster John Knox Press, 1994.

Rogasky, Barbara. *Smoke and Ashes: The Story of the Holocaust.* Holiday House, 1988.

Szner, Zvi and Alexander Sened, eds. *With A Camera In The Ghetto: Mendel Grossman.* Shocken Books, 1977.

Herschel Grynszpan

Born March 28, 1921
Hanover, Germany

Died 1942 or 1943 (?)
Germany

Jewish assassin

His shooting of a German was the excuse used for Kristallnacht, the evening when Jews were beaten and their stores were looted

Seventeen-year-old Herschel Grynszpan was a young man without a country, living illegally in Paris, France, when he learned his family had been deported (forcibly removed) from their home in Germany by the Nazis (the abbreviated term for members of the National Socialist German Workers' Party). As his family sought refuge in Poland, Grynszpan assassinated a minor German official stationed in Paris. Although a large-scale persecution of German Jews had already been planned by the Nazis, they used this assassination as their excuse for *Kristallnacht* ("Crystal Night"), also known as "The Night of Broken Glass" because of all the broken glass that scattered the streets. On that terrible evening, more than thirty thousand Jews were arrested without cause by the Nazis, and ninety-one were killed.

A Childhood in Poverty

Herschel Grynszpan was born in 1921, the sixth of eight children born to Sendel Siegmung and Rifka Silberberg Grynszpan. Herschel, an older brother, Mordechai Eliese (Marcus), and an older sister, Ester Beile (Berta), were the only three of the eight children who survived past childhood. Three other children were stillborn, one died of scarlet fever, and one died in an accident.

Both of Herschel's parents were born in Poland. They fled the country in 1911, a year after they were married, because of strong antisemitic (anti-Jewish) sentiments being expressed there. They settled in Hanover, Germany, where Sendel opened a tailoring shop in an extremely poor and unsavory area of the city. For years he barely made ends meet. Meanwhile, Germany lost World War I (1914–18) and was forced to pay huge penalties to the victors of that war. Economic conditions were bad and became even worse when the worldwide depression (economic downturn) began in 1929. Sendel was forced to give up his tailor shop and live mainly on welfare.

Herschel attended a public school until he was fourteen years old. His teachers considered him intelligent but lazy. He was surly (ill-humored), and although he was small (by the age of seventeen he was only five feet two inches tall and weighed one hundred pounds), he often instigated fights. He never received a diploma and later complained that his teachers had no interest in Jewish students, treating them as "outcasts." After leaving public school, he studied Hebrew for a year.

Nazi leader Adolf Hitler (see entry) became dictator (ruled with absolute power) of Germany in 1933. He promised to make Germany a great world power once again, as it had been before the loss of World War I. He blamed the loss of that war on the Jews and claimed Jews were a "poisonous" race. He said he would get rid of all Jews and win back the land lost by Germany in World War I. To succeed in these plans, Hitler began to build up the German army in violation of the Treaty of Versailles that ended the war. Under his leadership, the economic situation in Germany began to improve, and Sendel Grynszpan was able to reopen his tailor shop.

For a while the family lived in relative comfort. But by 1936 Nazi restrictions against German Jews began to take effect. These restrictions took away many rights, such as the

"Again and again I asked myself: 'What have we done to deserve such a fate?'"

right to own businesses. The Grynszpans were once again reduced to extreme poverty. Although his siblings found work, Herschel did not seem willing or interested in doing so. He said no one would hire him because he was Jewish.

Leaves Germany

One day Herschel Grynszpan met an old man at the synagogue (a Jewish place of worship). The old man told him to get out of Germany. "A boy like you can't stay here under such conditions. In Germany, a Jew is not a man, but is treated like a dog," the old man said. So it was decided that Grynszpan would go to live with an aunt and uncle in Paris, who promised to teach him a trade and perhaps adopt him.

Complications arose over his acquiring travel papers (he had been born in Germany but was a Polish citizen), so Grynszpan finally entered France illegally in late 1936. This illegal entry was later to cause him nightmarish problems.

In Paris, Grynszpan lived with his Uncle Abraham, a tailor, and his Aunt Chawa. They were a relatively poor couple who nevertheless made Grynszpan welcome and provided him with spending money. He entertained himself by going to dances and movies and by hanging out at a local coffee house. He continued to avoid looking for work because, he later wrote, "I didn't want to put myself in an illegal situation by working as an illegal immigrant.

Grynszpan's aunt and uncle finally grew tired of supporting him, and it was decided that Grynszpan should return to Germany. About this time the French authorities ordered him to leave the country, but German authorities said he was not welcome in Germany. As a result, Grynszpan was forced to go into hiding.

The News from Germany

The news from Germany was not good—Nazi treatment of the Jews grew worse every day. Moreover, in 1938 Hitler decided that all Jews in Germany who held Polish citizenship—some 15,000 to 17,000 people including the Grynszpan family—were to be deported back to Poland. But the Polish government did not want these unfortunate Jews either, and a law was passed in Poland revoking the Polish passports of all citizens who had lived out of the country for more than five years. Four days before that law went into effect, Heinrich Himmler (see entry), head of the SS, ordered that all Polish Jews in Germany should be rounded up and moved out. (The SS was the unit originally formed to act as bodyguards for Hitler.)

Without warning, on a freezing and rainy October night, German police seized the Polish Jews, herded them into boxcars, took them across the border, and dumped them in Poland. Each person was only allowed to carry one piece of luggage and a very small amount of money.

Grynszpan, who was already in a terrible predicament of his own, received a postcard from his sister on November 3, 1938. She wrote in part: "You have undoubtedly heard of our great misfortune. . . . We had to leave Germany before October 29 . . . I packed a valise [suitcase] with the most necessary clothes . . . That is all I could save. We don't have a cent." Grynszpan's father later told his family's story at the trial of Adolf Eichmann (see entry): "Finally we reached the border. We crossed it. The women went first because they began firing at us. The Poles had no idea why we were there or why there were so many of us. . . . They saw that we were all Polish citizens—we had special passports and they decided to let us into Poland . . . [we] were very hungry . . . they threw bread. . . . Then I wrote a letter to my son Herschel in Paris."

When he received the letter, Grynszpan decided to act. Although he knew nothing about guns, he was able to buy a small handgun at a neighborhood shop. On November 7, 1938, he proceeded to the German embassy and asked to speak to the ambassador, claiming he had a secret document to hand over. He was instead directed to the office of a fairly minor official, twenty-nine-year-old Ernst vom Rath. When vom Rath asked to see the secret document, Grynszpan cried: "You are a filthy kraut [a slang word for a German] and here in the name of twelve thousand persecuted Jews, is your document!" He then drew his small weapon from his pocket and shot vom Rath five times.

To Grynszpan's horror, vom Rath did not die. Instead he called for help while Grynszpan stood and watched. When the police came, Grynszpan calmly surrendered. He told the police: "I've just shot a man in his office. I do not regret it. I did it to avenge my parents, who are living in misery in Germany."

```
5   2   7   1   6

B i l d t e l e g r a m m   aus
         P a r i s :
as ist der jüdische Revolver-Attentäter
  Herschel Seibel  G r y n s z p a n !

nser (telegrafisch übermitteltes) Bild
us Paris zeigt den jüdischen polnischen
taatsangehörigen Herschel Seibel Grynsz
an, der am Montagvormittag in den Räu -
en der Deutschen Botschaft in Paris
inen Mordversuch an Legationssekretär
om Rath unternommen hatte, nach seiner
erhaftung auf dem Polizeikommissariat.
ort hatte der Verbrecher die Stirn, zu
rklären, dass er mit den beiden Revol
erschüssen auf Legationssekretär vom
ath seine jüdischen Rassegenossen rä
hen wollte.
ei Abdruck nennen: Scherl Bilderdienst
.11.19                          A V  5  2  7  1  6
```

Kristallnacht

The next day, Hitler was just leaving a party when his aide Joseph Goebbels (see entry) informed him of the shooting of vom Rath (who died on November 9). Hitler immediately promoted vom Rath, so the world would believe that Grynszpan had assassinated an important German official. Hitler saw the shooting not as the action of a desperate young man but as a conspiracy against Germany by the entire Jewish race. Vom Rath's death seemed the perfect opportunity for the Nazis to stage an act of mass revenge against the Jews.

The cable message that was sent to Berlin along with Grynszpan's photograph immediately after vom Rath's assassination.

An order went out that read in part: "Actions against the Jews and in particular against their synagogues will occur in a short time in all of Germany. . . . The seizure of some twenty to thirty thousand Jews . . . is to be prepared. Wealthy Jews above all are to be chosen" (so their money and goods could be taken and used by the Nazis). And so was launched the infamous pogrom (mass attack) on Germany's Jews that came to be called *Kristallnacht,* or "The Night of Broken Glass" because of the glow created by the broken glass from Jewish stores and buildings.

Back in Paris . . .

French authorities were horrified by the shooting—France's relations with Germany were already on shaky ground because there were rumors that Germany intended to take over countries such as France. News of the shooting and its aftermath, *Kristallnacht,* spread around the world. Grynszpan, too, was horrified to learn that his act had apparently triggered the Germans' attack against the Jews.

In the United States, fear that Grynszpan would be lynched (taken away by a mob and illegally hanged without a trial) led to the establishment of a fund to pay for lawyers to defend him. Preparations began for a major trial that would be attended by journalists from all the major world newspapers. Grynszpan was placed in a relatively comfortable prison for young offenders. He began to keep a journal, and he began to enjoy his celebrity. "For the first time in his life, he felt important," according to authors Anthony Read and David Fisher.

What followed was one delay after another. Grynszpan's lawyers were not sure how to handle his case. If they presented him as a "boy avenger attacking a brutal regime [government]," more Jews in Germany might suffer at the hands of the Nazis. No matter what his lawyers suggested, Grynszpan was unwilling to follow their advice. He began to write letters to famous people complaining about his situation—including one to Hitler himself. Hitler marched on Poland in September 1939, beginning World War II. He then continued his progress across Europe, reaching France in May 1940. Meanwhile, Grynszpan sat in jail.

France surrendered to Germany on June 17, 1940. Uncertain what to do with Grynszpan, and afraid to anger

Did Grynszpan Perform a Service?

Author Gerald Schwab was a fourteen-year-old witness to *Kristallnacht*. His father was arrested and spent five weeks in a concentration camp. Soon after his release the family moved to the United States. In 1946, Schwab was asked to serve as a translator at the International War Crimes Tribunal in Nuremberg, Germany, where Nazi leaders were tried for their crimes.

While he was in Berlin, Schwab became interested in the case of Herschel Grynszpan and later published a biography of him. In his biography, Schwab suggested that even though hundreds of Jews died as a result of Grynszpan's deed, many more lives were indirectly saved. The reason, he wrote, was that "many Jews who until that point [Crystal Night] had lived in the hope that Nazism would wither away or become more tolerant, suddenly found themselves face to face with another reality. They arrived at the realization that this evil was here to stay and that the conditions of Jews under Nazi domination could only get worse."

As a result, between 1933 and 1938, about 200,000 Jews left Germany, an action that saved their lives. Others argue, however, that Grynszpan's actions had no effect—that *Kristallnacht* would have happened with or without him.

the conquering Germans by seeming to protect him, French prison authorities released him. According to Read and Fisher: "Thus began what must be one of the most remarkable odysseys [wanderings] in penal [prison] history, as Herschel journeyed across France from prison to prison, from police station to police station, desperately seeking some jail that would take him in, some cell where he could be safely locked up" and hidden from the Nazis. He made no attempt to escape or save himself.

Even though they were preoccupied by a major war, the Germans had not forgotten Grynszpan. Under the terms of the agreement signed by France and Germany, France would "surrender on demand" anyone the Germans asked for, and they asked for Grynszpan. On July 18, 1940, France handed the hapless Grynszpan over to the Germans. He was taken to a concentration camp near Berlin, Germany. Concentration camps were places where Nazis confined people they regarded as "enemies of the state." The Nazis prepared to put him on trial for murder.

By this time Grynszpan had spent enough time in jail that he was no longer a naive young man. He concocted a story claiming that he had had homosexual relations (sexual relations with a member of the same gender) with his victim (vom Rath), who in return promised to see to it that Grynszpan's parents were not deported to Poland. When they were deported despite that promise, Grynszpan said, he killed vom Rath.

The Nazis were not at all pleased at the possibility of such a story coming out at trial. For vom Rath to be shown to the world as a seducer of a young boy would be very embarrassing, especially after he had been buried with a hero's funeral. The trial was postponed until at least late 1942. Then Grynszpan simply disappeared. What happened to him is not known for sure, but it is most unlikely he survived. His official date of death was later given as May 8, 1945, V-E Day, the day Germany surrendered in Europe.

Where to Learn More

Read, Anthony, and David Fisher. *Kristallnacht: The Nazi Night of Terror.* Random House, 1989.

Schwab, Gerald. *The Day the Holocaust Began: The Odyssey of Herschel Grynszpan.* Praeger, 1990.

Thalman, Rita, and Emmanuel Feinermann. *Crystal Night: 9–10 November 1938.* Translated from the French by Gilles Cremonesi. Coward, McCann and Geoghegan, 1974.

Rudolf Hess

Born April 26, 1894
Alexandria, Egypt

Died August 17, 1987
Spandau Prison, Berlin, Germany

Soldier, airplane pilot

Adolf Hitler's number three man

Rudolf Hess, loyal member of the inner circle surrounding German dictator (he ruled with absolute authority) Adolf Hitler (see entry), is best known for his surprise airplane flight to Scotland in 1941. He claimed to have been sent by Hitler to make peace with the British and convince them to fight with Germany against the Soviet Union (now Russia). He was branded a madman and imprisoned by the British. After the war he was taken from his British prison, tried by the victorious Allies (the United States, Great Britain, the Soviet Union, and France), and sentenced to life imprisonment in Germany. He was still in prison when he died in 1987. Some called his death suicide; others called it murder.

Childhood in Egypt

Rudolf Hess was born in 1894, the first of three children born to Friedrich and Clara

Muench Hess. A brother, Alfred, was born in 1897; his sister, Margarete, was born in 1908.

Hess's grandfather, who came from Bavaria (a German state), had started the family import-export business in Egypt. By the time Hess was born, his father had become wealthy from the business and the family lived in luxury, with a large home in Egypt and a summer home in Germany.

Hess's father was a strict and formal man. His children did not speak to him unless spoken to first. This story about the senior Hess, told by authors Roger Manvell and Heinrich Fraenkel, illustrates the hold he had over the household: "'I am not a goat,' he said once when served a salad, and no salad ever appeared again."

As was the German custom, Friedrich Hess oversaw the boys' education and directed their career choices. At the age of six, Hess attended a German school in Egypt. At age fourteen, he was sent to a Protestant boarding school in Germany. His teachers found him "responsive and intelligent." He was especially interested in German history, astronomy, physics, engineering, and mathematics. After three years at the boarding school, he requested that he be allowed to attend college. Instead, his father enrolled him in a Swiss business school to prepare him to take over the family company.

Young Manhood

Hess spent a year at business school and then signed on as a trainee at a German export house. Hess was rescued from an unwanted career in business by the start of World War I (1914–18). He immediately volunteered for the German army, was wounded twice, then transferred to the air corps, where he learned how to fly. When the war ended, 24-year-old Hess entered Munich University, where he fulfilled his dream of studying history, economics, and political science.

Like many young men who had served in the war, Hess was bitter about the conditions imposed on a defeated Germany. Forced to disband its mighty army, to give up territories it considered German property, and to pay huge penalties—known as reparations—Germany was poverty-stricken. Many people, including Hess, blamed Jews for such problems. They claimed that the Jews were "the enemies within" Germany who for their own devious reasons had brought

"We believe that the Führer [Hitler] is obeying a higher call to fashion German history. There can be no criticism of this belief."

about the loss of the war. Hess joined with others at the university who wished to see Germany great once again. One of their activities was to distribute anti-Jewish, or antisemitic, literature. Hess showed himself capable of more forceful action in 1919 when he took part in the armed uprising that overthrew the government of Bavaria.

Hess Listens and Obeys Hitler

In 1920, Hess attended a meeting of the National Socialist German Workers' Party (Nazi for short) and heard its leader, Adolf Hitler, speak for the first time. Hess was captivated and felt "as though overcome by a vision." In Hitler, Hess saw the only man who could restore Germany to its rightful position in the world. Hess became the sixteenth person to join the Nazi Party. According to author Eugene Bird, from that day forward, "he gave Hitler his loyalty and faith and followed him with a dog-like devotion."

Hess became a fixture at Nazi Party meetings, often engaging in brawls with those who attempted to disrupt Hitler's speeches. In 1923, he took part in the party's failed attempt to seize control of Germany and was imprisoned together with his idol, Hitler. While the two were in prison, Hess acted as Hitler's secretary, typing Hitler's book, *Mein Kampf* (meaning "My Struggle"), and making suggestions and corrections. As a reward, Hitler appointed Hess his personal secretary after they were released from prison in 1925.

Between 1925 and 1933, Hess was promoted several times for his loyal and obedient service. Hitler assumed control of Germany in 1933 and in 1934 appointed Hess Deputy Führer (pronounced Fyoor-uhr; it means "leader"). Hitler began issuing one demand after another having to do with the running of the country. These demands passed through Hess's office and from there to the people responsible for carrying them out. As Hitler's deputy, Hess signed the Nuremberg racial laws. These laws, which took effect in 1935, stripped German Jews of their citizenship and barred them from engaging in most professions.

Although Hess's job involved mountains of paperwork, he preferred actively working instead of just sitting at a desk. At first he tried to institute some actions on his own. Hitler usually ordered something different, though, and in time,

Hess greets Hitler at a Nazi conference in Nuremberg, Germany.

Hess grew unwilling to make any decisions, knowing Hitler would contradict them. He never had any major say in the decisions that Hitler made.

Hess became something of a joke to other Nazi leaders. Historian Roger Manvell wrote that they described Hess's attitude to his job this way: "Come unto me all ye that are weary and heavy laden, and I will do nothing." Hess exhibited other behaviors that his colleagues found odd. He was a vegetarian (didn't eat meat) who distrusted doctors and favored "nature cures and other weird beliefs," according to a Hess colleague quoted by Manvell. He was, however, one of the few men Hitler trusted completely, and in 1939 Hitler chose Hess as the number two man (behind Hermann Göring; see entry) to succeed him as head of Germany if anything should happen to Hitler.

Hess Takes Flight

World War II began when Germany attacked Poland in 1939, and Great Britain then declared war on Germany. With the war in full swing by 1941, Hitler set his sights on the Soviet Union (now Russia). Two years into the war, Great Britain was still courageously battling Germany without assistance. Hitler made a peace offer to Britain because he did not want to have to fight a war on two fronts (with Great Britain and the Soviet Union), but his offer was rejected.

Meanwhile, Hitler's circle of influence had expanded to include generals and others, who fought for the supreme leader's attention. Hess began to feel left out. He longed to perform some great act that would help further Hitler's aims, restore Hess to Hitler's esteem, and make him a hero too.

Hess was an accomplished pilot whose two flying heroes were American Charles Lindbergh and Great Britain's Duke of Hamilton, who had been the first pilot to fly over Mount Everest, the world's highest peak. Hess decided he would fly to the duke's home in Scotland and ask to be taken to see the king of England. There he hoped to persuade British leaders like Prime Minister Winston Churchill that it was in their best interests to join with Germany in the fight against their common enemy, the Soviet Union.

So it came about that on May 10, 1941, "the most loyal and unimaginative of Nazi leaders [attempted] a daring deed." Wearing an army uniform, Hess made the nine-hundred -mile flight to Scotland in five hours. About thirty miles from the home of the Duke of Hamilton, he parachuted out of the plane, which crashed and burst into flames, and landed in the path of a Scottish farmer. "I have an important message for the Duke of Hamilton," he said. He was turned over to authorities and treated as a prisoner of war.

Back in Germany, radio broadcasts announced that Hess, "'apparently in a fit of madness,' had taken possession of an aircraft contrary to Hitler's orders and had disap-

What the Charges Meant

The military tribunal that tried the Nazi criminals charged them with the following crimes:

1. Conspiracy: secretly planning to commit crimes against peace, war crimes, and crimes against humanity;

2. Crimes Against Peace: planning, preparing, starting, or waging aggressive war;

3. War Crimes: violations of the laws or customs of war;

4. Crimes Against Humanity: murder, extermination (total destruction), enslavement, persecution on political or racial grounds, involuntary deportment (forcibly removing people from their city or country), and inhumane acts against civilian (nonmilitary) populations.

Hess was found innocent of all crimes except crimes against peace.

peared." Churchill could hardly believe "that the Deputy Führer of Germany is in our hands." After listening to Hess's long and passionate praise of Hitler and his demands and proposals for peace, it was decided that Hess should be imprisoned in the Tower of London. Having seen the Nazis in action since 1939—their broken treaties, their lies, and their murder of innocent people—the British did not feel inclined to negotiate a peace with Germany. The war against Germany would continue.

Hess knew that his mission had failed—and Hitler hated failures. Hess was declared insane by Hitler and disowned by Nazi leaders. He attempted suicide but failed. Hess remained a prisoner of the British until the war ended. During this time he began to exhibit signs of mental instability and claimed that his food was being poisoned. At the war's end in 1945, Hess was returned to Nuremberg, Germany, to stand trial before a court of judges from all the victorious Allied countries. The Allies consisted of the United States, Great Britain, the Soviet Union, and France.

On Trial

On November 20, 1945, twenty-one Nazis appeared at the Palace of Justice in Nuremberg, Germany, to stand trial for conspiracy, crimes against peace, war crimes, and crimes against humanity (see box). At the trial, Hess scarcely seemed sane, although there are some people who believe his behavior was an act. Eugene Bird described him as "a pathetic thin figure [who] huddled in the dock [where accused prisoners sit] reading books and mumbling. . . . When, at last, Hess had the chance to get up and tell his story, he gave only a rambling [speech] on 'secret forces' and 'evil influences' being used to destroy him. He sat down, and was convicted [found guilty]."

All of the Allies except the former Soviet Union were inclined to let Hess go. The Soviets, however, were unwilling to forgive Hess for his attempt to talk the British into fighting against them; they called for his execution. A compromise was reached, and he was sentenced to life in prison at Spandau.

Imprisonment and Death

Spandau was a huge, high-security prison intended to hold more than six hundred prisoners. Groups of guards and soldiers from all the Allied countries took turns guarding the seven Nazi criminals confined there. One by one the six other prisoners, "many of them no less guilty," according to Manvell, were released, until there remained only the aging Hess. For twenty years he was the sole prisoner at Spandau; although the number of guards and soldiers remained the same as before.

By 1973, Hess was a "sick old man who while[d] away his time with books, gramophone records, and cups of instant coffee . . . too old any longer to work in the prison garden," according to Manvell. Hess lived for another 14 years until his death in 1987 at the age of 92. The official cause of death was listed as suicide.

His Legacy Lives On

Rudolf Hess remained loyal to Hitler to the end. He never expressed any remorse for the murders of millions of innocent people or for his part in it. He took with him to the

Hess's Son Defends Father

In 1991, Gerald L. Posner's book titled *Hitler's Children: Sons and Daughters of the Third Reich Talk about Their Fathers and Themselves* was published by Random House. In it Wolf Hess, son of Rudolf Hess, defended his father. Wolf Hess said his father always supported relocation of the Jews to their own homeland; he never favored the mass extermination that was actually carried out. Wolf Hess said his father had several Jewish friends, whom he helped escape from Germany. He pointed out that although his father held a powerful position in Hitler's cabinet, he never used it to enrich himself or his family, who lived very modestly. Wolf Hess believed his father's long imprisonment was "illegal." He stated that the courage his father displayed while imprisoned created a "spiritual bond between my father and myself [that] remained unsevered."

grave the secret of whether his flight to England was the act of a madman or a real mission on Hitler's behalf. Conspiracy theories about him continue to circulate. There are some (including Hess's son) who believe Hess was murdered. Yet another theory holds that Hess was executed while in England and a British secret agent posing as Hess died at Spandau.

Hess has become a cult figure to neo-Nazis, who apparently believe he was acting for Hitler and was not a traitor to the Nazi cause. Neo-Nazis are sometimes called "skinheads" because some have shaved heads. They are people who idolize the Nazis. Groups of them gather each August 17 in cities throughout Europe to mark the date of Hess's death. "Neo" means a new form. The neo-Nazi movement is a small but growing and violent movement in Germany and elsewhere, including the United States. Devoted to the memory of Adolf Hitler, neo-Nazis engage in such activities as the persecution of foreigners and the destruction of Jewish cemeteries.

Where to Learn More

Bird, Eugene K. *Prisoner #7 Rudolf Hess: The Thirty Years in Jail of Hitler's Deputy Führer* (originally published in England under the title of *The Loneliest Man in the World* by the American director of Spandau). Viking Press, 1974.

Douglas-Hamilton, James. *Motive for a Mission: The Story Behind Hess's Flight to Britain.* St. Martin's Press, 1971.

Manvell, Roger, and Heinrich Fraenkel. *Hess: A Biography.* Drake Publishers, 1973.

Reinhard Heydrich

Born March 7, 1904
Halle, Germany

Died June 4, 1942
Prague, Czechoslovakia

*Head of the SD, Deputy to
SS leader Heinrich Himmler*

*Known as "The Blonde Beast"
and "Hangman Heydrich"*

R einhard Heydrich (pronounced Rine-hard Hay-drick), one of the highest-ranking of Adolf Hitler's (see entry) followers, possessed the tall, fair-haired physical attributes of the Aryan (white, non-Jewish) superman. He was reported never to have had an affectionate personal relationship with anyone during his lifetime. As a chief organizer of the German plan to kill all the Jews of Europe, this cold, manipulative, and ambitious man was responsible for causing the suffering and deaths of millions of people.

Born into Wealth

Reinhard Eugen Heydrich was born near in Halle, Germany, in 1904. His father was an opera singer. His mother was a pianist, and the daughter of his father's music professor. Heydrich had an older sister, Maria, and a younger brother, Heinz Siegfried. As a child, Heydrich excelled at the violin, which he enjoyed playing all of his life. He and his brother enjoyed mock fights with wooden swords. Their childhood was spent in a handsome home living among the socially elite. However, Heydrich faced ridicule because of his high-pitched voice and devotion to the Catholic religion in a largely Protestant area. Because his grandmother's second husband had a Jewish-sounding name, he was also the target of gossip about his possibly having Jewish blood.

Heydrich grew up in a home where harsh attitudes and physical beatings were part of his everyday life. His father taught him to be fiercely antisemitic (anti-Jewish). Heydrich was a shy and unhappy child who felt a need to excel at all his undertakings. A gifted athlete, he was especially adept at fencing.

When World War I (1914–18) began, Heydrich was too young to join the military. Instead, he got involved with some anti-Jewish former soldiers who attacked communists in the streets. (Communism is an economic system that promotes the ownership of all property by the community as a whole.) He welcomed becoming part of a group that idealized people who looked like himself, as it helped to quiet the rumors about his lack of "racial purity."

Joins Nazi Party

Like many Germans, Heydrich's family lost most of its fortune following World War I. A lot of the German people blamed the Jews for the loss because of a false theory that the Jews were trying to take over the world by starting with the defeated Germany. The embittered young Heydrich became a German naval cadet in order to get an education. He advanced quickly, becoming a second lieutenant in 1926, but he proved unpopular because of his boastful ways. Heydrich was thrown out of the German navy for "conduct unbecoming an officer and a gentleman" after he got the daughter of a shipyard director pregnant and refused to marry her. Not sure where to turn, he joined the National Socialist German Workers' Party (Nazi for short) in 1931. That same year Heydrich married a 19-year-old student named Lina von Osten, who was also strongly antisemitic.

Heydrich's blue-eyed, typically Aryan looks helped earn him entrance into the SS (an abbreviation for *Shutzstaffeln* or

"The Führer has ordered the physical extermination of the Jews."

Security Squad that acted as Hitler's personal bodyguards). Impressed with his bearing and quick mind, Heinrich Himmler (see entry), Heydrich's boss, chose him for the task of building a new SS intelligence (spy) service, which became known as the SD. In a short time, the service became a massive spy network that reported on Hitler's opponents, especially anyone who was within the Nazi Party. Heydrich relished the use of secret cameras and hidden microphones. His success at this task helped his career to skyrocket. He became an SS major by the end of 1931, then an SS colonel with complete control of the SD by 1932. The following year, before he had even reached the age of 30, he was appointed SS brigadier general.

Despite recurrent rumors about his ancestry, Hitler decided not to force Heydrich out of the Nazi Party. Hitler described the six-foot-tall Nazi as "a highly gifted but also very dangerous man, whose gifts the movement had to retain . . . [he will be grateful that we did not expel him and he will] obey blindly."

Always haunted by the ever-present rumors that he might be Jewish, Heydrich's hatred toward the Jews grew even stronger. He also was tormented by a severe lack of self-esteem. One story tells of his returning home one night, drunk, seeing himself in the mirror, and using his pistol to shoot at his own reflection, shouting "filthy Jew."

At the beginning of 1933, Heydrich assisted Himmler in carrying out the large-scale arrest of opponents of the Nazis in Germany. These included religious leaders, communists, and trade union members who had spoken against Hitler. Great numbers of people were kept imprisoned at a converted munitions factory at Dachau, in Southern Germany. Dachau become the Nazis' first concentration camp, a place where people regarded as "enemies of the state" were kept. Workers were forced to toil up to 12 hours per day on very little food. They received lashings and other severe punishments for small crimes like stealing cigarettes. Similar camps for political prisoners were begun at Buchenwald and other sites around the country.

In April 1934, Himmler became head of a new secret state police force, popularly known as the Gestapo. Heydrich was made second in command. That same year, he and other

The Gestapo, SA, SD, and SS

During the Nazi era, the citizens of Germany were terrorized by a number of bullies who belonged to a variety of police-type organizations. The identities of these various units in the Third Reich (meaning "Third Empire," the name Hitler gave to his term as Germany's leader) can be quite confusing, especially because they are referred to by the initials for their German names.

The Gestapo is an abbreviation for the *Geheime Staats Politzei* or Secret State Police. The most famous of the German police groups, it was started by Hermann Göring in Prussia in 1933. The Gestapo men wore raincoats and slouch hats and were famous for their cruelty and violence. They had the power to follow, arrest, question, and imprison people, strictly on their own authority. The Gestapo inspired tremendous fear.

The SA stands for the *Sturmabteilung,* or Storm Troopers. The SA was founded at the very beginnings of the Nazi Party. The Storm Troopers were supposed to be a "means of defense" for the Nazis and "a training school for the coming struggle for liberty." The members were often referred to as the "Brownshirts" for the clothing they wore. The organization was headed by Ernst Röhm, a German homosexual. At its height, the SA numbered more than four million members.

The SA set up the first concentration camp at Dachau and marched around Berlin, rounding up political opponents and trade unionists. Röhm eventually grew drunk on power and began talking about merging the SA with the army. Hitler, afraid of a possible military takeover, had Röhm killed on what became known as the "Night of Long Knives" in 1934. After that, the SA declined in numbers and importance.

The SS stands for the *Shutzstaffeln,* the Security Squad. Members of the SS were Hitler's personal bodyguards. Led by Heinrich Himmler, the black-shirted group grew in size and importance following the murder of SA leader Ernst Röhm in 1934. In 1936, Himmler became head of all the police organizations in Germany, except the military intelligence group, the Abwehr. The SS provided guards at the various concentration camps and presided over the murders of millions of Jews, Roma (commonly called Gypsies), political prisoners, homosexuals, and others the Nazis deemed undesirable.

The SD stands for the *Sicherdienst* or Security Police. The SD, headed by Reinhard Heydrich, was started in 1931 to serve as the Intelligence (spy) Service of the SS. It was the job of the SD to spy on Hitler's enemies, especially those within the Nazi Party.

top Nazis engaged in an event known as the "Night of the Long Knives." On June 29, as writer Robert Leckie describes, "SA [which stands for *Sturmabteilung* or Storm Troopers] leaders and Adolf Hitler's enemies—private and public, real or imagined—old friends of the early days . . . co-conspirators and old collaborators, churchmen, generals and politicians,

Heydrich at work in his office at Gestapo headquarters.

as well as enemies of [other top Nazi officials] were put to death." Heydrich drew up the list of who was to be murdered that night. Among the hundreds killed was SA leader Ernst Röhm (see entry), head of four million Nazi Storm Troopers.

By 1936, Himmler controlled all of Germany's local police forces, as well as the SS and the Gestapo. The Gestapo was permitted to arrest anyone for any reason. People could even be imprisoned if it was thought that they might commit a crime in the future. The Gestapo, and the SD, headed by Heydrich, demanded bribes, and used torture and blackmail to control anyone opposed to the Nazis. As he grew in power, Heydrich became an object of fear throughout Germany. Even the highest-ranking Nazis shook in their boots when confronted by his evil glare. A man with no personal friends, Heydrich generally kept out of the public eye as much as possible.

Heydrich's lust for power and love of political scheming went beyond Germany. In 1937, he prepared forged documents that led to the overthrow of some important generals in the Soviet Union (now Russia). A year later, he ousted two powerful German generals who had expressed opposition to Hitler by forcing them into retirement as a result of phony scandals devised by Heydrich. He worked with Himmler to encourage pro-Nazis in Austria to commit terrorist acts and cause political unrest. When the Nazis gained rule over Austria in 1938, Heydrich's SD started the Gestapo Office of Jewish Emigration. Headed by an Austrian named Adolf Eichmann (see entry), the office was permitted to issue permits to Jews who wanted to leave the country. The office soon became a gold mine for Heydrich and other Nazis who provided the permits only after being bribed. More than 100,000 Jews sought the permits, many turning over all their goods and money to the SS. Heydrich set up a similar office in Berlin, Germany, further fattening the wallets of the SS.

On November 9 and 10, 1938, an event occurred referred to as *Kristallnacht* (meaning "Crystal Night" or "The Night of Broken Glass"). Those days marked the first widespread attacks on and mass arrests of Jewish people in Hitler's Germany. At Heydrich's order, more than 25,000 people were sent to concentration camps. The name *Kristallnacht* referred to the vast amount of shattered glass from Jewish-owned stores that filled the streets.

In 1939, Hitler gave Heydrich the responsibility of removing any "undesirables" from Poland by imprisoning or executing them. Polish people were considered inferior to the Germans. Heydrich formed five SS Special Action groups (*Einsatzgruppen*) to gather up and shoot the leading citizens, professionals, and clergymen of small Polish towns. They placed thousands of Polish citizens in jail on false charges, and some Poles were beheaded or burned alive. It is estimated that by the end of 1939 between 50,000 and 100,000 Polish citizens were exterminated under Heydrich's command.

It was also Heydrich's task to decide the fate of the three million Polish Jews. Heydrich first deported (forcibly removed) the Jews to German labor camps and then set up Jewish ghettos, crowded, walled sections of the cities where Jews were forced to live in poverty and apart from non-Jews. In the ghettos of Warsaw, Lódz, and Krakow, people were crowded together with very little food or medicine. By 1941, more than half a million Polish Jews had died there. Heydrich had Jewish leaders appointed to "Jewish councils" (*Judenrat*) that unwittingly led to the destruction of their own communities.

In 1941, after Hitler's invasion of the Soviet Union (now Russia), Heydrich sent four *Einsatzgruppen* units there to kill all the communist officials and anyone the Nazis thought to be a security risk. They also went into towns and villages, and told all the Jews to gather together in preparation for resettlement to another area. The Jews were commanded to hand over their valuable possessions, then to remove their clothing. Finally, they were marched to an area where trenches had been dug. Then they were shot, and their bodies were thrown into the open ditches. By the end of World War II more than 1.3 million people were murdered in this way in the Soviet Union.

On July 31, 1941, Hitler's right-hand man, Hermann Göring (see entry), gave the order that resulted in the extermination of millions of Jews. Göring's letter to Heydrich said, in part, "I hereby charge you with making all necessary preparations with regard to organizational and financial matters for bringing about a complete solution of the Jewish problem in the German sphere of influence in Europe."

Becomes Architect of Final Solution

On January 20, 1942, Heydrich met with other Nazi officials at the Berlin suburb of Wannsee. They came to discuss what they referred to as the "Final Solution," the plan to kill all the Jews of Europe. As head of the project, Heydrich explained that the so-called solution meant that able-bodied Jews would be worked to death building roads into the Soviet Union. The weak and sick would be put to death. Heydrich also suggested that marriages between Jews and non-Jews be declared invalid so that the Jewish spouse could be sent to a concentration camp. He also proposed that people who were part-Jews be sterilized (they would be made unable to have children). The story goes that following this meeting, Heydrich and SS Lieutenant Colonel Adolf Eichmann hopped up on the table and drank a toast.

Assassination

In 1941, Heydrich was chosen to be in charge of Moravia and Bohemia, sections of what was then Nazi-controlled Czechoslovakia. Believing that he had been named as Hitler's successor, the British launched a plan called "Daybreak." They trained two young Czech men and parachuted them into the region of Prague to assassinate Heydrich. When Heydrich's driver stopped at a red light in Prague, in May 1942, the gunmen appeared. One of them threw a grenade that severely injured Heydrich. The young men were later captured and killed. Because the Germans in Prague had no penicillin (medication to fight infection) to treat his wounds, Heydrich's medical situation became very serious. Even though Himmler sent his personal physician to Prague several days later to care for Heydrich, it was too late. He died of his wounds shortly thereafter.

The evil impact of Heydrich did not end with his death. Hitler, enraged that Heydrich had been murdered, decided to avenge the death of the man many believed was slated to be his successor. Hitler got a map of Czechoslovakia, focusing on Prague and the surrounding area. He randomly placed his finger on the village of Lidice and commanded that it be destroyed. As a result, all of the men of Lidice were murdered, the women were sent to concentration camps, and the children were relocated to an area in Germany to be raised as Nazis.

Where to Learn More

"Biography of SS Leader Reinhard Heydrich." http://www.historyplace.com/worldwar2/biographies.htm

Calic, Edouard. *Reinhard Heydrich.* Translated by Loell Bair. William Morrow, 1982.

Deschner, Gunther. *Reinhard Heydrich: A Biography.* Stein and Day, 1977.

Gilbert, Martin. *The Holocaust.* Holt, Rinehart & Winston, 1985.

Leckie, Robert. *Delivered from Evil: The Saga of World War II.* Harper & Row, 1987.

Neville, Peter. *Life in the Third Reich.* B. T. Batsford, 1992.

Wiener, Jan G. *The Assassination of Heydrich.* Grossman, 1969.

Wighton, Charles. *Heydrich: Hitler's Most Evil Henchman.* Chilton, 1962.

Heinrich Himmler

Born October 7, 1900
Munich, Germany

Died May 23, 1945
A British interrogation
camp near Lüneburg, Germany

Farmer, fertilizer analyst, Chief of the SS,
Reichminister of the Interior, a chief
architect of the Final Solution

Heinrich Himmler was a sickly and unimpressive man who dreamed of being a soldier but instead became one of the worst mass murderers in history. Under his command, the SS grew to be the most powerful and evil organization in Germany during World War II (1939–45). SS is an abbreviation for *Shutzstaffeln* or Security Squad. They were Hitler's personal body guards and acted as guards at the various concentration camps (places where the Nazis confined people they regarded as "enemies of the state"). SS guards enslaved and murdered millions of innocent people.

Childhood in Munich

Born in Munich, Germany, on October 7, 1900, Heinrich Himmler (pronounced Heyen-rikh Him-luhr) was the second of three sons born to Gebhard and Anna Maria Heyder Himmler. Anna was a pious Catholic and dedicated homemaker. Gebhard was the son of a poor soldier whose family roots extended far back in German history. The family lived a comfortable life, employed a full-time maid, and was considered solidly middle class. Gebhard believed that it was important to establish relationships with higher social classes, a belief he passed on to his sons, and he was especially proud to be employed as a tutor for a member of the royal family.

Himmler was often sick as a child and nearly died of a lung infection at the age of four. His father was a stern man who took an active interest in his sons' education and insisted on excellence. So, although Himmler was not an especially bright student, he worked hard and often managed to excel. When he was ten years old, Himmler's father encouraged his son to begin keeping a diary—his father even wrote the first entry in the diary as a model. Himmler dutifully followed his father's instructions; later, when he became a high-ranking member of the National Socialist German Workers' Party (Nazi for short), he used this early training to keep detailed records of his murderous activities.

When Himmler was thirteen years old, his father became headmaster of a school in Landshut, Germany, a town with its own castle located fifty miles from Munich. All three Himmler boys attended the school. The adolescent Himmler was short and plump, poor at sports, and wore thick glasses over unusually small eyes to correct his severe nearsightedness (unable to see distant objects clearly). He worked hard at his studies, though, and exercised in an effort to overcome his physical shortcomings. He often complained in his diaries about his poor health.

World War I (1914–18) was an event of great excitement for Himmler, who developed an interest in the military that stayed with him into adulthood. By working extremely hard, he managed to complete officer training but not in time to serve in the war. He left the military and decided to learn about farming. He was employed on a farm for a short time before he fell ill with typhoid fever, an infectious disease caused by unsanitary conditions. His doctor prescribed a less strenuous activity than farming for at least a year, so Himmler decided to go to college.

"You see, I did not deem myself justified in exterminating the men ... while allowing their children to grow up to avenge themselves on our sons and grandchildren. The hard decision had to be taken--this people [the Jews] must disappear from the face of the earth."

Gets Involved in Politics

Himmler enrolled in the agriculture program at the University of Munich. He gave up his dream of a military career, but he spent his school breaks playing soldier in groups organized like the regular military. Eager to be accepted socially, he took up fencing and dancing, which he did not enjoy but felt he needed to master to get ahead. He was never comfortable socially, though, especially with women. Because of a weak stomach that would plague him for the rest of his life, he could not drink beer with the other college boys, and they made fun of this weakness.

It was during his college years that Himmler began to display anti-Jewish or antisemitic feelings, confiding in his diary the opinion that Jews should be excluded from college clubs. The political climate of the time was also strongly antisemitic. Himmler heard the popular political speeches blaming the Jews for Germany's loss of World War I, and he found himself drawn to politics. He also developed a mistrust of doctors (many of whom were Jewish), so he turned to alternative forms of medical treatment for his frequent ailments. Interest in his own poor health and in alternative medicine later led Himmler to authorize gruesome medical experiments on concentration camp prisoners (see Josef Mengele entry).

When he completed his schooling with a diploma in agriculture in 1922, Himmler obtained a job with a fertilizer company. He continued his soldiering activities too, and in 1923 he joined the Nazi Party. The party was considered quite radical at the time because of its 1923 attempt to take over the German government by force. As a result, Himmler's association with it cost him his job.

In 1927, Himmler met a Polish nurse named Margarete (Marga) Concerzowo, who was seven or eight years older than he was. Marga, the owner of a Berlin nursing home, had an interest in herbal medicine and a thrifty nature that appealed to Himmler. The couple were married in 1928, and with the proceeds from the sale of Marga's nursing home they bought a small house and farm near Munich. There they kept hens and sold produce while Himmler continued his Nazi Party activities.

Although he had little personality, Himmler was efficient and paid careful attention to detail; he was finally rewarded with a promotion to *Reichsführer* (a rank equivalent to a U.S. Army general) of the SS in 1929. That same year his daughter, Gudrun, was born.

Builds SS into Powerful Organization

In his 16 years in charge, Himmler built the SS into a vast empire, and in the process he acquired the power of life and death over millions. The SS was originally intended to protect Nazi leader Adolf Hitler (see entry) and other important party members and to defend Germany against attack. Himmler, however, made the SS an organization that carried out anything Hitler ordered, including the punishment and murder of "enemies of the state." A timid man himself, Himmler became an object of fear to his countrymen and even to some of his fellow Nazis, and rose to become one of Hitler's inner circle. In a mere four years, he expanded the SS, a bodyguard unit whose membership originally totaled 280, into an enormous, cold-blooded military and economic empire totaling 50,000 members. Along the way, he acquired a number of new titles, including Chief of Police, Reich Commissioner for the Solidification of German Peoplehood, and Commander of the Political Police.

Hitler assigned Himmler the special task of building the SS into an organization of carefully selected men who would become the leaders of a new German race. He became obsessed with his assignment. Borrowing the ideas from a book written by German agricultural expert, Walter Darré, Himmler began by setting down the rules regarding marriage of SS members. Darré wrote that the future of Europe depended on the survival of the German race, and that the German race should reproduce and outnumber Jews and other groups. To help achieve that goal, SS men who wished to marry had to obtain a certificate approving their choice of brides so the couples would not produce children of "contaminated" blood. Himmler set up SS Bride Schools where brides were taught what was expected of them in the new Nazi tradition. It was not long before the push to build a pure, master race included the extermination of everyone Himmler and Hitler considered "racially impure." These "racially impure" people included Jews, Roma (dark-haired, dark-skinned people who are believed to have originated in India and are often called Gypsies), the physically and mentally

Heinrich Himmler **225**

Himmler (second from the left) on an inspection of the Auschwitz concentration camp in Poland.

handicapped, homosexuals, and Jehovah's Witnesses (a religious group).

The Move Toward a Pure German Race

The pure German person as Himmler saw him or her was tall, blond, and blue-eyed. According to Elizabeth Wiskemann, writing in *Anatomy of the SS State,* "Himmler really believed that he could breed better Germans and arrange for all the sub-humans to die out or rot away or, in plain language, be murdered." Author Robert E. Conot pointed out how ironic it was that Himmler pushed the idea of the superiority of that type when "he was a myopic, slope-shouldered, spindle-chested weakling who wanted to be an eagle-eyed warrior; a darkhaired, stub-chinned . . . [German] who dreamed of reincarnation as a . . . blond . . . ." Himmler found his ideal German type in Reinhard Heydrich (see entry), one of the most prominent in a string of cruel, cold men he recruited for the SS (others included Adolf Eichmann and

Rudolf Höss (see entries). On Himmler's orders, concentration camps were set up to interrogate, torture, and kill millions of "enemies of the state." The Jews, he said, were the cause of too much trouble in Europe. The sacrifice of these people, he reasoned, was necessary for the future of the German people. According to biographer Roger Manvell, Himmler believed that: "Just as the Americans had exterminated the Indians [Native Americans], so the Germans must wipe out the Jews."

Himmler, who preferred to remain in the background, had SS men act as his agents in a reign of terror that swept through country after country after World War II began in 1939. Gangs of SS soldiers dressed in black caps, swastika (a Nazi symbol) armbands with black borders, crisply pressed uniforms, and gleaming black boots rampaged through ghettos full of Jews, raping, robbing, murdering, and rounding up people to send to concentration camps. (Ghettos were crowded, walled sections of cities where Jews were forced to live apart from non-Jews in inferior conditions.)

In spite of his many activities, Himmler found time to adopt a son, sell the farm, and move his family to a small town by a lake, where he seldom visited them. He bought himself a modest house in Berlin, Germany, and had two children by his secretary. He began to suffer from severe headaches and stomach cramps and hired a masseur (a professional who gives massages) to treat him because he still mistrusted doctors.

The Final Solution Begins

In 1941, Himmler and other Nazi leaders received the order to begin the Final Solution of the Jewish problem. The Final Solution was the Nazi code for the complete elimination of European Jews. On January 20, 1942, Himmler's second-in-command, Reinhard Heydrich, headed the meeting called the Wannsee Conference, where fifteen top Nazis agreed upon the terms of the Final Solution. Up until this time, the Nazi plan was to force European Jews to leave Germany and German-occupied territories in Europe. The Final Solution, however, involved rounding up all Jews throughout Europe, transporting them to Poland, and organizing them into labor gangs at concentration camps. The plan called for camp conditions so bad that large numbers of Jews would

Albert Speer: Himmler's Partner in the War Factories

Albert Speer (pronounced Shpayr) was born into a wealthy family in Mannheim, Germany, in 1905. He lived in luxury in a large home with a staff of servants and was a gifted student. As the son and grandson of prominent architects, he decided to take up architecture too. Unable to find a job in his chosen profession, he became an architecture teacher. In his autobiography, Speer described himself as having no interest in politics as a young man. One day, at the urging of some of his students, though, he went to hear Adolf Hitler, leader of the National Socialist German Workers' or Nazi Party, speak. At first Speer found Hitler "engaging" and full of "South German charm"; as he listened further, he became aware of Hitler's "hypnotic persuasiveness." "I was carried away," he wrote. Speer joined the Nazi Party soon after, as did his mother.

With his professional life going nowhere, Speer became more and more involved in politics. He was given the task of redecorating a Nazi headquarters building; later he designed decorations for rallies that promoted the Nazi cause. Soon Speer's work was noticed by Hitler, himself a frustrated architect. Hitler had grand plans for buildings and monuments that would be suitable for his great German Empire, and Speer became Hitler's architect. "For the commission to do [design] a great building, I would have sold my soul," Hitler later wrote.

The building projects Hitler had in mind required laborers, and Heinrich Himmler's concentration camps (places to confine "enemies of the state") were full of idle hands. So began the first collaboration between Himmler and Speer. In 1942, Hitler named Speer his Minister of Armaments, in charge of arms production. With all able-bodied Germans off fighting the war, Speer needed workers for mass production of weapons, and his projects required secrecy. Himmler suggested that a work force made up entirely of concentration camp prisoners would guarantee secrecy, since they had absolutely no contact with the outside world. Before the war ended, Speer had 14 million unwilling workers under his control.

In 1946, after the end of World War II, at the Palace of Justice in Nuremberg, Germany, 21 captured Nazi leaders were brought together for what became known as "the greatest trial in history." Among the men being tried for crimes against peace, war crimes, and crimes against humanity was Speer. Like many of the Nazi criminals on trial, Speer tried to blame his crimes on the people who worked for him. He claimed that he was sick when many of the crimes occurred. In his autobiography *Inside the Third Reich*, Speer claimed that he was unaware of Hitler's anti-semitism (discrimination and hatred of Jews) and his plans to expand the German Empire. In his book about the trials, Robert Conot paints a picture of Speer as a "masterful liar" and manipulator of the truth, a man so attractive, intelligent, and convincing that he eventually received a sentence of only 20 years in prison for his crimes, when other less attractive criminals were sentenced to hang. While in prison Speer wrote his memoirs, which were later gathered together into a valuable insider's look at the Nazi reign. He went on to write several other books about his experiences. He died in 1981.

die. Those too old or young to work would be "treated accordingly," which really meant killed.

Himmler continued to make plans for carrying out the Final Solution and stepped up the activity at the concentration camps. He showed a special concern for the feelings of SS men who might have qualms about the unspeakably brutal acts that took place in the camps. He instructed that the killings not be photographed because "in time of war, executions are unfortunately necessary. But to take snapshots of them only shows bad taste." To raise money for the war effort, he ordered that gold teeth be removed from the bodies of dead prisoners and even, sometimes, from the living. Because of Himmler's passion for secrecy, the full extent of the horrors that took place was not known to the world until after the war ended in 1945.

War Winds Down

During the last days of the war, Himmler became concerned about Hitler's increasingly odd behavior, which he feared would lead Europe into disaster. It occurred to him that if Germany were to lose the war, the Allies (United States, Great Britain, the Soviet Union, and France) would overrun the concentration camps and tell a revolted world of his major role in them. Himmler hoped a friendly gesture on his part would lead the Allies to overlook his past activities (and perhaps put him in charge of a new Germany without Hitler). So, as the Allies approached Germany, Himmler decided to disregard Hitler's orders to blow up the concentration camps along with their inmates. His attempt to reach an agreement with the Allies failed, however, and resulted in Hitler's disfavor and the loss of Himmler's rank and offices. On May 21, 1945, while disguised as a low-ranking soldier, Himmler was stopped by British soldiers as he was attempting to flee the country. By May 23, when it became obvious to him that he was not going to receive special treatment, he bit open a cyanide (poison) capsule he had concealed in his mouth. Despite efforts to revive him, he died 15 minutes later. Himmler was buried in a secret grave so it could not become a gathering place for Nazi-lovers.

Where to Learn More

Breitman, Richard. *The Architect of Genocide: Himmler and the Final Solution.* Knopf, 1991.

Conot, Robert E. *Justice at Nuremberg.* Harper & Row, 1983.

Krausnick, Helmut, Hans Buchheim, and others. *Anatomy of the SS State.* Translated from the German by Richard Barry and others. Walker & Company, 1968.

Manvell, Roger, and Heinrich Fraenkel. *Himmler.* Putnam, 1965.

Speer, Albert. *Inside the Third Reich: Memoirs by Albert Speer.* Translated from the German by Richard and Clara Winston. Macmillan, 1970.

Magnus Hirschfeld

Born May 14, 1868
Kolberg, Prussia
(now Poland)

Died May 15, 1935
Nice, France

*Physician, writer, promoter of
homosexual rights*

*One of the twentieth-century's
foremost sex researchers*

Even though there were known homosexuals (persons attracted to members of the same sex) among the highest-ranking officials of the National Socialist German Workers' Party (Nazi for short), the Nazis publicly criticized homosexuals and even sent tens of thousands of them to the death camps. Magnus Hirschfeld, a German physician, pioneered large-scale research on human sexuality, especially homosexuality. Although he had gained worldwide acclaim for his work, threats of harm by the Nazis forced Hirschfeld into exile.

Childhood and Education

Robert Magnus Alexander Hirschfeld was born into a Jewish family in Kolberg, Prussia (then part of Germany) in 1868. The son of a doctor, he was the seventh of eight children. As a student, young Magnus couldn't decide if he wanted to be a physician or a writer. After attending several different schools in Germany, he received his medical degree.

Begins Study of Homosexuality

Shortly after beginning his medical practice, Hirschfeld received a letter written by an army officer who had committed suicide the day before his wedding. The soldier sent the letter to Hirschfeld hoping it would help other homosexuals who were undergoing similar stresses as he was, trying to make them fit into a heterosexual (attracted to members of the opposite sex) way of life. In his letter, the soldier stated that he could no longer deny that he was a homosexual and could not go through with the marriage. He asked that his story be publicized so that others could benefit from it. This incident prompted Hirschfeld to begin the study of homosexuality, and eventually to campaign for homosexual rights.

Becomes Esteemed Scholar

The Hirschfeld theories first came to the world's attention in 1896 when, using the name Theodor Ramien, he published a famous article on human sexuality. Throughout his lifetime, Hirschfeld wrote many books and articles on human sexuality, especially focusing on homosexuality. Hirschfeld also wrote on a variety of other subjects, including love, crime, prostitution (trading sexual favors for money), sex crimes, and alcoholism. He invented the term "transvestite" (someone who dresses in the clothing of the opposite sex) and was the first to explain that there was a difference between that practice and homosexuality.

On May 14, 1897, his twenty-ninth birthday, Magnus Hirschfeld founded the Scientific-Humanitarian Committee, the first homosexual rights organization in the world. Its purpose was to conduct research on homosexuality and to promote the ending of legal and social intolerance of homosexuals. Hirschfeld, himself a homosexual, conducted a thirty-year campaign to repeal the German law that had made homosexuality a criminal offense in Germany.

Hirschfeld's committee also advocated birth control (limiting the number of children a woman bears) and making divorces easier to obtain. The committee's work was supported over the years by a number of groups in Germany that had a variety of different political beliefs. It was opposed by

"[It should not be assumed] that reversed sex drive is a sign of degeneration, just as we do not assume this of a hare-lip."

conservative groups (who did not believe in drastic changes), including the Nazi Party, although Hirschfeld himself was very conservative and pro-German in most matters.

Starts Journals on Sexuality

In 1899, Hirschfeld edited a 23-volume series of books regarding sexuality. It was the world's first such publication devoted to investigating all aspects of homosexual life. In 1908, he edited the *Journal of Sexual Science,* the first scholarly publication that dealt with a wide variety of sexual issues.

Terms Homosexuality Valid

In Hirschfeld's younger days, he believed that homosexuals were a "third sex," intermediate between males and females. He based this idea on the work of two writers from the 1860s who had written that homosexuality was both natural and inborn. In order to advance his "third sex" theory, Hirschfeld had to ignore the fact that most homosexuals are in no way physically different in appearance from heterosexuals. As of 1910, Hirschfeld had established a medical practice in Berlin, Germany. By this time he was placing much less emphasis on his earlier "third sex" idea, and recognizing that, at least physically, most homosexuals resemble others of their gender.

From his own research Hirschfeld learned, however, that homosexuals vary in terms of their mental makeup from those who possess characteristics very like their own sex to those who display characteristics more common to the opposite gender. He believed that all varieties of these sexual preferences were normal and valid.

Founds Institute

Hirschfeld's major work of writing, *The Homosexuality of Men and Women,* was published in 1914. Written after Hirschfeld had studied more than 10,000 homosexual individuals, it is one of the most comprehensive books ever written on the topic. Critics say that the book and its three indexes contain everything that was known about homosexuality by the time the Nazis started coming to power.

In 1919, Hirschfeld was a consultant for, and acted in, the first film designed to inform people about homosexual-

A frame from a Nazi propaganda film showing Hirschfeld.

ity, *Different From Others*. That same year he founded the Institute for Sexual Science in Berlin. Located in an old mansion, the institute offered Germany's first marital counseling services, research facilities, a medical department, and a library on the topic of human sexuality with more than 20,000 books, 35,000 photographs, and 40,000 biographical letters. The institute also counseled homosexuals, which is why the antihomosexual Nazis termed it "a singular breeding ground for filth and dirt."

During its first year, the institute served more than 4,000 people from around the world. In 1924, Hirschfeld turned the facility over to the government of Germany. He remained as director and the institute's policies hardly changed.

Beliefs on Homosexuality

Hirschfeld believed that the causes of homosexuality should be the object of scientific investigation. He said that it was not homosexuality as such, but the secrecy that often surrounds it, that is unhealthy. He explained that it was very stressful to keep secret something that was so much a part of a person's makeup, especially something that has been considered sinful, abnormal, criminal, or even a sign of mental illness. He pointed out that some people spend much of their lives fighting their own homosexual orientation, in "the eternal battle between willing spirit and weak flesh; that the perpetual fear of being discovered, of blackmail, arrest, court sentences, loss of social status and respect from family and friends . . . greatly affects one's disposition, must surely be nerve-racking, and could bring on [a nervous breakdown, depression,] . . . and thoughts of suicide."

Hirschfeld taught that most homosexuals are not sick. In fact, because most remain hidden, he wrote, it is only the most mentally unhealthy homosexuals who come to be known by the medical profession. Hirschfeld often quoted the English writer, Eduard Carpenter, who stated: "In the vast majority of cases, loving persons of one's own sex bears a character of normalcy and healthfulness."

Hirschfeld and his colleagues spoke glowingly of the period in ancient Greece when homosexuality was totally accepted and even seen as blessed by the pagan gods. Hirschfeld worked hard throughout his lifetime to promote a healthy and positive image of homosexual relationships between consenting adults. He also campaigned to have the age of legal consent (the age in which it is legal to engage in sexual relations) in Germany raised from age 14 to age 16, as he believed that a person needed to reach that age before he was mature enough to decide whether and with whom to become sexually active.

Efforts Meet With Partial Success

Hirschfeld's efforts to promote homosexual rights were hard fought. The negative image of homosexuality that had existed for centuries in Europe made it almost impossible for Hirschfeld's movement to gain acceptance. The traditional theory, passed down by the Romani Catholic Church, held that homosexuality was acquired by a lack of mature mental development during a childhood stage, or by a child's being seduced (lured into sexual activity) by a homosexual during adolescence. Instead, Hirschfeld sought to spread the idea that homosexuality was inborn, spontaneous, and unchangeable.

Homosexuality Under the Nazis

Even in its earliest days, the National Socialist German Workers' Party, or Nazis, declared homosexuality unnatural and spoke against it on the grounds that it interfered with the natural increase in population and stood in opposition to "proper family life." In 1935 the Nazi penal code (laws) declared friendship between males who were homosexuals, even with no sexual activity involved, to be an offense.

According to author Elisha Shaul: "The Nazi position on homosexuality, however, was inconsistent. . . . Officially, homosexuality was sharply denounced, but its practice in certain Nazi circles was tolerated or ignored."

For years, Nazi leader Adolf Hitler ignored the fact that Ernst Röhm, head of the SA (the Storm Troopers who fought Nazi opponents in the early days of the Nazi Party) was a homosexual. Röhm was just one of several prominent people whose sexual preferences were used as an excuse for them to be killed when they fell out of favor with Nazi leaders.

The Nazis punished tens of thousands of people for being homosexuals. They were forced to wear pink triangular patches and were placed in concentration camps (places where the Nazis confined "enemies of the state"), where many of them died.

During the 1920s, Hirschfeld presided over the conferences of the World League for Sexual Reform on a Scientific Basis. The conferences took place in Berlin, Germany, in 1921; Copenhagen, Denmark, in 1928; London, England, in 1929; and Vienna, Austria in 1930.

Between 1930 and 1931, with Nazi power on the rise in Germany (see Adolf Hitler entry), Hirschfeld left on a world tour during which he lectured and collected material for Berlin's Institute for Sexual Science. He traveled to Japan, China, the United States, Egypt, India, and Palestine (now Israel), among other places, delivering both academic and public speeches.

Institute Destroyed

While Hirschfeld was still abroad, on May 6, 1933, Nazi soldiers broke into the institute he had founded, and caused major damage. The entire building was burned down four days later. The Nazis defended their actions by saying that they were fighting against the undermining of "morality in sexual life."

Exile and Death

In 1933, fearful for his own safety, Hirschfeld fled to Switzerland, then to Paris, France. In Paris, he founded the French Institute for Sexual Science, but it never attained the prominence of the institute in Germany. In 1934, Hirschfeld closed the French institute. He relocated to the French city of Nice, where in 1935 he died, and where his cremated ashes were buried. Some of Hirschfeld's papers were saved and are now in the archives of the Kinsey Institute for Sex Research in Indiana.

Where to Learn More

Bullough, Vern L., and Bonnie Bullough, eds. *Human Sexuality: An Encyclopedia.* Garland Publishing, 1994.

Elisheva, Shaul. "Homosexuality and the Third Reich." In *Encyclopedia of the Holocaust,* Macmillan, 1990.

"Magnus Hirschfield." *Contemporary Authors.* Vol. 148. Gale Research, 1996.

Russell, Paul Elliott. *The Gay 100: A Ranking of the Most Influential Gay Men and Lesbians, Past and Present.* Carol, 1994.

Streakley, James D. *The Writings of Dr. Magnus Hirschfeld: A Bibliography.* Canadian Gay Archives, 1985.

Wolff, Charlotte. *Magnus Hirschfeld: A Portrait of a Pioneer in Sexology.* Quarter Books, 1986.

Zentner, Christian, and Friedemann Bedurftig. *The Encyclopedia of the Third Reich.* Translation edited by Amy Hackett. Macmillan, 1991.

Adolf Hitler

Born April 20, 1889
Braunau, Austria

Died April 30, 1945
Berlin, Germany

*Dictator of Nazi Germany
from 1934 to 1945*

*Known as Führer
(meaning "my leader")*

Adolf Hitler, leader of the National Socialist German Workers' Party (Nazi for short), believed that the Germans were a superior race destined to rule the world. He hated the Jews, in part because he blamed them for the punishing terms of the Treaty of Versailles that had ended World War I (1914–18), and for the humiliation Germany suffered in the period afterwards. He also believed that mixing with their bloodlines would pollute the Aryan (white, non-Jewish) race. He dreamed of a period of Nazi rule lasting more than a thousand years and surpassing the glories of all that came before. In the 1920s, as head of the then-tiny Nazi Party, he was viewed by his opponents as a comic figure, not to be taken seriously. However, by the 1930s, through the use of masterful persuasion and violent tactics, he became Germany's dictator (he held absolute rule). His dream of a thousand-year empire ended in 1945. It had lasted only 12 years, but left more than 50 million people dead.

Born into a Troubled Family

Adolf Hitler was born in a small town in Austria near the German border in 1889. He was the son of Alois Hitler, a customs inspector, and his third wife, Klara, who had formerly been Alois's maid. Klara was the daughter of Alois's first cousin and, at 28, nearly half her husband's age.

Alois, who provided a comfortable living for the family, was a violent man who terrorized his family members, demanded perfection, and did not allow laughter in his presence. Hitler was quoted as saying he never loved his father. Klara Hitler was a frail, gentle woman who was an excellent housekeeper. She had lost several children during their infancy. She had a daughter named Paula, two stepsons, and Adolf, the youngest, who was her favorite. She pampered him and is reported to have catered to his every whim. Klara was the most important person in Hitler's life and, wherever he was, her portrait hung above his bed.

Hitler's family moved several times when he was in grade school. He was a well-behaved child who earned high grades. He was also a good artist, enjoyed writing poetry, and loved music, especially the operas of the German composer Richard Wagner.

Young Manhood

As a youngster Hitler had dreams of becoming a professional artist. His father was completely opposed to this idea, calling artists lazy and not respectable. During his adolescence, Hitler's behavior changed. He rebelled against his bullying father, ridiculed his teachers, and worked only on subjects that he found interesting. Alois Hitler died in 1903 when Hitler was fourteen. Hitler begged his mother to allow him to quit school. When he had finished the ninth grade, she finally agreed. For the next three years Hitler did only what he wished, sketching, walking through the town of Linz where he then lived, visiting the library, and attending the opera and the theater in the evenings. It has been said that Hitler never held a steady job until he became the leader of Germany.

"I have a historic mission, and this mission I will fulfill . . . Who is not with me will be crushed."

In 1907, at age 18, Hitler traveled to Vienna, Austria, to take the entrance examination at the Academy of Fine Arts painting school. The pictures he painted in his effort to gain entrance to the school were judged inadequate. This both shocked and disappointed the young Hitler. The director of the academy, who saw some merit in Hitler's drawings, suggested that he apply to enter the School of Architecture. This would have involved doing remedial work to finish his high school studies, and Hitler refused. Hitler's devoted mother, Klara, died that same year, which devastated the young man. He attempted to gain entrance to the painting school for a second time a year later, but was again rejected.

Hitler then found occasional work as a portrait artist and creator of postcard scenes. Although he could have made a reasonable living as a commercial artist, the young man proved quite lazy. Each time he had earned enough money to provide food he stopped working.

The empire of Austria-Hungary, into which Hitler was born, was struggling to modernize in an age of increasing industrial growth and socialism. (Socialism is an economic system in which the production and distribution of goods are controlled by the government, and in which cooperation rather than competition is stressed.) One of the country's chief problems was relations among the mix of ethnic peoples who lived there. This included Germans, many types of Eastern Europeans, Slavs, Italians, and others. There was a growing move to nationalism (excessive patriotism) among many of these groups. Conflicts were most common in Vienna, the capital, where Hitler was spending some of his formative years. It was at this time that his antisemitic (anti-Jewish) beliefs became deeply entrenched.

Unable to accept his failure to gain access to art school, Hitler now blamed this on the people who refused him entrance. He said that they were Jews in disguise who were jealous of his talent and wanted to ruin his career. Each day, it seemed, his hatred for Jews grew stronger and stronger. His anti-Jewish opinions were supported by many of his associates. Anti-Jewish beliefs and behavior had been common in Austrian and Eastern European society for centuries.

For the next few years, Hitler spent his time daydreaming and discussing politics with other unemployed people, wearing ragged clothing, and sleeping wherever he could. He eventually began to believe that all people were motivated merely by selfishness and that one had to act like an animal in a jungle in order to survive.

Becomes a Soldier

After moving to Munich, Germany, in 1913, Hitler was called back to Austria to take a physical examination for the army. There he was declared too weak and medically unfit to serve. In 1914, at the start of World War I, Hitler volunteered to join the German army, whose acceptance gave him a new start in life. Spending four years on the front lines, Hitler proved a courageous soldier, who avoided injury and death many times. He was wounded in battle once, and twice earned the Iron Cross. Life in the army provided him with some stability, and he described this period as "the greatest and most unforgettable" of his lifetime.

When World War I ended in 1918, and Germany was forced to sign the strict Treaty of Versailles (which strongly limited Germany's power), Hitler cried. It was the first time he had done so since his mother's death 11 years earlier. He convinced himself that Germany had not lost on the battle-field. Rather, it had been brought down by "un-German" forces including promoters of socialism, liberals (who favor political reforms that promote democracy and personal free-dom), and especially Jews.

In 1919, Hitler became one of several soldiers chosen for training as political agents. They were supposed to instill German troops with strong feelings of loyalty to their native land. His great success at this task marked the first recognition of Hitler's outstanding talents as a speaker.

Entrance into the Nazi Party

In his long and rambling autobiography, *Mein Kampf* ("My Struggle"), Hitler stated that right after World War I he came to believe that God had chosen him for a special mission. As a result, he had decided to go into politics. In 1920, Hitler visited the newly formed German Workers Party. It was a poorly organized, anti-Jewish, anti-Communist group with fewer than 100 members. (Communism is an economic system that promotes the ownership of al property by the community as a whole.) Hitler took over recruitment duties for the group. In a short time he produced leaflets, brochures, and news releases, and presided over public meetings. He created a newspaper and gave the group a new name, the National Socialist German Workers' Party (Nazi Party for short).

Hitler retired from the army to devote all his energies to the party. He wanted to establish a new Nazi rule of order for all of Europe.

Appointed Head of the Nazis

In 1921, Hitler quit the Nazi Party. He said he would return only if he were named its leader. Since Hitler's energy and public speaking skills held the party together, the members agreed and Hitler took over. By the end of the year, followers were required to refer to him as "mein führer" (pronounced mine fyoor-uhr; a popular name for Hitler, meaning "my leader"). At that time, the Nazi Party held that all German Jews were to be deprived of their civil rights and many ought to be banished from the country.

In 1923, Hitler was in charge of an armed attempt to seize power in Germany. In a beer hall outside of Munich, important government officials were speaking to a large gathering. Suddenly, Hitler and his Nazi militia (called Storm Troopers) burst in. Their *putsch* (attempt to seize power) failed when the officials escaped. Following this unsuccessful effort, the Nazi Party was banned in Germany, and Hitler was sentenced to jail for five years. His cell was really a rather attractive room where he entertained visitors and received various gifts including food. During his imprisonment, Hitler wrote the first part of his autobiographical work, *Mein Kampf,* which proclaimed the racial prejudices that had became central to his personal beliefs and political message. He stated that Aryans were the highest "creators of culture" in the world and should be its master. All other races were to serve them. He said that some races, especially Jews, were "destroyers of culture." Unfit even to serve, they needed to be eliminated. Hitler was released from jail after only nine months, and he reestablished the Nazi Party in 1925.

The Nazi Party Comes to Power

Hitler and his party now devoted themselves to gaining

Hitler on the Jews, from *Mein Kampf*

Hitler first published his book, *Mein Kampf* ("My Struggle"), in 1925. Many have considered the book practically unreadable, because of its rambling style and boring repetitions. But the document is important because its pages contain the ideas that form the basis of so many of the Nazis' policies.

Although Jews had lived among the Germans for centuries, and had become part of the fabric of society, in *Mein Kampf* Hitler says that they are an "alien race" and must never be considered part of the German people.

In the following excerpts from *Mein Kampf,* Hitler comments on the rise of the Jew in Germany over the centuries, refers to the Jews having a secret agenda of world domination, and talks about a "race problem" and "the Jewish question" that will eventually find its remedy in the Nazi's "Final Solution of the Jewish Problem"—that is, the mass murder of the Jews:

> In the course of a thousand years [the Jew] has learned to master the language of his host people to such an extent as to believe that he can in the future risk to accent his Judaism a little less and to put his "Germanity" more into the foreground; for no matter how ridiculous, nay, absurd, it may seem at first, yet he permits himself the impudence of changing himself into a 'Germanic'; in this case therefore a 'German.' Thereby begins one of the most infamous lies conceivable. Since of Germanity he possesses really nothing but the ability to speak its language, badly in the most terrible manner, since for the rest, however, he never blended with it, therefore his whole Germanity rests only on the language. The race, however, is not based upon the language, but upon the blood exclusively . . . [The Jew's] character qualities have remained the same . . . He is always the same Jew.
>
> The reason why the Jew decides now suddenly to become a 'German' is obvious. He feels that the power of the monarchs [rulers] begins slowly to tumble, and therefore he seeks to get a platform under his feet in time. Further, his financial rule of the entire business life has already progressed so far that, without the possession of all the 'civil' rights, he is no longer able to support the whole enormous building, in any case no further increase of his influence can take place. But he wishes both; for the higher he climbs, the more alluringly rises out of the veil of the past his old goal, once promised to him, and with feverish greed he watches in his brightest heads the dream of world domination step into tangible proximity. Therefore, his sole endeavor is aimed at putting himself into complete possession of the 'civil' rights.
>
> He who wants to redeem the German people from the qualities and vices which are alien to its original nature will have to redeem it first from the alien originators of these expressions.
>
> Without the clearest recognition of the race problem and, with it, of the Jewish question, there will be no rise of the German nation.

power through legal means. The economic depression that beset the entire western world in the early 1930s also increased the suffering of the German people. Many Germans, now without jobs, began to listen to Hitler's opinions. Playing on their fears, he became very effective at stirring up his listeners with his frantic, hateful, and irrational speeches. Men in his audiences were said to groan with emotion, and women fainted. The Nazi Party increased its influence in the German national elections, gaining 2 percent of the votes in 1928, and 18.3 percent by 1930. In 1932, running against Germany's president, Paul von Hindenberg, Hitler won nearly 37 percent of the votes. Still, he failed to beat von Hindenberg.

In 1933, von Hindenberg appointed Hitler chancellor of Germany. (Although the president served as chief of state, the chancellor ran the day-to-day business of the government.) Civil unrest seemed to grow worse daily. Some of Hitler's opponents who were then in power were afraid to ban the Nazis, even though they considered them a threat to the existing government. They felt such a ban would set off large-scale and violent protests by fervent Nazi supporters. These opponents also believed that the Nazis could be used to keep the population under control if there were an uprising by other rival political groups. They were under the mistaken belief that they could keep the Nazis in line.

To their dismay, Hitler and the Nazis moved quickly and brutally to seize power. On February 27, 1933, a fire destroyed part of the building of the German law-making body called the *Reichstag* (Parliament). Hitler used this as an excuse to begin a reign of terror against all other political enemies. It worked: the *Reichstag* granted the Nazis "legal" powers allowing them to take over the country. In a short time the Nazis burned huge piles of books they considered "un-German."

By the end of the year Hitler had ended both civil rights and rules of law. The civil rights of German citizens were taken away when the German Secret State Police (Gestapo) was given authority to arrest and imprison anyone it wished. Citizens lost the right to be protected by laws when the *Reichstag* was transformed into a body of men hand-picked by the Nazis. These men would pass whatever policy Hitler wanted. In addition, the Nazi Party became the only legal party in Germany.

The Nazis soon provoked pogroms (massive attacks against the Jews). In 1933, Jews were officially eliminated from all public functions in the country. Hitler's power increased when he took Germany out of the League of Nations (the forerunner of the United Nations) and began renewing the strength of the German military, a violation of the Treaty of Versailles. Hitler forged an agreement in which he promised to rearm the military if they would keep silent about any other policies he wished to pursue. During the next five years, according to author Dennis Wepaman, the armed forces became "a thoroughly submissive instrument of Nazi policy."

Hitler (standing) giving the Nazi salute during a meeting of the Reichstag *in 1932.*

Hitler Becomes "Führer"

At the death of von Hindenberg, Hitler became the head of state, commander of all military forces, and leader and Reich Chancellor of Germany. Now he was in complete control of Germany. He declared that henceforth he should be referred to by all citizens as "Führer."

Music always played an important role in Hitler's life. A boyhood friend described Hitler's reaction as a teenager to watching Richard Wagner's opera, *Rienzi*. The opera portrays the life of a youth of ancient Rome who achieves heroic stature by leading his people into revolution (the overthrow of the existing government). Hitler vowed that he would someday "lead his people out of servitude, to the heights of freedom." His appearances in large halls and stadiums, as well as his radio addresses, were always preceded by the playing of a military piece called "The Badenweiler March." At home Hitler enjoyed listening to music on the record player and hearing tunes played on the accordion by his butler. One of "the Führer's" favorite songs was "Who's Afraid of the Big Bad Wolf?"

Hitler's rise to power had positive economic effects on Germany. Within three years, German unemployment virtually ceased and the national income doubled. In addition, Hitler greatly increased Germany's supply of weapons. A national vote reflected the support of his policies by more than 90 percent of the public.

Nevertheless, Hitler chose to insure his power through the use of violence. He created a secret police force, popularly known as the Gestapo. Anyone opposed to it was tortured or killed. Hitler also had his own private bodyguard unit, the SS (known as the "blackshirts") which were headed by longtime Hitler supporter Heinrich Himmler (see entry).

Start of World War II

Hitler began building his German Empire in 1938 by taking control of Austria and the German-speaking regions of Czechoslovakia. The British and French governments, wishing to avoid war, agreed to let him have those regions. The dictator of Italy, Benito Mussolini (see entry), signed the "Pact of Steel" with Hitler in 1939. The pact allowed Mussolini to take over the country of Albania for Italy. "Guns before butter" became the Nazi rallying cry, meaning that Germans had to sacrifice luxuries in favor of rebuilding their army. Great Britain and France soon began to see that their policy of giving in to Nazi demands to try to avoid further trouble was resulting in Hitler demanding even more territory. They decided that if Germany attacked Poland, they would be forced to fight back. Hitler was mistaken in his belief that Great Britain and France would not help Poland, since they had not helped Czechoslovakia. On September 3, 1939, Hitler attacked Poland. Great Britain and France then declared war on Germany. Hitler announced it was now time for the "master race" (the name he gave to the German people) to claim its destiny.

The Final Solution

For years, Hitler had been going forward with the policies of "racial purity" so central to his personal and political beliefs. Hitler held the Jews responsible for the growth of democratic and socialistic ideas, which he believed would lead to Germany's ruin. He also believed that their elimination would free land for the use of the Aryan peoples, the only ones worthy to occupy the German Empire.

At the beginning of 1939, Hitler stated that all of the Jews in Europe would be done away with as the result of a new world war. Jews had already been stripped of their rights to vote, forbidden to marry Germans, and entirely eliminated from any official positions in German society, of which they had been an accepted part for centuries. Nearly 150,000 Jews left Germany in 1937, about one-third of the entire Jewish population. However, when Hitler united Austria with Germany in 1938, the Jewish population of the newly created state totaled approximately 500,000.

Starting in 1939, Jews in territories taken over by Hitler were segregated and some were sent to work camps in Poland. Then, in 1941, Hitler ordered what he called "the Final Solution to the Jewish Question"—the mass killing of all European Jews. Several concentration camps, where the Nazis confined people they regarded as "enemies of the state," were built to Hitler's specifications.

Over the next four years, millions of Jews were relocated to the camps, forced to work for no wages and very little food, and eventually killed in gas chambers, sealed rooms in which the Nazis release poisonous gas in order to kill the people locked inside. Their bodies were disposed of in enormous ovens called crematoriums. This despicable event in human history is known as the Holocaust. Its goal was genocide, the destruction of an entire race. Members of other groups killed in the death camps included Catholics, Roma (often called

Gypsies), homosexuals, socialists, and other political opponents to Nazism. Hitler's hatred was so deeply rooted that even in his will he left funds to "Continue to fight the Jews."

The Tide Turns

The early part of World War II was successful for the Nazis as they marched on and conquered Denmark, Norway, Belgium, Luxembourg, the Netherlands, and finally France. By 1940, Nazi Germany had nearly doubled in land area, and the population had grown from 65 million to more than 105 million.

In 1940, Great Britain, which up until then had been fighting Nazi Germany alone and had heroically survived tremendous punishment from Nazi bombs, finally had its first great success. The bombing of Berlin led by British prime minister Winston Churchill, gave the lie to Hitler's promise that no bombs would ever fall on the German capital. However, that same year, Nazi Germany went on to conquer Bulgaria, Hungary, and Romania. Hitler decided to extend his domination of Eastern Europe by turning against the Soviet Union (now called Russia). His invasion of the Soviet Union in June 1940 betrayed the nonaggression pact he had made with the Soviets in 1939. It also proved his biggest and most disastrous gamble.

For the Nazis, 1942 was a difficult year. There were numerous battles, with the opposing sides holding the advantage at different times. Nazi soldiers were unequipped for the horrible Soviet winters, and Hitler was unprepared for the tremendous resistance by the Soviet people, which thwarted his plans for an easy victory. The same year, the United States entered the war after Japan—Germany's ally—bombed Pearl Harbor, Hawaii. The defeat of Hitler's forces in Africa under General Erwin Rommel (see entry) soon followed. Germany surrendered to the Soviet Union in 1943. That same year Germany's ally, Italy, surrendered to the Allies (United States, Great Britain, the Soviet Union, and France), marking the beginning of the end for Hitler.

Assassination Attempts and Defeat

Hitler's political opponents had unsuccessfully tried to take his life several times. However, on July 20, 1944, knowing that their cause was lost, some of Hitler's own military leaders tried to assassinate him. Their attempt failed. Hitler took vicious revenge, killing about 5,000 people he believed were involved in the plot. Beginning in 1945, he never left the underground bunker in Berlin from which he continued to direct Nazi war efforts. Before long, even Hitler had to come to the realization that the end of Nazi rule was at hand.

Throughout his lifetime, Hitler suffered from digestive disorders and stomach cramps, as well as gas. His general health was excellent, although he remained overly concerned about it. During the last years of the war his health began to deteriorate. He experienced a leg rash, tremors in his arms and legs, and in 1945 he suffered a minor stroke. By the end of the war he had a pronounced stoop and had become increasingly irrational. He talked nonstop, repeatedly cursing all those in his life who he believed had betrayed him.

Hitler had met Eva Braun (see entry), an athletic young woman who worked as a photographer's assistant, in 1929. By 1936, she was invited to move in with him at his villa. It has been said that problems in their relationship played a major role in her two suicide attempts. On April 29, 1945, Hitler married Braun. The next day, to escape falling into the hands of approaching Soviet troops, Hitler killed his pet dog and put a bullet in his own brain. His new wife, seated beside him on a sofa, killed herself by ingesting poison. At Hitler's request their bodies were burned. The rule of the Nazis came to an end with their surrender to the Allies on May 7, 1945.

Some Germans refused to believe the news of Hitler's death. For years, rumors persisted that he was living in Argentina. Even the leader of the Soviet Union, Josef Stalin, said that reports of Hitler's death left him "dubious" (doubtful), and voiced his belief that Hitler must have escaped and gone into hiding.

In 1972, a dental forensic expert (a dental expert whose examinations and conclusions can be used for legal purposes) compared pictures of the dentures taken from a body found near Hitler's bunker and X-ray head plates of Hitler that were taken in 1943. The two were a perfect match. The dental expert told the Sixth International Meeting of Forensic Sciences that this was conclusive proof that Hitler had died in Germany as reported.

Where to Learn More

Carr, William. *Hitler: A Study in Personality and Politics*. St. Martin's Press, 1979.

Fuchs, Thomas. *The Hitler Fact Book*. Fountain Books, 1990.

Haas, Gerda.*Tracking the Holocaust*. Runestone Press, 1995.

Harris, Nathaniel. *Hitler*. B.T. Batsford Ltd., 1989.

Marrin, Albert. *Hitler*. Viking Kestrel, 1987.

Neville, Peter. *Life in the Third Reich*. B.T. Batsford, 1992.

Shirer, William L. *The Rise and Fall of Adolf Hitler*. Random House, 1961.

Speer, Albert. *Inside the Third Reich*. Macmillan, 1970.

Toland, John. *Adolf Hitler*. Doubleday, 1976.

Wepman, Dennis. *Adolf Hitler*. Chelsea House Publishers, 1985.

Rudolf Höss

Born November 25, 1900
Baden, Germany

Died April 7, 1947
Auschwitz Concentration Camp,
Poland

*Soldier, Commandant at Auschwitz
from 1940 through 1943*

*Supervised the executions of at least
1.3 million Jews at the Auschwitz-Birkenau
concentration camp*

R udolf Höss was an unremarkable man who accepted a job as a guard at Dachau concentration camp (a place where people regarded as "enemies of the state are confined). He did so well, moving swiftly up the ranks of the National Socialist German Workers' Party (Nazis), that after only four years he was promoted to commander of his own camp. He was responsible for turning a small army barracks in Poland into Auschwitz-Birkenau camp, the one of the largest and deadliest of the camps. Höss was singled out for special praise by his supervisors for his work at Auschwitz; they called him "a true pioneer . . . because of his new ideas and educational methods."

Joins Army to Escape Unhappy Home

Rudolf Höss was born in 1900 in Baden, Germany, a small town near the country's border with France. His father was a German army

"The killing
. . . did not
concern me
much at the
time. I must
even admit
that this
gassing set
my mind
at rest."

officer who had served in Africa. Höss seems to have had a rather peculiar childhood. According to author Robert Conot, "his father had been a bigoted [prejudiced] . . . Catholic, who, after fathering Höss and his younger sister, had taken an oath of celibacy [he did not have sexual relations] and dedicated [Höss] to God, intending that he should become a priest." The senior Höss declared further that Höss's sister was an angel. Höss's boyhood was such a misery to him that he developed a lasting hatred for both his father and his sister. He ran away at the age of 17 and became a soldier in the German army during World War I (1914–18).

When he returned to Germany after the war, Höss joined a group of former soldiers who "found themselves misfits in German life," he wrote in his autobiography. In 1922, he joined the Nazi Party, which was then in its infancy. It was headed by Adolph Hitler (see entry), who had not yet ascended to a position of national power. Hitler hated Jews and often shouted anti-Jewish or antisemitic accusations in his speeches. At the time Höss joined the party, though, the full-scale persecution of the Jews had not yet begun.

In 1923, Höss participated in the killing of a school teacher suspected of being a traitor to the Nazi cause. Höss was sentenced to serve at least ten years in prison but was released after serving only five years. (Although information is scarce, it appears that he married a woman by the name of Hedwig shortly after his release from prison.) Höss then joined a youth movement devoted to farming and country living—preferably in the east on land that belonged to Poland. (Part of the Nazis' political agenda was to enlarge Germany by taking land from neighboring countries.) Heinrich Himmler (see entry) was also a member of this group, and it was at Himmler's suggestion that Höss joined the SS. (The SS is an abbreviation for *Shutzstaffeln* or Security Squad. They were Hitler's personal bodyguards and provided guards for the various concentration camps.) When Himmler (head of the SS) established the Dachau concentration camp in 1933, Höss was chosen to become one of its guards.

Begins Career in Concentration Camps

Dachau was set up by Himmler in a former war materials factory. Dachau was in the state of Bavaria in southwestern Germany, where Hitler had begun his rise to power.

Dachau was intended to hold Bavaria's "undesirables"—that is, people who disagreed with the Nazi Party. At Dachau the undesirables could be "reeducated" to fit back into Nazi society. Höss "saw it as his main task to teach them the value of hard work, which would bring structure and endurance to an unstable life," according to authors Deborah Dwork and Robert Jan Van Pelt. Höss would later claim in his autobiography that he disliked the methods used against Dachau prisoners by the other guards, but he "had become too fond of the black uniform" to object. (The SS wore black uniforms and were often called "blackshirts.") He said he was too sensitive for the work at first, and wrote: "I wished to appear hard, lest I should appear weak." Soon he grew used to the brutality, though, and performed his job well.

Over the years, Dachau and the other concentration camps that were built performed many functions, from labor camps to farms to killing centers. Höss never forgot the lessons he learned at Dachau. The phrase *Arbeit macht frei* (Work makes one free) became his motto. Auschwitz concentration camp was established in 1940 and Höss was put in charge; one of his first acts was to have this motto nailed above the entrance.

Auschwitz was the name of a small town in Poland and also the name of the Polish army barracks at the edge of town. The town was ideally situated for a concentration camp as far as the Nazis were concerned. The area was thinly populated, so few outsiders would know what was going on in the camp, and it was situated on a direct railroad line to Germany. Hitler had taken over Poland in 1939, and Polish citizens who objected to German rule were sent to Auschwitz to be terrorized. Auschwitz also served as a center where captured Poles and later Soviets (now called Russians) were sent to determine their suitability for slave labor in other camps and factories.

Auschwitz Becomes Industrial and Farming Site

Hitler had grand plans for building a German empire, and the need for building materials became critical. Auschwitz had an abundance of sand and gravel, which could be made into concrete. It was decided to enlarge the camp, which became an outpost of the German Earth and Stone Works. Slave laborers from conquered countries

The gate to the Auschwitz concentration camp bearing the motto Arbeit Macht Frei *("Work Makes One Free").*

throughout Europe were used in this enterprise. A prison was built to hold the laborers, and a crematorium was built to dispose of the bodies of those who died from the brutal working conditions. The crematorium was a room with huge ovens that were used to burn the remains of dead workers.

Höss complained that his coworkers at Auschwitz were untrustworthy, which made him uncomfortable, and he began drinking in secret. His wife tried to help by inviting people to their home outside the camp for social evenings, but Höss had little interest. He wrote: "I lived only for my work. I was absorbed, I might say obsessed. . . . Every fresh difficulty only increased my zeal. . . . [A]ll human emotions were forced into the background."

Inspired by his interest in farming, Höss drew up maps, plans, and diagrams for an agricultural complex to be built at Auschwitz. Höss, a man who took pride in his devotion to his five children and his pets, designed the complex to include a farm for his family. To his delight, his superior, Heinrich Himmler, was enchanted with the idea. When female prisoners began to arrive at Auschwitz in 1942, they were set to work cultivating the heavy clay soil surrounding the camp. Working 12 hours a day with very little to eat, and beaten by guards if they faltered, the women and girls built greenhouses, barns, and roads, while the male prisoners were occupied at the sand and gravel pits.

As Hitler prepared for his assault on the Soviet Union (now called Russia), Himmler ordered Höss to prepare Auschwitz to accept 100,000 Soviet prisoners of war. A group of 12,000 Soviet prisoners was sent to the camp in December 1941 to construct facilities for this purpose. So it came about that a new part of the camp was built in an area thickly forested with birch trees. It was called Birkenau ("in the birches"). The 12,000 Soviets worked so hard that by April 1942 there were only 150 still alive. Ironically, Hitler's march into the Soviet Union failed, and the large numbers of Soviet prisoners never arrived at Auschwitz.

Author Robert Conot described an incident in Höss's life that happened at the end of 1942. At a dinner party, a man asked Höss's wife what she thought about her husband's work. He then went on to describe that work for her (she had previously only heard rumors). Later that evening, she asked her husband if what she had heard was true. When he admitted it was, she was so upset she refused to sleep with him from that day forward. Soon after, Höss forced a camp inmate to become his mistress.

Gets Orders to Prepare for "Final Solution"

According to Höss, in 1941 or 1942 he was ordered by Himmler to transform Auschwitz into a killing site. This order was to fulfill the Nazis' plans for the Final Solution. (The "Final Solution" was the Nazi code for the total elimination of European Jews.) Höss claimed Himmler told him that if the Jews of Europe were not killed right away, the Jews would later exterminate the German people. Höss later told a psychologist about this order: "I had nothing to say; I could only say *Jawohl*! [Yes, I will!]" Höss claimed he tried to get Himmler to do something about the terrible conditions at the camp—overcrowding, lack of drainage for sanitation purposes, and lack of a reliable water supply—but Himmler was not interested. By Himmler's will, said Höss, "Auschwitz became the greatest human extermination [killing] center of all time."

By the winter of 1943, Höss had equipped the facility with four new crematoriums, each with a gas chamber that could kill 2,000 people at one time. A gas chamber was a sealed room that was filled with poisonous gas in order to suffocate the people locked inside. As new transports of "undesirables" (Jews, Roma [often called Gypsies], homosexuals, Jehovah's Witnesses [a religious group]) arrived at the camps, Höss and his coworkers would select as many people as they needed for camp labor (more were needed as farmhands in the summer), and the rest were killed. Obviously, the selection favored the young and strong who could do heavy field work. Those who died were the sick, the elderly, and small children.

The Horrors Described

According to author Abram Sachar, when Höss testified at the Nuremberg Trials (1945–46) of Nazi war criminals (people accused of violating the laws and customs of war) after the war ended, he did so "with the dispassion [lack of emotion] of a robot." His voice was described by author Robert Conot as high-pitched and almost boyish. His sworn statement read in part: "The 'final solution' of the Jewish question meant the complete extermination of all Jews in Europe. I had the order to produce extermination facilities in Auschwitz in June 1942. . . . When I built the . . . building in Auschwitz, I therefore used Zyklon B, a crystallized hydrocyanic acid, which we threw into the death chamber through a small opening. It took three to fifteen minutes, depending on the climatic conditions, in order to kill the people in the death chamber. We knew when the people were dead because their screaming stopped. We waited usually a half hour before we opened the doors and removed the bodies. After the bodies were brought forth, our special commandos [troops] took off the rings and pulled the gold out of the teeth of the bodies." The jewelry and gold were stored to later be transferred into money to support the German war effort.

Höss estimated that during his command of Auschwitz, which lasted until December 1, 1943, "at least 2.5 million victims were put to death and exterminated there through gassing; at least a further half million died through hunger

Postcards from Auschwitz

William L. Shirer (1904–1993) was an American journalist and historian who was working in Berlin, Germany, as a radio correspondent when World War II began in 1939. He was often at Adolf Hitler's side during the dictator's rise to power, and detailed his experiences in his massive book, *The Rise and Fall of the Third Reich: A History of Nazi Germany.* The book won the National Book Award.

Shirer offered this description of the selection process that took place under Rudolf Höss's command, based on accounts given by jailers and inmates who survived Auschwitz concentration camp:

> The "selection," which decided which Jews were to be [put to work] and which ones immediately gassed, took place at the railroad siding as soon as the victims had been unloaded from the freight cars in which they had been locked without food or water for as much as a week—for many came from such distant parts as France, Holland and Greece. Though there were heart-rending scenes as wives were torn away from husbands and children from parents, none of the captives, as Höss testified [at a trial after the war was over] and survivors agree, realized just what was in store for them. In fact some of them were given pretty picture postcards . . . to be signed and sent back home to their relatives with a printed inscription saying:
>
> "We are doing very well here. We have work and we are well treated. We await your arrival."

and sickness." Other estimates put the number of Jews killed under his command at 1.13 million. Höss performed his job so well that he was promoted to chief of the Central Administration for Camps, a job that took him to Berlin, Germany, location of the Nazis' headquarters.

The War Winds Down

By the time Höss had moved to Berlin, it was obvious that Germany was losing the war. The order came down to destroy the concentration camps so the conquering Allied armies would not learn of the horrors that had taken place in them (the Allies were United States, Great Britain, the Soviet Union, and France). As the Soviets closed in on Auschwitz, officials there were ordered to kill as many inmates as possible before the Soviet troops arrived. The remainder were to be transported to other camps not in the path of the Allies. Höss tried to get to Auschwitz to supervise the murders, but he apparently decided it was unwise to put himself in the path of the conquering Soviets. Instead, he joined a group who were fleeing in the direction of Denmark. "It was a gruesome journey," he later wrote, "as the enemy's low flying planes continually machine-gunned the escape route." When the news reached them that Hitler himself had committed suicide, anything resembling order and discipline among the fleeing Germans collapsed.

Thousands of Germans—including Höss—were captured by the British, but Höss managed to conceal his identity and was released. He took a job on a farm and escaped arrest for nearly a year before the British—who had been looking for him—caught up with him in 1945. He was imprisoned and forced to testify at two trials of Nazi criminals. During his imprisonment, he wrote his autobiography. In it he simultaneously denied responsibility for many of the crimes he was accused of, yet accepted responsibility for and described many horrific acts. He was finally handed over to authorities in Poland, the scene of his crimes. In 1947, he was tried and condemned to death. He was hanged on April 7, 1947, at Auschwitz.

Where to Learn More

Conot, Robert E. *Justice at Nuremberg.* Harper & Row, 1983.

Dwork, Deborah, and Robert Jan Van Pelt. *Auschwitz: 1270 to the Present.* W. W. Norton, 1996.

Manvell, Roger, and Heinrich Fraenkel. *Himmler.* Putnam, 1965.

"Rudolf Höss Testimony." http://www.writething.com/cybrary/Facts.aft.tri.nur.html

Sachar, Abram L. *The Redemption of the Unwanted.* St. Martin's/Marek, 1983.

Index

Italic type indicates volume numbers;
boldface types indicates entries and their page numbers;
(ill.) indicates illustrations.

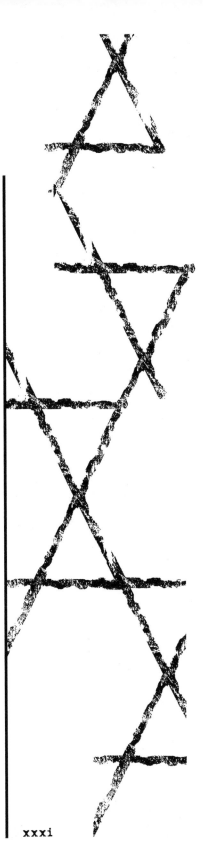

E

Edelstein, Jacob *1:* 16
Eichmann, Adolf *1:* 15, **112-20**, 112 (ill.), 117 (ill.), 200, 219-20, 226; *2:* 271, 319, 449, 485-86, 488, 495, 505-07
Eichmann in Jeresalem 1: 119
Eichmann in My Hands 1: 118
"Eichmann's Hobby Shops" *1:* 115
Einsatzgruppen 1: 219-20; *2:* 324
Eisenhower, Dwight D. *1:* 162; *2:* 341, 345
Elie Wiesel Foundation for Humanity *2:* 498
Emalia camp *2:* 419
Emergency Rescue Committee *1:* 150
Encyclicals *2:* 351
England *1:* 22; *2:* 259, 263, 408
Epenstein, Hermann von *1:* 181
Ernst, Max *1:* 151
Essen, Germany *2:* 291, 298-99
The Essence of Judaism 1: 10
Ethiopia *2:* 332
Europe *1:* 20, 24-25; *2:* 297, 302, 316, 325, 329, 336, 368, 396, 398, 409, 413, 446-47, 452, 458, 462, 468, 478, 493, 495, 508
Euthanasia *1:* 65, 67; *2:* 472

F

"Faith Movement" *1:* 50
Farago, Ladislas *1:* 63
Fasci di Combattimento 2: 330
Fascism *2:* 328, 331-33, 335, 351, 493
Fascist Party *2:* 493
"Fat Bertha" *2:* 294
"Fat Gustav" *2:* 294
Federal Republic of Germany *2:* 257
Federal Republic of Yugoslavia *2:* 480
Feingold, Henry L. *2:* 397
Fénelon, Fania *2:* 375
Ferdinand, Francis *2:* 475
Fermi, Laur *2:* 329
Fest, Joachim C. *1:* 130; *2:* 381
Feuchtwanger, Lion *1:* 151
The Fighting Pioneer 1: 108
Final Solution *1:* 14, 56, 87, 115, 191, 220, 227, 229, 243, 247, 255; *2:* 313, 321, 325, 334, 349, 367-69, 395, 438-39, 505
Finland *1:* 32; *2:* 355
"The Firm" *2:* 410
Fisher, David *1:* 202-03
Florence, Italy *2:* 453
Flossenburg *1:* 52
Flying Corps *2:* 295
Fock-Kantzoa, Carin von *1:* 182, 184
Foot, M. R. D. *2:* 261
Fraenkel, Heinrich *1:* 206
Fragments of Isabella 2: 309
France *1:* 19, 21-22, 27, 147, 149, 152, 202-03, 248; *2:* 262-63, 268-70, 272, 326, 336, 339, 342-43, 388, 408, 410-11, 428, 441, 446, 469, 475, 484, 496

V

W

World League for Sexual Reform on a Scientific Basis *1:* 236
World War I *1:* 9, 14, 20, 48-49, 57, 66, 81, 89-90, 95, 121, 139, 156-57,
    165, 173, 180-81, 191, 198, 206, 215, 223-24, 238, 241, 252; *2:* 285,
    287, 293, 302-03, 312, 322, 324, 330, 332, 348, 363, 379, 385-86, 408,
    427, 436, 475-76, 483, 494, 501
World War II *1:* 1-2, 13, 19, 21-22, 32, 34, 47, 53, 56, 59, 62, 65, 67, 74-75,
    85-86, 88, 90, 95-96, 105-07, 112, 128, 131, 137, 147, 155, 159, 164,
    167, 172, 176-77, 185, 196, 202, 209, 220, 222, 227-28, 248; *2:* 259-61,
    263, 265-67, 270, 272, 277, 283, 285, 287, 291, 294-95, 297, 299,
    301-03, 311, 313, 321, 324-25, 328, 334, 339-40, 342, 344-45, 347,
    349, 351-52, 354, 359, 366, 368-69, 372, 384, 392, 397-98, 413, 415,
    422, 425-26, 428, 434, 436, 440, 443, 451, 467-69, 474, 478-80, 485,
    489-91, 494-95, 498, 500, 502
Wroblewski, Michal (Misha) *2:* 289
Wulf, Josef *1:* 109-11
Wyman, David S. *2:* 439

Y

Yad Vashem *1:* 53, 94, 153; *2:* 423, 489
Yahil, Leni *1:* 119
Yiddish *1:* 114; *2:* 496
Young, Desmond *2:* 388
Young Germans *2:* 427
Yugoslav Communist Party *2:* 479
Yugoslavia *2:* 448, 474, 476, 479, 481-82

Z

Zegreb, Yugoslavia *2:* 477
Zeilsheim *2:* 398
Zelkowicz, Josef *1:* 194
Zionism *1:* 114; *2:* 287, 372, 445
Zionists *2:* 375, 449
Zyklon B *1:* 115, 256